Sunnyvale Middle S
1080 Mango Avenue
Sunnyvale, Calif. 94087

W9-CCO-593

WHERE THE RED FERN GROWS
The story of two dogs and a boy

with Connections

WHERE THE RED FERN GROWS

The story of two dogs and a boy

Wilson Rawls

with Connections

HOLT, RINEHART AND WINSTON
Harcourt Brace & Company

Austin · New York · Orlando · Atlanta · San Francisco
Boston · Dallas · Toronto · London

All of the characters in this book are fictitious,
and any resemblance to actual persons, living or dead,
is purely coincidental.

Copyright © by Holt, Rinehart and Winston

All rights reserved. No part of this publication may be reproduced or transmitted in any form or by any means, electronic or mechanical, including photocopy, recording, or any information storage and retrieval system, without permission in writing from the publisher.

Requests for permission to make copies of any part of the work should be mailed to the following address: Permissions Department, Holt, Rinehart and Winston, 1120 South Capital of Texas Highway, Austin, Texas 78746-6487.

For permission to reprint copyrighted material, grateful acknowledgment is made to the following sources:

Bantam Doubleday Dell Books for Young Readers, a division of Bantam Doubleday Dell Publishing Group, Inc., New York, New York: *Where the Red Fern Grows* by Wilson Rawls. Copyright © 1961 by Woodrow Wilson Rawls; copyright © 1961 by The Curtis Publishing Company. All rights reserved.

The Emma Courlander Trust: "Paul Bunyan's Cornstalk" from *Ride with the Sun* by Harold Courlander. Copyright © 1983 by Harold Courlander. **John R. Erickson:** From *The Original Adventures of Hank the Cowdog* by John R. Erickson (A Maverick book). Copyright © 1988 by John Erickson. **Harcourt Brace & Company:** "The Saddest Day the Summer Had" from *Raymond and Me That Summer* by Dick Perry. Copyright © 1964 and renewed © 1992 by Dick Perry. **HarperCollins Publishers:** "Princess" from *El Bronx Remembered: A Novella and Stories* by Nicholasa Mohr. Copyright © 1975 by Nicholasa Mohr. **Ashley Deal Matin:** "The Christmas Hunt" by Borden Deal. First appeared in *The Saturday Evening Post*. **G. P. Putnam's Sons, a division of Penguin Putnam Inc.:** "The Pine of Akoya" from *Mysterious Tales of Japan* by Rafe Martin. Copyright © 1996 by Rafe Martin. **Random House, Inc.:** Excerpt (retitled "Momma's Store") from *I Know Why the Caged Bird Sings* by Maya Angelou. Copyright © 1969 and renewed © 1997 by Maya Angelou. **Simon & Schuster and Simon & Schuster Books for Young Readers:** Excerpt (retitled "Him") from *Bambi* by Felix Salten. Copyright 1928 and renewed © 1956 by Simon & Schuster Inc. **University of Illinois Press:** "Mart Moody's Bird Dog" adapted from *Adirondack Voices: Woodsmen and Woods Lore.* Copyright © 1981 by the Board of Trustees of the University of Illinois.

Cover illustration by Lori Lohstoeter/Lindgren & Smith Represents

HRW is a registered trademark licensed to Holt, Rinehart and Winston.

Printed in the United States of America

ISBN 0-03-054774-1

7 8 9 10 11 043 06 05 04 03

*To my wonderful wife
without whose help this book
would not have been
written*

Contents

WHERE THE RED FERN GROWS
The story of two dogs and a boy

with Connections

I

WHEN I LEFT MY OFFICE that beautiful spring day, I had no idea what was in store for me. To begin with, everything was too perfect for anything unusual to happen. It was one of those days when a man feels good, feels like speaking to his neighbor, is glad to live in a country like ours, and proud of his government. You know what I mean, one of those rare days when everything is right and nothing is wrong.

I was walking along whistling when I heard the dogfight. At first I paid no attention to it. After all it wasn't anything to get excited about, just another dogfight in a residential section.

As the sound of the fight grew nearer, I could tell there were quite a few dogs mixed up in it. They boiled out of an alley, turned, and headed straight toward me. Not wanting to get bitten or run over, I moved over to the edge of the sidewalk.

I could see that all the dogs were fighting one. About twenty-five feet from me they caught him and down he went. I felt sorry for the unfortunate one. I knew if something wasn't done quickly the sanitation department would have to pick up a dead dog.

I was trying to make up my mind to help when I got a surprise. Up out of that snarling, growling, slashing mass reared an old redbone hound. For a second I saw him. I caught my breath. I couldn't believe what I had seen.

Twisting and slashing, he fought his way through the pack and backed up under the low branches of a hedge. Growling and snarling, they formed a half-moon circle around him. A big bird dog, bolder than the others, darted in. The hedge shook as he tangled with the hound. He came out so fast he fell over backwards. I saw that his right ear was split wide open. It was too much for him and he took off down the street, squalling like a scalded cat.

A big ugly cur tried his luck. He didn't get off so easy. He came out with his left shoulder laid open to the bone. He sat down on his rear and let the world know that he had been hurt.

By this time, my fighting blood was boiling. It's hard for a man to stand and watch an old hound fight against such odds, especially if that man has memories in his heart like I had in mine. I had seen the time when an old hound like that had given his life so that I might live.

Taking off my coat, I waded in. My yelling and scolding didn't have much effect, but the swinging coat did. The dogs scattered and left.

Down on my knees, I peered back under the hedge. The hound was still mad. He growled at me and showed his teeth. I knew it wasn't his nature to fight a man.

In a soft voice, I started talking to him. "Come on, boy," I said. "It's all right. I'm your friend. Come on now."

The fighting fire slowly left his eyes. He bowed his head and his long, red tail started thumping the ground. I kept coaxing. On his stomach, an inch at a time, he came to me and laid his head in my hand.

I almost cried at what I saw. His coat was dirty and mud-caked. His skin was stretched drum-tight over his bony frame. The knotty joints of his hips and shoulders stood out a good three inches from his body. I could tell he was starved.

I couldn't figure it out. He didn't belong in town. He was far out of place with the boxers, poodles, bird dogs, and other breeds of town dogs. He belonged in the country. He was a hunting hound.

I raised one of his paws. There I read the story. The pads were worn down slick as the rind on an apple. I knew he had come a long way, and no doubt had a long way to go. Around his neck was a crude collar. On closer inspection, I saw it had been made from a piece of check-line leather. Two holes had been punched in each end and the ends were laced together with bailing wire.

As I turned the collar with my finger, I saw something else. There, scratched deep in the tough leather, was the name

"Buddie." I guessed that the crude, scribbly letters had probably been written by a little boy.

It's strange indeed how memories can lie dormant in a man's mind for so many years. Yet those memories can be awakened and brought forth fresh and new, just by something you've seen, or something you've heard, or the sight of an old familiar face.

What I saw in the warm gray eyes of the friendly old hound brought back wonderful memories. To show my gratitude, I took hold of his collar and said, "Come on, boy, let's go home and get something to eat."

He seemed to understand that he had found a friend. He came willingly.

I gave him a bath and rubbed all the soreness from his muscles. He drank quarts of warm milk and ate all the meat I had in the house. I hurried down to the store and bought more. He ate until he was satisfied.

He slept all that night and most of the next day. Late in the afternoon he grew restless. I told him I understood, and as soon as it was dark, he could be on his way. I figured he had a much better chance if he left town at night.

That evening, a little after sundown, I opened the back gate. He walked out, stopped, turned around, and looked at me. He thanked me by wagging his tail.

With tears in my eyes, I said, "You're more than welcome, old fellow. In fact, you could've stayed here as long as you wanted to."

He whined and licked my hand.

I was wondering which way he would go. With one final whimper he turned and headed east. I couldn't help smiling as I watched him trot down the alley. I noticed the way his hind quarters shifted over to the right, never in line with the front, yet always in perfect rhythm. His long ears flopped up and down, keeping time with the jogging motion of his body. Yes, they were all there, the unmistakable marks of a hunting hound.

Where the alley emptied into the street, he stopped and looked back. I waved my hand.

As I watched him disappear in the twilight shadows, I whispered these words: "Good-bye, old fellow. Good luck, and good hunting!"

I didn't have to let him go. I could have kept him in my back yard, but to pen up a dog like that is a sin. It would have broken his heart. The will to live would have slowly left his body.

I had no idea where he had come from or where he was going. Perhaps it wasn't too far, or maybe it was a long, long way. I tried to make myself believe that his home was in the Ozark Mountains somewhere in Missouri, or Oklahoma. It wasn't impossible even though it was a long way from the Snake River Valley in Idaho.

I figured something drastic must have happened in his life, as it is very unusual for a hound to be traveling all alone. Perhaps he had been stolen, or maybe he had been sold for some much-needed money. Whatever it was that had interrupted his life, he was trying to straighten it out. He was going home to the master he loved, and with the help of God, he would make it.

To him it made no difference how long the road, or how rough or rocky. His old red feet would keep jogging along, on and on, mile after mile. There would be no crying or giving up. When his feet grew tired and weary, he would curl up in the weeds and rest. Water from a rain puddle or a mountain stream would quench his thirst and cool his hot dry throat. Food found along the highway, or the offerings from a friendly hand would ease the pangs of hunger. Through the rains, the snows, or the desert heat, he would jog along, never looking back.

Some morning he would be found curled up on the front porch. The long journey would be over. He would be home. There would be a lot of tail-wagging and a few whimpering cries. His warm moist tongue would caress the hand of his master. All would be forgiven. Once again the lights would shine in his dog's world. His heart would be happy.

After my friend had disappeared in the darkness, I stood and stared at the empty alley. A strange feeling came over me. At first I thought I was lonely or sad, but I realized that wasn't it at all. The feeling was a wonderful one.

Although the old hound had no way of knowing it, he had stirred memories, and what priceless treasures they were. Memories of my boyhood days, an old K. C. Baking Powder can, and two little red hounds. Memories of a wonderful love, unselfish devotion, and death in its saddest form.

As I turned to enter my yard I started to lock the gate, and then I thought, "No, I'll leave it open. He might come back."

I was about halfway to the house when a cool breeze drifted down from the rugged Tetons. It had a bite in it and goose-pimples jumped out on my skin. I stopped at the woodshed and picked up several sticks of wood.

I didn't turn on any lights on entering the house. The dark, quiet atmosphere was a perfect setting for the mood I was in. I built a fire in the fireplace and pulled up my favorite rocker.

As I sat there in the silence, the fire grew larger. It crackled and popped. Firelight shadows began to shimmer and dance around the room. The warm, comfortable heat felt good.

I struck a match to light my pipe. As I did, two beautiful cups gleamed from the mantel. I held the match up so I could get a better look. There they were, sitting side by side. One was large with long, upright handles that stood out like wings on a morning dove. The highly polished surface gleamed and glistened with a golden sheen. The other was smaller and made of silver. It was neat and trim, and sparkled like a white star in the heavens.

I got up and took them down. There was a story in those cups—a story that went back more than a half century.

As I caressed the smooth surfaces, my mind drifted back through the years, back to my boyhood days. How wonderful the memories were. Piece by piece the story unfolded.

II

I SUPPOSE THERE'S A TIME in practically every young boy's life when he's affected by that wonderful disease of puppy love. I don't mean the kind a boy has for the pretty little girl that lives down the road. I mean the real kind, the kind that has four small feet and a wiggly tail, and sharp little teeth that can gnaw on a boy's finger; the kind a boy can romp and play with, even eat and sleep with.

I was ten years old when I first became infected with this terrible disease. I'm sure no boy in the world had it worse than I did. It's not easy for a young boy to want a dog and not be able to have one. It starts gnawing on his heart, and gets all mixed up in his dreams. It gets worse and worse, until finally it becomes almost unbearable.

If my dog-wanting had been that of an ordinary boy, I'm sure my mother and father would have gotten me a puppy, but my wants were different. I didn't want just one dog. I wanted two, and not just any kind of a dog. They had to be a special kind and a special breed.

I had to have some dogs. I went to my father and had a talk with him. He scratched his head and thought it over.

"Well, Billy," he said, "I heard that Old Man Hatfield's collie is going to have pups. I'm sure I can get one of them for you."

He may as well have poured cold water on me. "Papa," I said, "I don't want an old collie dog. I want hounds—coon hounds—and I want two of them."

I could tell by the look on his face that he wanted to help me, but couldn't.

He said, "Billy, those kind of dogs cost money, and that's something we don't have right now. Maybe some day when we can afford it, you can have them, but not right now."

I didn't give up. After my talk with Papa, I went to Mama. I fared no better there. Right off she said I was too young to be hunting with hounds. Besides, a hunter needed a gun, and that was one thing I couldn't have, not until I was twenty-one anyway.

I couldn't understand it. There I was sitting right in the middle of the finest hunting country in the world and I didn't even have a dog.

Our home was in a beautiful valley far back in the rugged Ozarks. The country was new and sparsely settled. The land we lived on was Cherokee land, allotted to my mother because of the Cherokee blood that flowed in her veins. It lay in a strip from the foothills of the mountains to the banks of the Illinois River in northeastern Oklahoma.

The land was rich, black, and fertile. Papa said it would grow hair on a crosscut saw. He was the first man to stick the cold steel point of a turning plow into the virgin soil.

Mama had picked the spot for our log house. It nestled at the edge of the foothills in the mouth of a small canyon, and was surrounded by a grove of huge red oaks. Behind our house one could see miles and miles of the mighty Ozarks. In the spring the aromatic scent of wild flowers, redbuds, papaws, and dogwoods, drifting on the wind currents, spread over the valley and around our home.

Below our fields, twisting and winding, ran the clear blue waters of the Illinois River. The banks were cool and shady. The rich bottom land near the river was studded with tall sycamores, birches, and box elders.

To a ten-year-old country boy it was the most beautiful place in the whole wide world, and I took advantage of it all. I roamed the hills and the river bottoms. I knew every game trail in the thick canebrakes, and every animal track that was pressed in the mud along the riverbanks.

The ones that fascinated me the most were the baby-like tracks of a river coon. I'd lie for hours examining them. Before leaving, I'd take a switch and sweep them all away. These I called my "trail looks." The next day I'd hurry back, and sure enough, nine times out of ten, there in the clean-swept ground I would again find the tracks of a ringtail coon.

I knew he had passed over the trail during the night. I could close my eyes and almost see him, humped up and waddling along, fishing under the banks with his delicate little paws for crawfish, frogs, and minnows.

I was a hunter from the time I could walk. I caught lizards on the rail fences, rats in the corn crib, and frogs in the little creek that ran through the fields. I was a young Daniel Boone.

As the days passed, the dog-wanting disease grew worse. I began to see dogs in my sleep. I went back to my father and mother. It was the same old story. Good hounds cost money, and they just didn't have it.

My dog-wanting became so bad I began to lose weight and my food didn't taste good any more. Mama noticed this and she had a talk with Papa.

"You're going to have to do something," she said. "I never saw a boy grieve like that. It's not right, not right at all."

"I know," said Papa, "and I feel just as badly as you do, but what can I do? You know we don't have that kind of money."

"I don't care," said Mama. "You've got to do something. I can't stand to see him cry like that. Besides he's getting to be a problem. I can't get my work done. He follows me around all day long begging for hounds."

"I offered to get him a dog," said Papa, "but he doesn't want just any kind of dog. He wants hounds, and they cost money. Do you know what the Parker boys paid for those two hounds they bought? Seventy-five dollars! If I had that much money, I'd buy another mule. I sure do need one."

I had overheard this conversation from another room. At first it made me feel pretty good. At least I was getting to be a problem. Then I didn't feel so good. I knew my mother and father were poor and didn't have any money. I began to feel sorry for them and myself.

After thinking it over, I figured out a way to help. Even though it was a great sacrifice, I told Papa I had decided I didn't want two hounds. One would be enough. I saw the hurt in his eyes. It made me feel like someone was squeezing water out of my heart.

Papa set me on his lap and we had a good talk. He told me how hard times were, and that it looked like a man couldn't get a fair price for anything he raised. Some of the farmers had quit farming and were cutting railroad ties so they could feed their families. If things didn't get better, that's what he'd have to do. He said he'd give anything if he could get some good hounds for me, but there didn't seem to be any way he could right then.

I went off to bed with my heart all torn up in little pieces, and cried myself to sleep.

The next day Papa had to go to the store. Late that evening I saw him coming back. As fast as I could, I ran to meet him, expecting a sack of candy. Instead he handed me three small steel traps.

If Santa Claus himself had come down out of the mountains, reindeer and all, I would not have been more pleased. I jumped up and down, and cried a whole bucketful of tears. I hugged him and told him what a wonderful papa he was.

He showed me how to set them by mashing the spring down with my foot, and how to work the trigger. I took them to bed with me that night.

The next morning I started trapping around the barn. The first thing I caught was Samie, our house cat. If this didn't cause a commotion! I didn't intend to catch him. I was trying to catch a rat, but somehow he came nosing around and got in my trap.

My sisters started bawling and yelling for Mama. She came running, wanting to know what in the world was going on. None of us had to tell her. Samie told her with his spitting and squalling.

He was mad. He couldn't understand what that thing was that was biting his foot, and he was making an awful fuss about it. His tail was as big as a wet corncob and every hair on his small body was sticking straight up. He spit and yowled and dared anyone to get close to him.

My sisters yelled their fool heads off, all the time saying, "Poor Samie! Poor Samie!"

Mama shushed them up and told me to go get the forked stick from under the clothesline. I ran and got it.

Mama was the best helper a boy ever had. She put the forked end over Samie's neck and pinned him to the ground.

It was bad enough for the trap to be biting his foot, but to have his neck pinned down that way was too much. He threw a fit. I never heard such a racket in all my life.

It wasn't long until everything on the place was all spooked up. The chickens started cackling and flew way up on the hillside. Daisy, our milk cow, all but tore the barn lot up and refused to give any milk that night. Sloppy Ann, our hog, started running in circles, squealing and grunting.

Samie wiggled and twisted. He yowled and spit, but it didn't do him any good. Mama was good and stout. She held him down, tight to the ground. I ran in and put my foot on the trap spring, mashed it down, and released his foot. With one loud squall, he scooted under the barn.

After it was all over, Mama said, "I don't think you'll have any more trouble with that cat. I think he has learned his lesson."

How wrong Mama was. Samie was one of those nosy kind of cats. He would lie up on the red oak limbs and watch every move I made.

I found some slick little trails out in our garden down under some tall hollyhocks. Thinking they were game trails, and not knowing they were Samie's favorite hunting trails, I set my traps. Samie couldn't understand what I was doing out there, messing around his hunting territory. He went to investigate.

It wasn't long until I had him limping with all four feet. Every time Papa saw Samie lying around in the warm sun with his feet wrapped up in turpentine rags, he would laugh until big tears rolled down his cheeks.

Mama had another talk with Papa. She said he was going to have to say something to me, because if I caught that cat one more time, it would drive her out of her mind.

Papa told me to be a little more careful where I set my traps.

"Papa," I said, "I don't want to catch Samie, but he's the craziest cat I ever saw. He sees everything I do, and just has to go sniffing around."

Papa looked over at Samie. He was lying all sprawled out in the sunshine with all four paws bandaged and sticking straight up. His long tail was swishing this way and that.

"You see, Papa," I said, "he's watching me right now, just waiting for me to set my traps."

Papa walked off toward the barn. I heard him laughing fit to kill.

It finally got too tough for Samie. He left home. Oh, he came in once in a while, all long and lean looking, but he never was the same friendly cat any more. He was nervous and wouldn't let anyone pet him. He would gobble down his milk and then scoot for the timber.

Once I decided to make friends with him because I felt bad about catching him in my traps. I reached out my hand to rub his back. He swelled up like a sitting hen. His eyeballs got all green, and he growled way down deep. He spat at me, and drew back his paw like he was going to knock my head off. I decided I'd better leave him alone.

In no time at all I cleaned out the rats. Then something bad happened. I caught one of Mama's prize hens. I got one of those "young man peach tree" switchings over that.

Papa told me to go down in the canebrakes back of our fields and trap. This opened up all kinds of new wonders. I caught opossums, skunks, rabbits, and squirrels.

Papa showed me how to skin my game. In neat little rows I tacked the hides on the smokehouse wall. I'd stand for hours and admire my magnificent trophies.

There was only one thing wrong. I didn't have a big coonskin to add to my collection. I couldn't trap old Mister Ringtail. He was too smart for me. He'd steal the bait from the traps, spring the triggers, and sometimes even turn them over.

Once I found a small stick standing upright in one of my traps. I showed it to Papa. He laughed and said the stick must have fallen from a tree. It made no difference what Papa said. I was firmly convinced that a smart old coon had deliberately poked that stick in my trap.

The traps helped my dog-wanting considerably, but like a new toy, the newness wore off and I was right back where I started from. Only this time it was worse, much worse. I had been exposed to the feel of wildlife.

I started pestering Mama again. She said, "Oh, no! Not that again. I thought you'd be satisfied with the traps. No, Billy, I don't want to hear any more about hounds."

I knew Mama meant what she said. This broke my heart. I

decided I'd leave home. I sneaked out a quart jar of peaches, some cold corn bread, and a few onions, and started up the hollow back of our house. I had it all figured out. I'd go away off to some big town, get a hundred dogs, and bring them all back with me.

I made it all right until I heard a timber wolf howl. This stopped my home-leaving.

When the hunting season opened that fall, something happened that was almost more than I could stand. I was lying in bed one night trying to figure out a way I could get some dogs when I heard the deep baying of a coon hound. I got up and opened my window. It came again. The deep voice rang loud and clear in the frosty night. Now and then I could hear the hunter whooping to him.

The hound hunted all night. He quit when the roosters started crowing at daybreak. The hunter and the hound weren't the only ones awake that night. I stayed up and listened to them until the last tones of the hound's voice died away in the daylight hours.

That morning I was determined to have some hounds. I went again to Mama. This time I tried bribery. I told her if she'd get me a hunting dog, I'd save the money I earned from my furs, and buy her a new dress and a boxful of pretty hats.

That time I saw tears in her eyes. It made me feel all empty inside and I cried a little, too. By the time she was through kissing me and talking to me, I was sure I didn't need any dogs at all. I couldn't stand to see Mama cry.

The next night I heard the hound again. I tried to cover my head with a pillow to shut out the sound. It was no use. His voice seemed to bore its way through the pillow and ring in my ears. I had to get up and again go to the window. I'm sure if that coon hunter had known that he was slowly killing a ten-year-old boy, he would have put a muzzle on his hound.

Sleep was out of the question. Even on nights when I couldn't hear the hound, I couldn't sleep. I was afraid if I did, he would come and I would miss hearing him.

By the time hunting season was over, I was a nervous wreck. My eyes were red and bloodshot. I had lost weight and was as thin as a bean pole. Mama checked me over. She looked at my tongue and turned back one of my eyelids.

"If I didn't know better," she said, "I'd swear you weren't sleeping well. Are you?"

"Why, Mama," I said, "I go to bed, don't I? What does a boy go to bed for if it isn't to sleep?"

By the little wrinkles that bunched up on her forehead, I could tell that Mama wasn't satisfied. Papa came in during one of these inspections. Mama told him she was worried about my health.

"Aw," he said, "there's nothing wrong with him. It's just because he's been cooped up all winter. A boy needs sunshine, and exercise. He's almost eleven now, and I'm going to let him help me in the fields this summer. That will put the muscles back on him."

I thought this was wonderful. I'd finally grown up to be a man. I was going to help Papa with the farm.

III

THE DOG-WANTING DISEASE never did leave me altogether. With the new work I was doing, helping Papa, it just kind of burned itself down and left a big sore on my heart. Every time I'd see a coon track down in our fields, or along the riverbanks, the old sore would get all festered up and start hurting again.

Just when I had given up all hope of ever owning a good hound, something wonderful happened. The good Lord figured I had hurt enough, and it was time to lend a helping hand.

It all started one day while I was hoeing corn down in our field close to the river. Across the river, a party of fishermen had been camped for several days. I heard the old Maxwell car as it snorted and chugged its way out of the bottoms. I knew they were leaving. Throwing down my hoe, I ran down to the river and waded across at a place called the Shannon Ford. I hurried to the camp ground.

It was always a pleasure to prowl where fishermen had camped. I usually could find things: a fish line, or a forgotten fish pole. On one occasion, I found a beautiful knife stuck in the bark of a sycamore tree, forgotten by a careless fisherman. But on that day, I found the greatest of treasures, a sportsman's magazine, discarded by the campers. It was a real treasure for a country boy. Because of that magazine, my entire life was changed.

I sat down on an old sycamore log, and started thumbing through the leaves. On the back pages of the magazine, I came to the "For Sale" section—"Dogs for Sale"—every kind of dog. I read on and on. They had dogs I had never heard of, names I couldn't make out. Far down in the right-hand corner, I found an ad that took my breath away. In small letters, it read: "Registered redbone coon hound pups—twenty-five dollars each."

The advertisement was from a kennel in Kentucky. I read it over and over. By the time I had memorized the ad, I was seeing dogs, hearing dogs, and even feeling them. The magazine was forgotten. I was lost in thought. The brain of an eleven-year-old boy can dream some fantastic dreams.

How wonderful it would be if I could have two of those pups. Every boy in the country but me had a good hound or two. But fifty dollars—how could I ever get fifty dollars? I knew I couldn't expect help from Mama and Papa.

I remembered a passage from the Bible my mother had read to us: "God helps those who help themselves." I thought of the words. I mulled them over in my mind. I decided I'd ask God to help me. There on the banks of the Illinois River, in the cool shade of the tall white sycamores, I asked God to help me get two hound pups. It wasn't much of a prayer, but it did come right from the heart.

When I left the camp ground of the fishermen, it was late. As I walked along, I could feel the hard bulge of the magazine jammed deep in the pocket of my overalls. The beautiful silence that follows the setting sun had settled over the river bottoms. The coolness of the rich, black soil felt good to my bare feet.

It was the time of day when all furried things come to life. A big swamp rabbit hopped out on the trail, sat on his haunches, stared at me, and then scampered away. A mother gray squirrel ran out on the limb of a burr oak tree. She barked a warning to the four furry balls behind her. They melted from sight in the thick green. A silent gray shadow drifted down from the top of a tall sycamore. There was a squeal and a beating of wings. I heard the tinkle of a bell in the distance ahead. I knew it was Daisy, our milk cow. I'd have to start her on the way home.

I took the magazine from my pocket and again I read the ad. Slowly a plan began to form. I'd save the money. I could sell stuff to the fishermen: crawfish, minnows, and fresh vegetables. In berry season, I could sell all the berries I could pick at my grandfather's store. I could trap in the winter. The more I planned, the more real it became. There was the way to get those pups—save my money.

I could almost feel the pups in my hands. I planned the little doghouse, and where to put it. Collars I could make myself. Then the thought came, "What could I name them?" I tried name after name, voicing them out loud. None seemed to fit. Well, there would be plenty of time for names.

Right now there was something more important—fifty dollars—a fabulous sum—a fortune—far more money than I had ever seen. Somehow, some way, I was determined to have it. I had twenty-three cents—a dime I had earned running errands for my grandpa, and thirteen cents a fisherman had given me for a can of worms.

The next morning I went to the trash pile behind the barn. I was looking for a can—my bank. I picked up several, but they didn't seem to be what I wanted. Then I saw it, an old K. C. Baking Powder can. It was perfect, long and slender, with a good tight lid. I took it down to the creek and scrubbed it with sand until it was bright and new-looking.

I dropped the twenty-three cents in the can. The coins looked so small lying there on the shiny bottom, but to me it was a good start. With my finger, I tried to measure how full it would be with fifty dollars in it.

Next, I went to the barn and up in the loft. Far back over the hay and up under the eaves, I hid my can. I had a start toward making my dreams come true—twenty-three cents. I had a good bank, safe from the rats and from the rain and snow.

All through that summer I worked like a beaver. In the small creek that wormed its way down through our fields, I caught crawfish with my bare hands. I trapped minnows with an old screen-wire trap I made myself, baited with yellow corn bread from my mother's kitchen. These were sold to the fishermen, along with fresh vegetables and roasting ears. I tore my way through the blackberry patches until my hands and feet were scratched raw and red from the thorns. I tramped the hills seeking out the huckleberry bushes. My grandfather paid me ten cents a bucket for my berries.

Once Grandpa asked me what I did with the money I earned. I told him I was saving it to buy some hunting dogs. I asked him if he would order them for me when I had saved enough. He said he would. I asked him not to say anything to my father. He promised me he wouldn't. I'm sure Grandpa paid little attention to my plans.

That winter I trapped harder than ever with the three little traps I owned. Grandpa sold my hides to fur buyers who came to his store all through the fur season. Prices were cheap: fifteen cents for a large opossum hide, twenty-five for a good skunk hide. Little by little, the nickels and dimes added up. The old K. C. Baking Powder can grew heavy. I would heft its weight in the palm of my hand. With a straw, I'd measure from the lip of the can to the money. As the months went by, the straws grew shorter and shorter.

The next summer I followed the same routine.

"Would you like to buy some crawfish or minnows? Maybe you'd like some fresh vegetables or roasting ears."

The fishermen were wonderful, as true sportsmen are. They seemed to sense the urgency in my voice and always bought my wares. However, many was the time I'd find my vegetables left in the abandoned camp.

There never was a set price. Anything they offered was good enough for me.

A year passed. I was twelve. I was over the halfway mark. I had twenty-seven dollars and forty-six cents. My spirits soared. I worked harder.

Another year crawled slowly by, and then the great day came. The long hard grind was over. I had it—my fifty dollars! I cried as I counted it over and over.

As I set the can back in the shadowy eaves of the barn, it seemed to glow with a radiant whiteness I had never seen before. Perhaps it was all imagination. I don't know.

Lying back in the soft hay, I folded my hands behind my head, closed my eyes, and let my mind wander back over the two long years. I thought of the fishermen, the blackberry patches, and the huckleberry hills. I thought of the prayer I had said when I asked God to help me get two hound pups. I knew He had surely helped, for He had given me the heart, courage, and determination.

Early the next morning, with the can jammed deep in the pocket of my overalls, I flew to the store. As I trotted along, I whistled and sang. I felt as big as the tallest mountain in the Ozarks.

Arriving at my destination, I saw two wagons were tied up at the hitching rack. I knew some farmers had come to the store, so I waited until they left. As I walked in, I saw my grandfather behind the counter. Tugging and pulling, I worked the can out of my pocket and dumped it out in front of him and looked up.

Grandpa was dumbfounded. He tried to say something, but it wouldn't come out. He looked at me, and he looked at the pile of coins. Finally, in a voice much louder than he ordinarily used, he asked, "Where did you get all this?"

"I told you, Grandpa," I said, "I was saving my money so I could buy two hound pups, and I did. You said you would order them for me. I've got the money and now I want you to order them."

Grandpa stared at me over his glasses, and then back at the money.

"How long have you been saving this?" he asked.

"A long time, Grandpa," I said.

"How long?" he asked.

I told him, "Two years."

His mouth flew open and in a loud voice he said, "Two years!"

I nodded my head.

The way my grandfather stared at me made me uneasy. I was on needles and pins. Taking his eyes from me, he glanced back at the money. He saw the faded yellow piece of paper sticking out from the coins. He worked it out, asking as he did, "What's this?"

I told him it was the ad, telling where to order my dogs.

He read it, turned it over, and glanced at the other side.

I saw the astonishment leave his eyes and the friendly-old-grandfather look come back. I felt much better.

Dropping the paper back on the money, he turned, picked up an old turkey-feather duster, and started dusting where there was no dust. He kept glancing at me out of the corner of his eye as he walked slowly down to the other end of the store, dusting here and there.

He put the duster down, came from behind the counter, and walked up to me. Laying a friendly old work-calloused hand on my head, he changed the conversation altogether, saying, "Son, you need a haircut."

I told him I didn't mind. I didn't like my hair short; flies and mosquitoes bothered me.

He glanced down at my bare feet and asked, "How come your feet are cut and scratched like that?"

I told him it was pretty tough picking blackberries barefoot. He nodded his head.

It was too much for my grandfather. He turned and walked away. I saw the glasses come off, and the old red handkerchief come out. I heard the good excuse of blowing his nose. He stood for several seconds with his back toward me. When he turned around, I noticed his eyes were moist.

In a quavering voice, he said, "Well, Son, it's your money. You worked for it, and you worked hard. You got it honestly, and you want some dogs. We're going to get those dogs. Be damned! Be damned!"

That was as near as I ever came to hearing my grandfather curse, if you can call it cursing.

He walked over and picked up the ad again, asking, "Is this two years old, too?"

I nodded.

"Well," he said, "the first thing we have to do is write this outfit. There may not even be a place like this in Kentucky any more. After all, a lot of things can happen in two years."

Seeing that I was worried, he said, "Now you go on home. I'll write to these kennels and I'll let you know when I get an answer. If we can't get the dogs there, we can get them someplace else. And I don't think, if I were you, I'd let my Pa know anything about this right now. I happen to know he wants to buy that red mule from Old Man Potter."

I told him I wouldn't, and turned to leave the store.

As I reached the door, my grandfather said in a loud voice, "Say, it's been a long time since you've had any candy, hasn't it?"

I nodded my head.

He asked, "How long?"

I told him, "A long time."

"Well," he said, "we'll have to do something about that."

Walking over behind the counter, he reached out and got a sack. I noticed it wasn't one of the nickel sacks. It was one of the quarter kind.

My eyes never left my grandfather's hand. Time after time, it dipped in and out of the candy counter: peppermint sticks, jawbreakers, horehound, and gumdrops. The sack bulged. So did my eyes.

Handing the sack to me, he said, "Here. First big coon you catch with those dogs, you can pay me back."

I told him I would.

On my way home, with a jawbreaker in one side of my mouth and a piece of horehound in the other, I skipped and hopped, making half an effort to try to whistle and sing, and couldn't for the candy. I had the finest grandpa in the world and I was the happiest boy in the world.

I wanted to share my happiness with my sisters but decided not to say anything about ordering the pups.

Arriving home, I dumped the sack of candy out on the bed. Six little hands helped themselves. I was well repaid by the love and adoration I saw in the wide blue eyes of my three little sisters.

IV

Day after day, I flew to the store. Grandpa would shake his head. Then on a Monday, as I entered the store, I sensed a change in him. He was in high spirits, talking and laughing with half a dozen farmers. Every time I caught his eye, he would smile and wink at me. I thought the farmers would never leave, but finally the store was empty.

Grandpa told me the letter had come. The kennels were still there, and they had dogs for sale. He said he had made the mail buggy wait while he made out the order. And, another thing, the dog market had gone downhill. The price of dogs had dropped five dollars. He handed me a ten-dollar bill.

"Now, there's still one stump in the way," he said. "The mail buggy can't carry things like dogs, so they'll come as far as the depot at Tahlequah, but you'll get the notice here because I ordered them in your name."

I thanked my grandfather with all my heart and asked him how long I'd have to wait for the notice.

He said, "I don't know, but it shouldn't take more than a couple of weeks."

I asked how I was going to get my dogs out from Tahlequah.

"Well, there's always someone going in," he said, "and you could ride in with them."

That evening the silence of our supper was interrupted when I asked my father this question: "Papa, how far is it to Kentucky?"

I may as well have exploded a bomb. For an instant there was complete silence, and then my oldest sister giggled. The two little ones stared at me.

With a half-hearted laugh, my father said, "Well, now, I don't know, but it's a pretty good ways. What do you want to know for? Thinking of taking a trip to Kentucky?"

"No," I said. "I just wondered."

My youngest sister giggled and asked, "Can I go with you?" I glared at her.

Mama broke into the conversation, "I declare, what kind of a question is that? How far is it to Kentucky? I don't know what's gotten into that mind of yours lately. You go around like you were lost, and you're losing weight. You're as skinny as a rail, and look at that hair. Just last Sunday they had a haircutting over at Tom Rolland's place, but you couldn't go. You had to go prowling around the river and the woods."

I told Mama that I'd get a haircut next time they had a cutting. And I just heard some fellows talking about Kentucky up at the store, and wondered how far away it was. Much to my relief, the conversation was ended.

The days dragged by. A week passed and still no word about my dogs. Terrible thoughts ran through my mind. Maybe my dogs were lost; the train had a wreck; someone stole my money; or perhaps the mailman lost my order. Then, at the end of the second week, the notice came.

My grandfather told me that he had talked to Jim Hodges that day. He was going into town in about a week and I could ride in with him to pick up my dogs. Again I thanked my grandfather.

I started for home. Walking along in deep thought, I decided it was time to tell my father the whole story. I fully intended to tell him that evening. I tried several times, but somehow I couldn't. I wasn't scared of him, for he never whipped me. He was always kind and gentle, but for some reason, I don't know why, I just couldn't tell him.

That night, snuggled deep in the soft folds of a feather bed, I lay thinking. I had waited so long for my dogs, and I so desperately wanted to see them and hold them. I didn't want to wait a whole week.

In a flash I made up my mind. Very quietly I got up and put on my clothes. I sneaked into the kitchen and got one of Mama's precious flour sacks. In it I put six eggs, some leftover corn bread, a little salt, and a few matches. Next I went to the smokehouse and cut off a piece of salt pork. I stopped at the barn and picked up a gunny sack. I put the flour sack inside the gunny sack. This I rolled up and crammed lengthwise in the bib of my overalls.

I was on my way. I was going after my dogs.

Tahlequah was a small country town with a population of about eight hundred. By the road it was thirty-two miles away, but as the crow flies, it was only twenty miles. I went as the crow flies, straight through the hills.

Although I had never been to town in my life, I knew what direction to take. Tahlequah and the railroad lay on the other side of the river from our place. I had the Frisco Railroad on my right, and the Illinois River on my left. Not far from where the railroad crossed the river lay the town of Tahlequah. I knew if I bore to the right I would find the railroad, and if I bore to the left I had the river to guide me.

Some time that night, I crossed the river on a riffle somewhere in the Dripping Springs country. Coming out of the river bottoms, I scatted up a long hogback ridge, and broke out on top in the flats. In a mile-eating trot, I moved along. I had the wind of a deer, the muscles of a country boy, a heart full of dog love, and a strong determination. I wasn't scared of the darkness, or the mountains, for I was raised in those mountains.

On and on, mile after mile, I moved along. I saw faint gray streaks appear in the east. I knew daylight was close. My bare feet were getting sore from the flint rocks and saw briers. I stopped beside a mountain stream, soaked my feet in the cool water, rested for a spell, and then started on.

After leaving the mountain stream, my pace was much slower. The muscles of my legs were getting stiff. Feeling the pangs of hunger gnawing at my stomach, I decided I would stop and eat at the next stream I found. Then I remembered I had forgotten to include a can in which to boil my eggs.

I stopped and built a small fire. Cutting off a nice thick slab of salt pork, I roasted it, and with a piece of cold corn bread made a sandwich. Putting out my fire, I was on my way again. I ate as I trotted along. I felt much better.

I came into Tahlequah from the northeast. At the outskirts of town, I hid my flour sack and provisions, keeping the gunny sack. I walked into town.

I was scared of Tahlequah and the people. I had never seen such a big town and so many people. There was store after store, some of them two stories high. The wagon yard had wagons on top of wagons; teams, buggies, and horses.

Two young ladies about my age stopped, stared at me, and then giggled. My blood boiled, but I could understand. After all, I had three sisters and they were giggling all the time, too. I went on.

I saw a big man coming up the street. The bright shiny star on his vest looked as big as a bucket. I saw the long, black gun at his side and I froze in my tracks. I'd heard of sheriffs and marshals, but had never seen one. Stories repeated about them in the mountains told how fast they were with a gun, and how many men they had killed.

The closer he came, the more frightened I got. I knew it was the end for me. I could just see him aiming his big, black gun and shooting me between the eyes. It seemed like a miracle that he passed by, hardly glancing at me. Breathing a sigh, I walked on, seeing the wonders of the world.

Passing a large store window, I stopped and stared. There in the window was the most wonderful sight I had ever seen; everything under the sun; overalls, jackets, bolts of beautiful cloth, new harnesses, collars, bridles; and then my eyes did pop open. There were several guns and one of them had two barrels. I couldn't believe it—two barrels. I had seen several guns, but never one with two barrels.

Then I saw something else. The sun was just right, and the plate glass was a perfect mirror. I saw the full reflection of myself for the first time in my life.

I could see that I did look a little odd. My straw-colored hair was long and shaggy, and was bushed out like a corn tassle that had been hit by a wind. I tried to smooth it down with my hands. This helped some but not much. What it needed was a good combing and I had no comb.

My overalls were patched and faded but they were clean. My shirt had pulled out. I tucked it back in.

I took one look at my bare feet and winced. They were as brown as dead sycamore leaves. The spider-web pattern of raw, red scratches looked odd in the saddle-brown skin. I thought, "Well, I won't have to pick any more blackberries and the scratches will soon go away."

I pumped up one of my arms and thought surely the muscle was going to pop right through my thin blue shirt. I stuck out my tongue. It was as red as pokeberry juice and anything that color was supposed to be healthy.

After making a few faces at myself, I put my thumbs in my ears and was making mule ears when two old women came by. They stopped and stared at me. I stared back. As they turned to go on their way, I heard one of them say something to the other. The words were hard to catch, but I did hear one word: "Wild." I couldn't help grinning. They sounded just like Mama.

As I turned to leave, my eyes again fell on the overalls and the bolts of cloth. I thought of my mother, father, and sisters. Here was an opportunity to make amends for leaving home without telling anyone.

I entered the store. I bought a pair of overalls for Papa. After telling the storekeeper how big my mother and sisters were, I bought several yards of cloth. I also bought a large sack of candy.

Glancing down at my bare feet, the storekeeper said, "I have some good shoes."

I told him I didn't need any shoes.

He asked if that would be all.

I nodded.

He added up the bill. I handed him my ten dollars. He gave me my change.

After wrapping up the bundles, he helped me put them in my sack. Lifting it to my shoulder, I turned and left the store.

Out on the street, I picked out a friendly-looking old man and asked him where the depot was. He told me to go down to the last street and turn right, go as far as I could, and I couldn't miss it. I thanked him and started on my way.

Leaving the main part of town, I started up a long street through the residential section. I had never seen so many beautiful houses, and they were all different colors. The lawns were neat and clean and looked like green carpets. I saw a man pushing some kind of a mowing machine. I stopped to watch the whirling blades. He gawked at me. I hurried on.

I heard a lot of shouting and laughing ahead of me. Not wanting to miss anything, I walked a little faster. I saw what was making the noise. More kids than I had ever seen were playing around a big red brick building. I thought some rich man lived there and was giving a party for his children. Walking up to the edge of the playground, I stopped to watch.

The boys and girls were about my age, and were as thick as flies around a sorghum mill. They were milling, running, and jumping. Teeter-totters and swings were loaded down with them. Everyone was laughing and having a big time.

Over against the building, a large blue pipe ran up on an angle from the ground. A few feet from the top there was a bend in it. The pipe seemed to go into the building. Boys were crawling into its dark mouth. I counted nine of them. One boy stood about six feet from the opening with a stick in his hand.

Staring goggle-eyed, trying to figure out what they were doing, I got a surprise. Out of the hollow pipe spurted a boy. He sailed through the air and lit on his feet. The boy with the stick marked the ground where he landed. All nine of them came shooting out, one behind the other. As each boy landed, a new mark was scratched.

They ganged around looking at the lines. There was a lot of loud talking, pointing, and arguing. Then all lines were erased and a new scorekeeper was picked out. The others crawled back into the pipe.

I figured out how the game was played. After climbing to the top of the slide, the boys turned around and sat down. One at a time, they came flying down and out, feet first. The one that shot out the furthest was the winner. I thought how wonderful it would be if I could slide down just one time.

One boy, spying me standing on the corner, came over. Looking me up and down, he asked, "Do you go to school here?"

I said, "School?"

He said, "Sure. School. What did you think it was?"

"Oh. No, I don't go to school here."

"Do you go to Jefferson?"

"No. I don't go there either."

"Don't you go to school at all?"

"Sure I go to school."

"Where?"

"At home."

"You go to school at home?"

I nodded.

"What grade are you in?"

I said I wasn't in any grade.

Puzzled, he said, "You go to school at home, and don't know what grade you're in. Who teaches you?"

"My mother."

"What does she teach you?"

I said, "Reading, writing, and arithmetic, and I bet I'm just as good at it as you are."

He asked, "Don't you have any shoes?"

I said, "Sure, I have shoes."

"Why aren't you wearing them?"

"I don't wear shoes until it gets cold."

He laughed and asked where I lived.

I said, "Back in the hills."

He said, "Oh, you're a hillbilly."

He ran back to the mob. I saw him pointing at me and talking to several boys. They started my way, yelling, "Hillbilly, hillbilly."

Just before they reached me, a bell started ringing. Turning, they ran to the front of the building, lined up in two long lines, and marching like little tin soldiers disappeared inside the school.

The playground was silent. I was all alone, and felt lonely and sad.

I heard a noise on my right. I didn't have to turn around to recognize what it was. Someone was using a hoe. I'd know that sound if I heard it on a dark night. It was a little old white-headed woman working in a flower bed.

Looking again at the long, blue pipe, I thought, "There's no one around. Maybe I could have one slide anyway."

I eased over and looked up into the dark hollow. It looked scary, but I thought of all the other boys I had seen crawl into it. I could see the last mark on the ground, and thought, "I bet I can beat that."

Laying my sack down, I started climbing up. The farther I

went, the darker and more scary it got. Just as I reached the top, my feet slipped. Down I sailed. All the way down I tried to grab on to something, but there was nothing to grab.

I'm sure some great champions had slid out of that pipe, and no doubt more than one world record had been broken, but if someone had been there when I came out, I know the record I set would stand today in all its glory.

I came out just like I went in, feet first and belly down. My legs were spread out like a bean-shooter stalk. Arms flailing the air, I zoomed out and up. I seemed to hang suspended in air at the peak of my climb. I could see the hard-packed ground far below.

As I started down, I shut my eyes tight and gritted my teeth. This didn't seem to help. With a splattering sound, I landed. I felt the air whoosh out between my teeth. I tried to scream, but had no wind left to make a sound.

After bouncing a couple of times, I finally settled down to earth. I lay spread-eagled for a few seconds, and then slowly got to my knees.

Hearing loud laughter, I looked around. It was the little old lady with the hoe in her hand. She hollered and asked how I liked it. Without answering, I grabbed up my gunny sack and left. Far up the street, I looked back. The little old lady was sitting down, rocking with laughter.

I couldn't understand these town people. If they weren't staring at a fellow, they were laughing at him.

V

On ARRIVING AT THE DEPOT, my nerve failed me. I was afraid to go in. I didn't know what I was scared of, but I was scared.

Before going around to the front, I peeked in a window. The stationmaster was in his office looking at some papers. He was wearing a funny little cap that had no top in it. He looked friendly enough but I still couldn't muster up enough courage to go in.

I cocked my ear to see if I could hear puppies crying, but could hear nothing. A bird started chirping. It was a yellow canary in a cage. The stationmaster walked over and gave it some water. I thought, "Anyone that is kind to birds surely wouldn't be mean to a boy."

With my courage built up I walked around to the front and eased myself past the office. He glanced at me and turned back to the papers. I walked clear around the depot and again walked slowly past the office. Glancing from the corner of my eye, I saw the stationmaster looking at me and smiling. He opened the door and came out on the platform. I stopped and leaned against the building.

Yawning and stretching his arms, he said, "It sure is hot today. It doesn't look like it's ever going to rain."

I looked up at the sky and said, "Yes, sir. It is hot and we sure could do with a good rain. We need one bad up where I come from."

He asked me where I lived.

I told him, "Up the river a ways."

"You know," he said, "I have some puppies in there for a boy that lives up on the river. His name is Billy Colman. I know his dad, but never have seen the boy. I figured he would be in after them today."

On hearing this remark, my heart jumped clear up in my throat. I thought surely it was going to hop right out on the depot platform. I looked up and tried to tell him who I was, but something went wrong. When the words finally came out they sounded like the squeaky old pully on our well when Mama drew up a bucket of water.

I could see a twinkle in the stationmaster's eyes. He came over and laid his hand on my shoulder. In a friendly voice he said, "So you're Billy Colman. How is your dad?"

I told him Papa was fine and handed him the slip my grandpa had given me.

"They sure are fine-looking pups," he said. "You'll have to go around to the freight door."

I'm sure my feet never touched the ground as I flew around the building. He unlocked the door, and I stepped in, looking for my dogs. I couldn't see anything but boxes, barrels, old trunks, and some rolls of barbed wire.

The kindly stationmaster walked over to one of the boxes.

"Do you want box and all?" he asked.

I told him I didn't want the box. All I wanted was the dogs.

"How are you going to carry them?" he asked. "I think they're a little too young to follow."

I held out my gunny sack.

He looked at me and looked at the sack. Chuckling, he said, "Well, I guess dogs can be carried that way same as anything else, but we'll have to cut a couple of holes to stick their heads through so that they won't smother."

Getting a claw hammer, he started tearing off the top of the box. As nails gave way and boards splintered, I heard several puppy whimpers. I didn't walk over. I just stood and waited.

After what seemed like hours, the box was open. He reached in, lifted the pups out, and set them down on the floor.

"Well, there they are," he said. "What do you think of them?"

I didn't answer. I couldn't. All I could do was stare at them. They seemed to be blinded by the light and kept blinking their eyes. One sat down on his little rear and started crying. The other one was waddling around and whimpering.

I wanted so much to step over and pick them up. Several times I tried to move my feet, but they seemed to be nailed to the floor. I knew the pups were mine, all mine, yet I couldn't move. My heart started acting like a drunk grasshopper. I tried to swallow and couldn't. My Adam's apple wouldn't work.

One pup started my way. I held my breath. On he came until I felt a scratchy little foot on mine. The other pup followed. A warm puppy tongue caressed my sore foot.

I heard the stationmaster say, "They already know you."

I knelt down and gathered them in my arms. I buried my face between their wiggling bodies and cried. The stationmaster, sensing something more than just two dogs and a boy, waited in silence.

Rising with the two pups held close to my chest, I asked if I owed anything.

He said, "There is a small feed bill but I'll take care of it. It's not much anyway."

Taking his knife he cut two slits in the sack. He put the pups in it and worked their heads through the holes. As he handed the sack to me, he said, "Well, there you are. Good-bye and good hunting!"

Walking down the street toward town, I thought, "Now, maybe the people won't stare at me when they see what I've got. After all, not every boy owns two good hounds."

Turning the corner onto the main street, I threw out my chest.

I hadn't gone far before I realized that the reception I got wasn't what I thought it would be. People began to stop and stare, some even snickered. I couldn't understand why they were staring. Surely it couldn't be at the two beautiful hound pups sticking out of the gunny sack.

Thinking that maybe I had a hole in the seat of my britches, I looked over to my reflection in a plate-glass window. I craned my neck for a better view of my rear. I could see a patch there all right, and a few threadbare spots, but no whiteness was showing through. I figured that the people were just jealous because they didn't have two good hounds.

I saw a drunk coming. He was staggering all over the street.

Just as he was passing me I heard him stop. As I looked back I saw he was staring wide-eyed at my sack. Closing his eyes, he rubbed them with his hands. Opening them again he stared. Shaking his head, he staggered on down the street.

All around people began to roar with laughter. Someone shouted, "What's the matter, John? You seeing things today?"

I hurried on, wanting to get away from the stares and the snickers.

It wouldn't have happened again in a hundred years, but there they came. The same two old women I had met before. We stopped and had another glaring fight.

One said, "I declare."

The other one snorted, "Well, I never."

My face burned. I couldn't take any more. After all, a man can stand so much and no more. In a loud voice, I said, "You may have these people fooled with those expensive-looking feathers in your hats, but I know what they are. They're goose feathers painted with iodine."

One started to say something, but her words were drowned out by the roaring laughter from all around. Gathering up their long skirts, they swished on down the street.

All around me people began to shout questions and laugh. One wanted to know if I had the mother in the sack. Storekeepers stepped out and gawked. I could see the end of the street, but it looked as if it were a hundred miles away. My face was as red as a fox's tail. I ducked my head, tightened my grip on the sack, and walked on.

I don't know where they came from, but like chickens coming home to roost, they flocked around me. Most of them were about my age. Some were a little bigger, some smaller. They ganged around me, screaming and yelling. They started clapping their hands and chanting, "The dog boy has come to town. The dog boy has come to town."

My heart burst. Tears came rolling. The day I had waited for so long had turned black and ugly.

The leader of the gang was about my size. He had a dirty freckled face and his two front teeth were missing. I suppose he had lost them in a back alley fight. His shock of yellow sunburnt hair bobbed up and down as he skipped and jumped to the rhythm of the "dog boy" song. He wore a pair of cowboy boots. They were two sizes too big for him, no doubt handed down by an older brother.

He stomped on my right foot. I looked down and saw a drop of blood ooze out from under the broken nail. It hurt like the dickens but I gritted my teeth and walked on.

Freckle-face pulled the ear of my little girl pup. I heard her painful cry. That was too much. I hadn't worked two long hard years for my pups to have some freckle-faced punk pull their ears.

Swinging the sack from my shoulder, I walked over and set it down in a doorway. As I turned around to face the mob, I doubled up my fist, and took a Jack Dempsey stance.

Freckle-face said, "So you want to fight." He came in swinging.

I reached way back in Arkansas somewhere. By the time my fist had traveled all the way down to the Cherokee Strip, there was a lot of power behind it.

Smack on the end of Freck's nose it exploded. With a loud grunt he sat down in the dusty street. Grabbing his nose in both hands, he started rocking and moaning. I saw the blood squeeze out between his fingers.

Another one sailed in. He didn't want to fight. He wanted to wrestle. He stuck a finger in my mouth. I ground down. Shaking his hand and yelling like the hoot owls were after him, he ran across the street.

Another one bored in. I aimed for his eye, but my aim was a little low. It caught him in the Adam's apple. A sick look came over his face. Bending over, croaking like a bullfrog that had been caught by a water moccasin, he started going around in a circle.

But there were too many of them. By sheer weight and numbers, they pulled me down. I managed to twist over on my stomach and buried my face in my arms. I could feel them beating and kicking my body.

All at once the beating stopped. I heard loud cries from the gang. Turning over on my back, I was just in time to see the big marshal plant a number-twelve boot in the seat of the last kid. I just knew I was next. I wondered if he'd kick me while I was down.

I lay where I was. He started toward me. I closed my eyes.

I felt a hand as big as an anvil clamp on my shoulder. I thought, "He's going to stand me up, and then knock me down."

He raised me to a sitting position. His deep friendly voice said, "Are you all right, son?"

I opened my eyes. There was a smile on his wide rugged face. In a choking voice, I said, "Yes, sir. I'm all right."

He helped me to my feet. His big hands started brushing the dust from my clothes.

"Those kids are pretty tough, son," he said, "but they're really not bad. They'll grow up some day."

"Marshal," I said, "I wouldn't have fought them, but they pulled my pup's ears."

He looked over to my sack. One pup had worked its way almost out through the hole. The other one's head and two little paws were sticking out. Both of them were whimpering.

A smile spread all over the big marshal's face. "So that's what started the fight," he said.

Walking over, he knelt down and started petting the pups. "They're fine-looking dogs," he said. "Where did you get them?"

I told him I had ordered them from Kentucky.

"What did they cost you?" he asked.

"Forty dollars," I said.

He asked if my father had bought them for me.

"No," I said. "I bought them myself."

He asked me where I got the money.

"I worked and saved it," I said.

"It takes a long time to save forty dollars," he said.

"Yes," I said. "It took me two years."

"Two years!" he exclaimed.

I saw an outraged look come over the marshal's face. Reaching up, he pushed his hat back. He glanced up and down the street. I heard him mutter, "There's not a one in that bunch with that kind of grit."

Picking up my sack, I said, "Thanks for helping me out. I guess I'd better be heading for home."

He asked where I lived.

I said, "Up the river a way."

"Well, you've got time for a bottle of pop before you go, haven't you?"

I started to say "No," but looking at his big friendly smile, I smiled back and said, "I guess I have."

Walking into a general store, the marshal went over to a large red box and pulled back the lid. He asked what kind I wanted. I'd never had a bottle of pop in my life, and didn't know what to say.

Seeing my hesitation, he said, "This strawberry looks pretty good."

I said that would be fine.

The cool sweet pop felt wonderful to my hot dry throat. My dark little world had brightened up again. I had my pups, and had found a wonderful friend. I knew that the stories I had heard about marshals weren't true. Never again would I be scared when I saw one.

Back out on the street, I shook hands with the marshal, saying as I did, "If you're ever up in my part of the country come over and see me. You can find our place by asking at my grandfather's store."

"Store?" he asked. "Why, the only store upriver is about thirty miles from here."

"Yes," I said, "that's my grandpa's place."

He asked if I was afoot.

"Yes," I said.

"You won't make it tonight," he said. "Will you?"

"No," I said. "I intend to camp out somewhere."

I saw he was bothered.

"I'll be all right," I said. "I'm not scared of the mountains."

He looked at me and at my pups. Taking off his hat, he scratched his head. Chuckling deep down in his barrel-like chest, he said, "Yes, I guess you will be all right. Well, good-bye and good luck! If you're ever in town again look me up."

From far down the street, I looked back. The marshal was still standing where I had left him. He waved his hand. I waved back.

On the outskirts of town, I stopped and picked up a can and my provisions.

I hadn't gone far before I realized that I had undertaken a tough job. The sack became heavier and heavier.

For a while my pups cried and whimpered. They had long

since pulled their heads back in the sack. I would peek in at them every once in a while. They were doing all right. Curled up into two little round balls on my bundles, they were fast asleep.

Deep in the heart of the Sparrow Hawk Mountains, night overtook me. There, in a cave with a stream close by, I put up for the night.

Taking my pups and bundles from the gunny sack, I used it to gather leaves to make us a bed. My pups followed me on every trip, whimpering and crying, tumbling and falling over sticks and rocks.

After the bed was made I built a fire. In a can of water from the mountain stream, I boiled three eggs. Next, I boiled half of the remaining salt pork. Cutting the meat up in small pieces, I fed it to my pups. Each of us had a piece of candy for dessert. My pups enjoyed the candy. With their needle-sharp teeth, they gnawed and worried with it until it was melted away.

While they were busy playing, I dragged up several large timbers and built a fire which would last for hours. In a short time the cave grew warm and comfortable from the heat. The leaves were soft, and felt good to my tired body and sore feet. As I lay stretched out, my pups crawled all over me. I played with them. They would waddle up to the front of the cave, look at the fire, and come scampering back to roll and play in the soft leaves.

I noticed the boy dog was much larger than the girl dog. He was a deeper red in color. His chest was broad and solid. His puppy muscles knotted and rippled under the velvety skin. He was different in every way. He would go closer to the fire. I saw right away he was bold and aggressive.

Once he went around the fire and ventured out into the darkness. I waited to see if he would come back. He came wobbling to the mouth of the cave, but hesitated there. He made several attempts to come back, but the flames were leaping higher by the minute. The space between the fire and the wall of the cave was much hotter than when he had ventured out. Whimpering and crying, he kept trying to get around the fire. I said not a word; just watched.

Puppy though he was, he did something which brought a smile

to my face. Getting as close as he could to the side of the cave, he turned his rear to the fire. Hopping sideways, yipping at every jump, he made it through the heat and sailed into the pile of leaves. He had had enough. Curling up in a ball close to me, he went to sleep.

The girl pup was small and timid. Her legs and body were short. Her head was small and delicate. She must have been a runt in the litter. I didn't have to look twice to see that what she lacked in power, she made up in brains. She was a much smarter dog than the boy dog, more sure of herself, more cautious. I knew when the trail became tough, she would be the one to unravel it.

I knew I had a wonderful combination. In my dogs, I had not only the power, but the brains along with it.

I was a tired boy. My legs were stiff, and my feet sore and throbbing. My shoulders were red and raw from the weight of the sack. I covered my pups up in the leaves and moved my body as close to them as I could. I knew as night wore on, and the fire died down, the chill would come. Tired but happy, I fell asleep.

Along in the silent hours of night, I was awakened. I opened my eyes, but didn't move. I lay and listened, trying to figure out what it was that had aroused me. At first I thought one of my pups had awakened me by moving and whimpering. I discarded this thought for I could see that they were both fast asleep. I decided it was my imagination working.

My fire had burned down, leaving only a glowing red body of coals. The cave was dark and silent. Chill from the night had crept in. I was on the point of getting up to rebuild my fire, when I heard what had awakened me. At first I thought it was a woman screaming. I listened. My heart began to pound. I could feel the strain all over my body as nerves grew tighter and tighter.

It came again, closer this time. The high pitch of the scream shattered the silence of the quiet night. The sound seemed to be all around us. It screamed its way into the cave and rang like a blacksmith's anvil against the rock walls. The blood froze in my veins. I was terrified. Although I had never heard one, I knew what it was. It was the scream of a mountain lion.

The big cat screamed again. Leaves boiled and stirred where

my pups were. In the reflection of the glowing coals, I could see that one was sitting up. It was the boy dog. A leaf had become entangled in the fuzzy hair of a floppy ear. The ear flicked. The leaf dropped.

Again the hellish scream rang out over the mountains. Leaves flew as my pup left the bed. I jumped up and tried to call him back.

Reaching the mouth of the cave, he stopped. Raising his small red head high in the air, he bawled his challenge to the devil cat. The bawl must have scared him as much as it had startled me. He came tearing back. The tiny hairs on his back were standing on end.

My father had told me lions were scared of fire. I started throwing on more wood. I was glad I'd dragged up a good supply while making camp.

Hearing a noise from the bed, I looked back. The girl pup, hearing the commotion, had gotten up and joined the boy dog. They were sitting side by side with their bodies stiff and rigid. Their beady little eyes bored into the darkness beyond the cave. The moist tips of their little black noses wiggled and twisted as if trying to catch a scent.

What I saw in my pups gave me courage. My knees quit shaking and my heart stopped pounding.

I figured the lion had scented my pups. The more I thought about anything harming them, the madder I got. I was ready to die for my dogs.

Every time the big cat screamed, the boy dog would run to the mouth of the cave and bawl back at him. I started whooping and throwing rocks down the mountainside, hoping to scare the lion away. Through the long hours of the night, I kept this up.

The lion prowled around us, screaming and growling; first on the right, and then on the left, and above and below. In the wee hours of morning, he gave up and left to stalk other parts of the mountains. I'm sure he thought he didn't stand a chance against two vicious hounds and a big hunter.

VI

AFTER THE TERRIFYING NIGHT, the bright morning sun was a welcome sight. I fixed breakfast and soon we were on our way. I tried to get the pups to follow me, so as to lighten my load. They would for a way, and then, sitting down on their rears, they would cry and whimper. Back in the sack they would go, with their heads sticking out of the holes and their long ears flopping. I moved on.

About midday I entered country I knew. I wasn't far from home. I dropped down out of the mountains into the bottoms far above the place I had crossed the river on my way to town.

Staying on the left of the river, I followed its course past several campgrounds, but didn't stop until I came to the one where I had found the magazine. Here I took the pups out of the sack and sat down in the warm sand.

As the afternoon wore on, I sat there deep in thought. I was trying to think what I was going to tell my mother and father. I could think of nothing. Finally I decided I would just tell them the truth, and with the help of the new overalls, cloth, and candy, I would weather the storm.

My pups were having a big time playing. With their little front paws locked around each other, they were growling, rolling, and chewing on one another. They looked so cute, I laughed out loud.

While I was watching their romping, the thought came, "I haven't named them."

I went over the list of names. For him, I tried "Red," "Bugle," "Lead," name after name as before. For her, I tried "Susie," "Mabel," "Queen," all kinds of girl names. None seemed to fit.

Still mumbling names over and over, I glanced up. There, carved in the white bark of a sycamore tree, was a large heart. In the center of the heart were two names, "Dan" and "Ann." The name Dan was a little larger than Ann. It was wide and bold. The scar stood out more. The name Ann was small, neat, and even. I stared unbelieving—for there were my names. They were perfect.

I walked over and picked up my pups. Looking at him, I said, "Your name is Dan. I'll call you Old Dan." Looking at her, I said, "Your name, little girl, is Ann. I'll call you Little Ann."

It was then I realized it was all too perfect. Here in this fishermen's camp, I had found the magazine and the ad. I looked over at the old sycamore log. There I had asked God to help me get two hound pups. There were the pups, rolling and playing in the warm sand. I thought of the old K. C. Baking Powder can, and the fishermen. How freely they had given their nickels and dimes.

I looked up again to the names carved in the tree. Yes, it was all there like a large puzzle. Piece by piece, each fit perfectly until the puzzle was complete. It could not have happened without the help of an unseen power.

I stayed at the campground until dark. I knew I had to go home but I put it off as long as I could. The crying of the pups, telling me they were hungry, made up my mind for me. I knew the time had come for me to face my mother and father.

I sacked up my dogs and waded the river. As I came out of the bottoms, I could see the lamplight glow from the windows of our home. One of the small yellow squares darkened for an instant. Someone had walked across the floor. I wondered who it was. I heard Daisy, our milk cow, moo. I was thinking so hard of what I would say, it startled me for a second.

Reaching the gate to our house, I stopped. I had never thought our home very pretty, but that night it looked different. It looked clean and neat and peaceful, nestled there in the foothills of the Ozarks. Yes, on that night I was proud of our home.

My bare feet made no noise as I crossed the porch. With my free hand, I reached and pulled the leather that worked the latch. Slowly the door swung inward.

I couldn't see my father or sisters. They were too far to the right of me, but my mother was directly in front of the door, sitting in her old cane-bottom rocker, knitting.

She looked up. I saw all the worry and grief leave her eyes. Her head bowed down. The knitting in her hands came up to cover her face. I stepped inside the room. I wanted to run to her and comfort her and tell her how sorry I was for all the worry and grief I had caused her.

The booming voice of my father shook me from my trance. He said, "Well, what have you got there?"

Laughing, he got up from his chair and came over to me. He reached and took the sack from my shoulder.

"When we started looking for you," he said, "I went to the store and your grandpa told me all about it. It wasn't too hard to figure out what you had done, but you should have told us."

I ran to my mother and, dropping to my knees, I buried my face in her lap.

As Mama patted my head, I heard her say in a quavering voice, "Oh, why didn't you tell us? Why?"

I couldn't answer.

Between sobs, I heard the squeals of delight from my sisters as they fondled my pups.

I heard my father say, "What's this other stuff you've got?"

Without raising my head from my mother's lap, in a choking voice I said, "One is for you, one is for Mama, and the other is for the girls."

I heard the snapping of string and the rattle of paper. The oh's and ah's from my sisters were wonderful to hear.

Papa came over to Mama. Laying the cloth on the arm of her chair, he said, "Well, you've been wanting a new dress. Here is enough cloth to make half a dozen dresses."

Realizing that everything was forgiven, I stood up and dried my eyes. Papa was pleased with his new overalls. My sisters forgot the pups for the candy. The light that was shining from my mother's eyes, as she fingered the cheap cotton cloth, was something I will never forget.

Mama warmed some milk for the pups. They drank until their little tummies were tight and round.

As I ate, Papa sat down at the table and started talking man-talk to me. He asked, "How are things in town?"

I told him it was boiling with people. The wagon yard was full of wagons and teams.

He asked if I had seen anyone I knew.

I told him I hadn't, but the stationmaster had asked about him.

He asked me where I had spent the night.

I told him about the cave in the Sparrow Hawk Mountains. He said that must have been the one called "Robber's Cave."

My youngest sister piped up, "Did you stay all night with some robbers?"

My oldest sister said, "Silly, that was a long time ago. There aren't any robbers there now."

The other one put her nickel's worth in, "Weren't you scared?"

"No," I said, "I wasn't scared of staying in the cave, but I heard a mountain lion scream and it scared me half to death."

"Aw, they won't bother you," Papa said. "You had a fire, didn't you?"

I said, "Yes."

He said, "They'll never bother you unless they are wounded or cornered, but if they are, you had better look out."

Papa asked me how I liked town.

I said I didn't like it at all, and wouldn't live there even if they gave it to me.

With a querying look on his face, he said, "I'm afraid I don't understand. I thought you always wanted to go to town."

"I did," I said, "but I don't any more. I don't like the people there and couldn't understand them."

"What was wrong with them?" he asked.

I told him how they had stared at me, and had even laughed and made fun of me.

He said, "Aw, I don't think they were making fun of you, were they?"

"Yes, they were," I said, "and to beat it all, the boys jumped on me and knocked me down in the dirt. If it hadn't been for the marshal, I would have taken a beating."

Papa said, "So you met the marshal. What did you think of him?"

I told him he was a nice man. He had bought me a bottle of soda pop.

At the mention of soda pop, the blue eyes of my sisters opened wide. They started firing questions at me, wanting to know what color it was, and what it tasted like. I told them it was strawberry and it bubbled and tickled when I drank it, and it made me burp.

The eager questions of my three little sisters had had an effect on my father and mother.

Papa said, "Billy, I don't want you to feel badly about the people in town. I don't think they were poking fun at you, anyway not like you think they were."

"Maybe they weren't," I said, "but I still don't want to ever live in town. It's too crowded and you couldn't get a breath of fresh air."

In a sober voice my father said, "Some day you may have to live in town. Your mother and I don't intend to live in these hills all our lives. It's no place to raise a family. A man's children should have an education. They should get out and see the world and meet people."

"I don't see why we have to move to town to get an education," I said. "Hasn't Mama taught us how to read and write?"

"There's more to an education than just reading and writing," Papa said. "Much more."

I asked him when he thought we'd be moving to town.

"Well, it'll be some time yet," he said. "We don't have the money now, but I'm hoping some day we will."

From the stove where she was heating salt water for my feet, Mama said in a low voice, "I'll pray every day and night for that day to come. I don't want you children to grow up without an education, not even knowing what a bottle of soda pop is, or ever seeing the inside of a schoolhouse. I don't think I could stand that. I'll just keep praying and some day the good Lord may answer my prayer."

I told my mother I had seen the schoolhouse in town. Again I had to answer a thousand questions for my sisters. I told them it was made of red brick and was bigger than Grandpa's store, a lot bigger. There must have been at least a thousand kids going to school there.

I told all about the teeter-totters, the swings made out of log chains, the funny-looking pipe that ran up the side of the building, and how I had climbed up in it and slid out like the other kids. I didn't tell them how I came out.

"I think that was a fire escape," Papa said.

"Fire escape!" I said. "It looked like a slide to me."

"Did you notice where it made that bend up at the top?" he asked.

I nodded my head.

"Well, inside the school there's a door," he said. "If the school gets on fire, they open the door. The children jump in the pipe and slide out to safety."

"Boy, that's a keen way of getting out of a fire," I said.

"Well, it's getting late," Papa said. "We'll talk about this some other time. We'd better get to bed as we have a lot of work to do tomorrow."

My pups were put in the corn crib for the night. I covered them with shucks and kissed them good night.

The next day was a busy one for me. With the hampering help of my sisters I made the little doghouse.

Papa cut the ends off his check lines and gave them to me for collars. With painstaking care, deep in the tough leather I scratched the name "Old Dan" on one and "Little Ann" on the other. With a nail and a rock two holes were punched in each end of the straps. I put them around their small necks and laced the ends together with bailing wire.

That evening I had a talk with my mother. I told her about praying for the two pups, about the magazine and the plans I had made. I told her how hard I had tried to find names for them and how strange it was finding them carved in the bark of a sycamore tree.

With a smile on her face, she asked, "Do you believe God heard your prayer and helped you?"

"Yes, Mama," I said. "I know He did and I'll always be thankful."

VII

It seems that the worries and wants of a young boy never cease. Now that I had my pups another obstacle had cropped up. This one looked absolutely impossible. I had to have a coonskin so I could train them.

With my three little traps and a bulldogged determination, I set out to trap Mister Ringtail. For three solid weeks I practically lived on the river. I tried every trick I knew. It was no use. I just couldn't catch the wiley old coons.

In desperation I went to my grandfather. He smiled as he listened to my tale of woe. "Well, we'll have to do something about that," he said. "To train those dogs right, you'll need that coon hide, that's for sure. Now you watch the store while I go over to my tool shed. I'll be right back."

After what seemed like an eternity I saw him coming. He was carrying a brace and bit, that was all.

With a mischievous little smile on his face, he said, "You wouldn't think a fellow could catch a coon with this brace and bit, would you?"

I thought he was kidding me and it made me feel bad. "Why, Grandpa," I said, "you couldn't catch a coon in a jillion years with that thing. You just don't have any idea how smart they are."

"Yes, you can," he said. "You bet your boots you can. Why, when I was a boy I caught coons on top of coons with one of these things."

I saw Grandpa was serious and I got interested.

He laid the brace down on the counter, picked up a small paper sack, and filled it about half-full of horseshoe nails.

"Now you do everything exactly as I tell you," he said, "and you'll catch that coon."

"Yes, sir, Grandpa," I said, "I will. I'll do anything to catch one of them."

"Now the first thing you'll need is some bright objects," he said. "The best thing is bright shiny tin. Cut out some little round pieces, a little smaller than this bit. Do you understand?"

I nodded my head.

"Now," he said, "you go down along the river where there are a lot of coon tracks. Find a good solid log close by and bore a hole down about six inches. Drop one of the bright pieces of tin down in the hole, and be sure it's laying right on the bottom."

I was all ears. I didn't want to miss one word my grandfather said. Now and then I would glance at him to see if he was kidding me.

In a serious voice, he went on talking. "Now pay close attention," he said, "because this is the main part of the trap."

With eyes as big as a hoot owl's, I looked and listened.

He took four of the horseshoe nails from the sack. With the thumb and forefinger of his left hand he made a small "o" about the size of the bit, which was an inch and a half in diameter.

"Now, we'll say this is the hole you bored in the log," he said. "About an inch apart, drive these nails in on a slant opposite each other."

Holding one of the nails in his right hand, he showed me the right angle.

"The ends of the nails will enter the hole about halfway between the top and the piece of tin," he continued. "Leave an opening between the sharp points big enough for a coon to get his paw through."

He asked me if I understood.

Again I nodded my head and moved a little closer to him. "How is that going to catch a coon, Grandpa?" I asked.

"It'll catch him all right," he said, "and it won't fail. You see a coon is a curious little animal. Anything that is bright and shiny attracts him. He will reach in and pick it up. When his paw closes on the bright object it balls up, and when he starts to pull it from the hole, the sharp ends of the nails will gouge into his paw and he's caught."

He looked over at me.

"Well, what do you think of it?" he asked.

I closed my eyes and in my mind I could see the funnel-like entrance of the hole, and the sharp slanting points of the nails. I could see the coon reaching in for the shiny piece of metal. Naturally his paw would be much larger when closed than it was when he reached in. It would be impossible for it to pass the sharp nails.

It was all looking pretty good to me and I was on the point of saying so, when it hit me. Why, all the coon had to do was open his paw, drop the object, and he was free. It all blew up then and there. I just knew my grandfather was playing a joke on me.

I stepped back and almost cried as I said, "Grandpa, you're kidding me. That kind of a trap couldn't catch a coon. Why all he'd have to do is open his paw, drop the piece of tin, and he could pull it from the hole."

Grandpa started roaring with laughter. This did make me feel bad. With tears in my eyes, I started for the door.

"Wait a minute," Grandpa said. "I'm not kidding you. Oh, I know I like to have my jokes, same as any man, but I meant every word I said."

I turned around and looked at him. He had stopped laughing and there was a hurt expression on his face.

"I wasn't laughing at you," he said. "I was laughing more at myself than you. I just wanted to see if you were smart enough to see that there was a way the coon could free himself."

"A fellow wouldn't have to be very smart to see that," I said.

Grandpa started talking seriously again. "You know," he said, "a coon has more than one peculiarity about him. When I was a boy I had a pet coon. By watching him, I saw and learned a lot of things.

"He had a den in an old hollow tree in our front yard. I don't know the number of times I'd have to climb that tree and get my mother's scissors, buttons, needles, and thimble from his den. Why, he'd even carry out our knives, forks, and spoons. Anything that was bright and shiny, he took to his den."

Grandpa stopped talking for a few minutes. I could see a faraway look in his eyes. Once again he was living in those long-ago days. I waited in silence for him to go on with his story.

"One of the most peculiar things about that coon," he said, "was his front feet. Once he wrapped those little paws around something he would never let go.

"My mother had an old churn. It was one of those kind with a small hole in the lid for the dasher. When she would get through churning, she would take the dasher out to wash it. That crazy coon would climb up on top of the churn, poke his little front paw through the hole, and get a fistful of butter. The hole was small, and when he closed his paw, he couldn't get it back out. All he had to do was open it, drop the butter, and he would be free, but do you think he would? No, sir. He would carry that churn lid all over the house, squalling and growling. Why, it took everyone in the house to free him. I'd have to wrap him up in a gunny sack or an old coat and pry his claws loose from the butter. Seeing this time after time is what gave me the idea for this trap. Once he reaches in and gets hold of that tin, he's caught, because he will never open his paw."

With my confidence restored, it all sounded pretty good to me and I was anxious to try out this wonderful plan. I thanked him and, taking the brace and nails, I left the store.

By the time I reached home it was too late in the day to start making my traps. That night I talked the idea over with Papa.

"I've heard of coons being caught that way," he said, "but I never paid much attention to it. Your grandfather should know, though, for he was quite a coon hunter when he was a boy."

"From what he told me," I said, "it never fails."

Papa asked if I wanted him to help make my traps.

"No," I said, "I think I can do it myself."

I didn't sleep too well that night. I bored holes, drove nails, and fought coons practically all night.

Early the next morning I went to the trash pile. As I stirred around in the rusty old cans, I thought of another time I had searched for a can. Finally I found the one I wanted. It was bright and shiny.

Everything was going along just fine until Mama caught me cutting out the circles of tin with her scissors. I always swore she could find the biggest switches of any woman in the Ozarks. That time she overdid it. I was almost to the river before the stinging stopped.

It wasn't hard to find places for my traps. All along the river large sycamore logs lay partly submerged in the clear blue water. On one where I could see the muddy little tracks of the ringtails, I bored a hole, dropped in a piece of tin, and drove my nails.

On down the river I went, making my traps. I stopped when I ran out of nails. Altogether I had fourteen traps.

That night Papa asked me how I was making out.

"Oh, all right," I said. "I've got fourteen of them made."

He laughed and said, "Well, you can't ever tell. You may catch one."

The next morning I was up with the chickens. I took my pups with me as I just knew I'd have a big ringtail trapped and I wanted them to see it. I was a disappointed boy when I peeked out of a canebrake at my last trap and didn't see a coon. All the way home I tried to figure out what I had done wrong.

I went to Papa. He put his thinking cap on and thought the situation over. "Maybe you left too much scent around when you made those traps," he said. "If you did, it'll take a while for it to go away. Now I wouldn't get too impatient. I'm pretty sure you'll catch one sooner or later."

Papa's words perked me up just like air does a deflated inner tube. He was right. I had simply left too much scent around my traps. All I had to do was wait until it disappeared and I'd have my coon hide.

Morning after morning it was the same old disappointment; no coon. When a week had gone by and still no results from my traps, I gave up. What little patience I had was completely gone. I was firmly convinced that coons didn't walk on sycamore logs any more, and bright shiny objects had about as much effect on them as a coon hound would.

One morning I didn't get up to run my trap line. I stayed in bed. What was the use? It was just a waste of time.

When the family sat down to breakfast, I heard my oldest sister say, "Mama, isn't Billy going to get up for breakfast?"

"Why, is he in his room?" Mama asked. "I didn't know. I thought he was down looking at his traps."

I heard Papa say, "I'll go wake him up."

He came to the door and said, "You'd better get up, Billy. Breakfast is ready."

"I don't want any breakfast," I said. "I'm not hungry."

Papa took one look at me and saw I had a bad case of the ringtail blues. He came over and sat down on the bed.

"What's the matter?" he asked. "You having coon trouble?"

"Grandpa lied to me, Papa," I said. "I should've known better. Who ever heard of anyone catching a coon with a brace and bit and a few horseshoe nails."

"I wouldn't say that," Papa said. "I don't think your grandpa deliberately lied to you. Besides, I've heard of coons being caught that way."

"Well, I don't think I've done anything wrong," I said. "I've done everything exactly as he said, and I haven't caught one yet."

"I still think it's that scent," Papa said. "You know, someone told me, or I read it somewhere, that it takes about a week for scent to die away. How long has it been since you made those traps?"

"It's been over a week," I said.

"Well, the way I figure, it's about time for you to catch one. Yes, sir, I wouldn't be surprised if you came in with one any day now."

After Papa had left the room I lay thinking of what he had said. "Any day now." I got up and hurried into my clothes.

As soon as I was finished with breakfast, I called my pups and lit out for the river.

The first trap was empty. So was the second one. That old feeling of doubt came over me again. I thought, "It's no use. I'll never catch one and I so need the skin to train my pups."

On the way to my third trap I had to walk through a thick stand of wild cane. It was tough going and my pups started whimpering. I stopped and picked them up.

"We'll be out of this in a few minutes," I said, "and then you'll be all right."

I came plowing out of the matted mass and was right on the trap before I realized it. I was met by a loud squall. I was so surprised I dropped the pups. There he was, my first coon.

He was humped up on the sycamore log, growling and showing

his teeth. He kept jerking his front paw, which was jammed deep in the hole I had bored. He was trapped by his own curiosity.

I couldn't move and I felt like my wind had been cut off. I kept hearing a noise but couldn't make out what it was. The movement of the boy pup shook me from my trance. The unidentified sound was his bawling. He was trying to climb up on the log and get to the coon.

I yelled at him and darted in to get hold of his collar. On seeing my movement, the coon let out another squall. It scared me half to death. I froze in my tracks and started yelling again at my pup.

The girl pup worked around behind the coon and climbed up on the log. I screamed at her. She paid no attention to me.

Digging his sharp little claws in the bark, the boy pup made it to the top. He didn't hesitate. Straight down that sycamore log he charged. With teeth bared, the coon waited. When my pup was about two feet from him, he made a lunge. The coon just seemed to pull my pup up under his stomach and went to work with tooth and claw.

The girl pup saved him. Like a cat in a corn crib, she sneaked in from behind and sank her needle-sharp teeth in the coon's back.

It was too much for Old Ringy. He turned the boy pup loose, turned around, and slapped her clear off the log. She came running to me, yelping her head off. I grabbed her up in my arms and looked for the boy pup. When the coon had turned him loose, he too had fallen off the log. He was trying to get back to the coon. I darted in and grabbed him by the hind leg.

With a pup under each arm and running as fast as I could, I lit out for the house. Coming out of the bottoms into a fresh-plowed field I set my pups down so I could get a little more speed. I started yelling as soon as I came in sight of the house.

Mama came flying out with my sisters right behind her. Papa was out by the barn harnessing his team. Mama yelled something to him about a snake. He dropped the harness, jumped over the rail fence, and in a long lope started for me.

Mama reached me first. She grabbed me and shouted, "Where did it bite you?"

"Bite me?" I said. "Why Mama, I'm not bit. I've got him, Mama. I've got him."

"Got what?" Mama asked.

"A big coon," I said. "The biggest one in the river bottoms. He's this big, Mama." I made a circle with my arms as big as a twenty-gallon keg.

Mama just groaned way down deep and covered her face with her hands. Some big tears squeezed out between her fingers. Almost in a whisper, I heard her say, "Thank God; I thought you were snake-bitten."

My sisters, seeing Mama crying, puckered up and started bawling.

"He needs a whipping," the oldest one said, "that's what he needs, scaring Mama that way."

Something busted loose inside me and I cried a little, too.

"I didn't mean to scare Mama," I sniffed. "I just wanted everyone to know I caught a coon."

Up until this time Papa hadn't said a word. He just stood looking on.

"Here now," he said, "let's have none of this crying. He didn't mean to scare anyone."

Taking his handkerchief from his pocket, he stepped over to Mama, put his arm around her, and started drying her eyes.

Mama poked her head around him and glared at me. "Billy Colman," she shouted, "if you ever scare me like that again, I'll take a switch and wear you to a frazzle."

This hurt my feelings and I really did get tuned up. "Everyone's mad at me," I said, "and I haven't done anything but catch the biggest coon on the river."

Mama came over. "I'm sorry," she said. "I didn't mean to be cross, but you did scare me. I thought a rattlesnake had bitten you."

"Now that that's all settled," Papa said, "we had better go get that coon." Looking at Mama, he said, "Why don't you and the girls go with us. I don't think it'll take long."

Mama looked at me, smiled, and turned to the girls. "Would you like to go?" she asked.

Their only answer was a lot of squealing and jumping up and down.

On the way, Mama noticed some blood on my shirt. She stopped me and started looking me over.

"Where did that come from?" she asked. "Did that coon bite you?"

"No, Mama," I said. "I didn't get close enough for him to bite me."

With a worried look on her face, she jerked out my shirt. "You don't seem to be scratched anywhere," she said.

"Maybe this is where it came from," Papa said.

He reached down and picked up my boy pup. His little black nose was split wide open and was bleeding.

I saw a relieved look come over Mama's face.

Looking at me, she started shaking her head. "I don't know," she said. "I just don't know."

"Did that coon get hold of this pup?" Papa asked.

"He sure did, Papa," I said, "but it wasn't the coon's fault. If it hadn't been for Little Ann, he'd have eaten him up."

I told how my dogs had tied into the coon.

Papa laughed as he fondled my pup. "This dog is going to be a coon hound," he said, "and I mean a good one."

The coon started squalling as soon as we came in sight.

"My goodness," Mama said, "you wouldn't think anything so small would be so vicious."

Papa picked up a club. "Now everybody stand back out of the way," he said. "This won't take long."

My pups were wanting to get to the coon so badly that they were hard to hold. I had to squeeze them up tight to keep them from jumping right out of my arms.

My sisters, with eyes as big as blue marbles, got behind Mama and peeked around her.

Papa whacked the coon a good one across the head. He let out a loud squall, growled, and showed his teeth. He tried hard to get to Papa but the trap held him.

The girls buried their faces in Mama's dress and started bawling. Mama turned her back on the fight. I heard her say, "I wish we hadn't come. Poor thing."

Papa whacked him again and it was all over.

It was too much for Mama and the girls. They left. I heard the tall cane rattling as they ran for the house.

After the coon was killed, I walked over. Papa was trying to get the coon's paw from the trap. He couldn't do it. Taking a pair of pliers from his pocket, he said, "It's a good thing I had these along or we would have had to cut his foot off."

After Papa had pulled the nails, he lifted the coon's paw from the hole. There, clamped firmly in it, was the bright piece of tin.

In a low voice Papa said, "Well, I'll be darned. All he had to do was open it up and he was free, but he wouldn't do it. Your grandfather was right."

A sorrowful look came over Papa's face as he ran his fingers through the soft, yellow hair. "Billy," he said, "I want you to take a hammer and pull the nails from every one of those traps. It's summertime now and their fur isn't any good. Besides, I don't think this is very sportsmanlike. The coon doesn't have a chance. It's all right this time. You needed this one, but from now on I want you to catch them with your dogs. That way they have a fifty-fifty chance."

"I will, Papa," I said. "That's what I intended to do."

While we were skinning the coon, Papa asked me when I was going to start training my dogs.

"I don't know," I said. "Do you think they're too young?"

"No, I don't think so," he said. "I've heard that the younger they are the better it is."

"Well, in that case," I said, "I'll start tomorrow."

With the help of my oldest sister, we started giving my pups their first lessons. She would hold their collars while I made trails with the hide for them to follow.

I'd climb trees that leaned out over the river, jump out into the water, swim to the other side, and make trails up and down the bank. With a long pole and wire, I'd drag the hide on top of rail fences, swing it through the air, and let it touch the ground twenty or thirty feet away. I did everything with that hide a coon would do and probably a lot of things a coon couldn't do.

It was a beautiful sight to see my pups work those trails. At first they were awkward and didn't know what to do, but they would never quit trying.

Old Dan would get so eager and excited, he would overrun a trail. Where it twisted or turned, he would run straight on, bawling up a storm. It didn't take him long to realize that a smart old coon didn't always run in a straight line.

Little Ann never overran a trail. She would wiggle and twist, cry and whine, and pretty soon she would figure it out.

At first they were afraid of water. I never would admit it even to myself. I always said that they just didn't like to get wet. They would follow the trail to the stream and stop. Sitting down on their rears, they would cry and beg for help. With a pup under each arm, I'd wade out into the stream and set them down in the cool water. Nine times out of ten, one pup would swim one way and the other one would go just the opposite way. I had a time with this part of their training, but my persistence had no bounds.

It wasn't long until they loved the water. Old Dan would jump as far out as he could and practically knock the river dry. Little Ann would ease herself in and swim like a muskrat for the opposite shore.

I taught my dogs every trick I knew and any new ones I heard about. I taught them how to split up on a riverbank to search for the hidden trail, because it was impossible to tell where a coon would come out of the water. Sometimes he might swim downstream and other times he might swim upstream. Maybe he would come back to the bank he had just left, or he would cross over to the other side. Perhaps he would stop in the middle of the stream on an old drift.

Sometimes he would come out of the water by catching the dangling limbs of a leaning birch and climbing up, never touching the bank. Or he could come out on the same trail he used to go in, and backtrack. He would sometimes crawl up under an undermined bank or into an old muskrat den.

One of the favorite tricks of a smart old ringtail is the tree-barking trick. This he accomplished by running far up on the side of a tree and using his stout legs for leverage, springing twenty or thirty feet away before touching the ground. Dumb hounds trail up to the tree and start bawling treed. I taught my dogs to circle for a good hundred yards to be sure he was still in the tree before bawling.

In order to learn more about coon hunting, I'd hang around my grandfather's store and listen to the stories told by the coon hunters. Some of the tales I heard were long and tall, but I believed them all.

I could always tell when Grandpa was kidding me by the twinkle in his eyes. He told me how a coon could climb right up the fog and disappear in the stars, and how he could leap on a horse's back and run him over your dogs. I didn't care, for I loved to hear the tall tales. Anything that had a coon hair in it I believed completely.

All through that summer and into the late fall the training went on. Although I was worn down to a frazzle, I was a happy boy. I figured I was ready for the ringtails.

Late one evening, tired and exhausted, I sat down by a big sycamore and called my dogs to me. "It's all over," I said. "There'll be no more lessons. I've worked hard and I've done my best. From now on it's all up to you. Hunting season is just a few days away and I'm going to let you rest for I want you to be in good shape the night it opens."

It was wonderful indeed how I could have heart-to-heart talks with my dogs and they always seemed to understand. Each question I asked was answered in their own doggish way.

Although they couldn't talk in my terms, they had a language of their own that was easy to understand. Sometimes I would see the answer in their eyes, and again it would be in the friendly wagging of their tails. Other times I could hear the answer in a low whine or feel it in the soft caress of a warm flicking tongue. In some way, they would always answer.

VIII

THE DAY HUNTING SEASON OPENED, I was as nervous as Samie, our house cat. Part of that seemingly endless day was spent getting things ready for the coming night.

I cleaned my lantern and filled it full of oil. With hog lard I greased my boots until they were as soft as a hummingbird's nest. I was grinding my ax when Papa came around.

He smiled as he said, "This is the big night, isn't it?"

"It sure is, Papa," I said, "and I've waited a long time for it."

"Yes, I know," he said. "I've been thinking—there's not too much to do around here during the hunting season. I'm pretty sure I can take care of things, so you just go ahead and hunt all you want to."

"Thanks, Papa," I said. "I guess I'll be out pretty late at night, and I'll probably have to do a lot of sleeping in the daytime."

Papa started frowning. "You know," he said, "your mother doesn't like this hunting of yours very much. She's worried about you being out all by yourself."

"I can't see why Mama has to worry," I said. "Haven't I been roaming the woods ever since I was big enough to walk, and I'm almost fourteen now."

"I know," said Papa. "It's all right with me, but women are a little different than men. They worry more.

"Now just to be on the safe side, I think it would be a good idea for you to tell us where you'll be hunting. Then if anything happens, we'll know where to look."

I told him I would, but I didn't think anything was going to happen.

After Papa had left, I started thinking, "He doesn't even talk to me like I was a boy any more. He talks to me like I was a man." These wonderful thoughts made me feel just about as big as our old red mule.

I had a good talk with my dogs. "I've waited almost three years for this night," I said, "and it hasn't been easy. I've taught you everything I know and I want you to do your best."

Little Ann acted like she understood. She whined and saved me a wash job on my face. Old Dan may have, but he didn't act like it. He just lay there in the sunshine, all stretched out and limber as a rag.

During supper Mama asked me where I was going to hunt.

"I'm not going far," I said, "just down on the river."

I could tell Mama was worried and it didn't make me feel too good.

"Billy," she said, "I don't approve of this hunting, but it looks like I can't say no; not after all you've been through, getting your dogs, and all that training."

"Aw, he'll be all right," Papa said. "Besides, he's getting to be a good-size man now."

"Man!" Mama exclaimed. "Why, he's still just a little boy."

"You can't keep him a little boy always," Papa said. "He's got to grow up some day."

"I know," Mama said, "but I don't like it, not at all, and I can't help worrying."

"Mama, please don't worry about me," I said. "I'll be all right. Why, I've been all over these hills, you know that."

"I know," she said, "but that was in the daytime. I never worried too much when it was daylight, but at night, that's different. It'll be dark and anything could happen."

"There won't be anything happen," I said. "I promise I'll be careful."

Mama got up from the table saying, "Well, it's like I said. I can't say no and I can't help worrying. I'll pray every night you're out."

The way Mama had me feeling. I didn't know whether to go hunting or not. Papa must have sensed how I felt. "It's dark now," he said, "and I understand those coons start stirring pretty early. You had better be going, hadn't you?"

While Mama was bundling me up, Papa lit my lantern. He handed it to me, saying, "I'd like to see a big coonskin on the smokehouse wall in the morning."

The whole family followed me out on the porch. There we all got a surprise. My dogs were sitting on the steps, waiting for me.

I heard Papa laugh. "Why, they know you're going hunting," he said, "know it as well as anything."

"Well, I never," said Mama. "Do you really think they do? It does look like they do. Why, just look at them."

Little Ann started wiggling and twisting. Old Dan trotted out to the gate, stopped, turned around, and looked at me.

"Sure they know Billy's going hunting," piped the little one, "and I know why."

"How do you know so much, silly?" asked the oldest one.

"Because I told Little Ann, that's why," she said, "and she told Old Dan. That's how they know."

We all had to laugh at her.

The last thing I heard as I left the house was the voice of my mother. "Be careful, Billy," she said, "and don't stay out late."

It was a beautiful night, still and frosty. A big grinning Ozark moon had the countryside bathed in a soft yellow glow. The starlit heaven reminded me of a large blue umbrella, outspread and with the handle broken off.

Just before I reached the timber, I called my dogs to me. "Now the trail will be a little different tonight," I whispered. "It won't be a hide dragged on the ground. It'll be the real thing, so remember everything I taught you and I'm depending on you. Just put one up a tree and I'll do the rest."

I turned them loose, saying, "Go get 'em."

They streaked for the timber.

By the time I had reached the river, every nerve in my body was drawn up as tight as a fiddlestring. Big-eyed and with ears open, I walked on, stopping now and then to listen. The way I was slipping along anyone would have thought I was trying to slip up on a coon myself.

I had never seen a night so peaceful and still. All around me tall sycamores gleamed like white streamers in the moonlight. A prowling skunk came wobbling up the riverbank. He stopped when he saw me. I smiled at the fox-fire glow of his small, beady, red eyes. He turned and disappeared in the underbrush. I heard a sharp snap and a feathery rustle in some brush close by. A small rodent started squealing in agony. A night hawk had found his supper.

Across the river and from far back in the rugged mountains I heard the baying of a hound. I wondered if it was the same one I had heard from my window on those nights so long ago.

Although my eyes were seeing the wonders of the night, my ears were ever alert, listening for the sound of my hounds telling me they had found a trail.

I was expecting one of them to bawl, but when it came it startled me. The deep tones of Old Dan's voice jarred the silence around me. I dropped my ax and almost dropped my lantern. A strange feeling came over me. I took a deep breath and threw back my head to give the call of the hunter, but something went wrong. My throat felt like it had been tied in a knot. I swallowed a couple of times and the knot disappeared.

As loud as I could, I whooped, "Who-e-e-e. Get him, Dan. Get him."

Little Ann came in. The bell-like tones of her voice made shivers run up and down my spine. I whooped to her. "Who-e-e-e. Tell it to him, little girl. Tell it to him."

This was what I had prayed for, worked and sweated for, my own little hounds bawling on the trail of a river coon. I don't know why I cried, but I did. While the tears rolled, I whooped again and again.

They straightened the trail out and headed down river. I took off after them as fast as I could run.

A mile downstream the coon pulled his first trick. I could tell by my dogs' voices that they had lost the trail. When I came to them they were out on an old drift, sniffing around.

The coon had pulled a simple trick. He had run out on the drift, leaped into the water, and crossed the river. To an experienced coon hound, the crude trick would have been nothing at all, but my dogs were just big, awkward pups, trailing their first live coon.

I stood and watched, wondering if they would remember the training I had given them. Now and then I would whoop, urging them on.

Old Dan was having a fit. He whined and he bawled. He whimpered and cried. He came to me and reared up, begging for help.

"I'm not going to help you," I scolded, "and you're not going to find him out on that drift. If you would just remember some of the training I gave you, you could find the trail. Now go find that coon."

He ran back out on the drift and started searching.

Little Ann came to me. I could see the pleading in her warm gray eyes. "I'm ashamed of you, little girl," I said. "I thought you had more sense than this. If you let him fool you this easily, you'll never be a coon dog."

She whined, turned, and trotted downstream to search again for the lost trail.

I couldn't understand. Had all the training I had given them been useless? I knew if I waded the river they would follow me. Once on the other side, it would be easy for them to find the trail. I didn't want it that way. I wanted them to figure it out by themselves. The more I thought about it, the more disgusted I became. I sat down and buried my face in my arms.

Out on the drift, Old Dan started whining. It made me angry and I got up to scold him again.

I couldn't understand his actions. He was running along the edge of the drift, whimpering and staring downriver. I looked that way. I could see something swimming for the opposite shore. At first I thought it was a muskrat. In the middle of the stream, where the moonlight was the brightest, I got a good look. It was Little Ann.

With a loud whoop, I told her how proud I was. My little girl had remembered her training.

She came out on a gravel bar, shook the water from her body, and disappeared in the thick timber. Minutes later, she let me know she had found the trail. Before the tones of her voice had died away, Old Dan plowed into the water. He was so eager to join her I could hear him whining as he swam.

As soon as his feet touched bottom in the shallows, he started bawling and lunging. White sheets of water, knocked high in the moonlight by his churning feet, gleamed like thousands of tiny white stars.

He came out of the river onto a sand bar. In his eagerness, his feet slipped in the loose sand and down he went. He came out of his roll, running and bawling. Ahead of him was a log jam. He sailed over it and disappeared down the riverbank. Seconds later I heard his deep voice blend with the sharp cries of Little Ann.

At that moment no boy in the world could have been more proud of his dogs than I was. Never again would I doubt them.

I was hurrying along, looking for a shallow riffle so I could wade across, when the voices of my dogs stopped. I waited and listened. They opened up again on my side of the stream. The coon had crossed back over.

I couldn't help smiling. I knew that never again would a ring-tail fool them by swimming the river.

The next trick the old fellow pulled was a dandy. He climbed a large water oak standing about ten feet from the river and simply disappeared.

I got there in time to see my dogs swimming for the opposite shore. For half an hour they worked that bank. Not finding the trail, they swam back. I stood and watched them. They practically tore the riverbank to pieces looking for the trail.

Old Dan knew the coon had climbed the water oak. He went back, reared up on it, and bawled a few times.

"There's no use in doing that, boy," I said. "I know he climbed it, but he's not there now. Maybe it's like Grandpa said, he just climbed right on out through the top and disappeared in the stars."

My dogs didn't know it, but I was pretty well convinced that that was what the coon had done.

They wouldn't give up. Once again they crossed over to the other shore. It was no use. The coon hadn't touched that bank. They came back. Old Dan went up the river and Little Ann worked downstream.

An hour and a half later they gave up and came to me begging for help. I knelt down between their wet bodies. While I scratched and petted them, I let them know that I still loved them.

"I'm not mad," I said. "I know you did your best. If that coon can fool both of us, then we're just beat. We'll go someplace else to hunt. He's not the only coon in these bottoms."

Just as I picked up my ax and lantern, Little Ann let out a bawl and tore out down the riverbank. Old Dan, with a bewildered look on his face, stood for a moment looking after her. Then, raising his head high in the air, he made my eardrums ring with his deep voice. I could hear the underbrush popping as he ran to join her.

I couldn't figure out what had taken place. Surely Little Ann had heard or seen something. I could tell by their voices that whatever it was they were after, they were close enough to see it and were probably running by sight.

The animal left the bottoms and headed for the mountains. Whatever it was, it must have realized my dogs were crowding it too closely. At the edge of the foothills it turned and came back toward the river.

I was still trying to figure out what was going on, when I realized that on striking the river the animal had again turned and was coming straight toward me. I set my lantern down and tightened my grip on the ax.

I was standing my ground quite well when visions of bears, lions, and all kinds of other animals started flashing across my mind. I jumped behind a big sycamore and was trying hard to press my body into the tree when a big coon came tearing by. Twenty-five yards behind him came my dogs, running side by side. I saw them clearly when they passed me, bawling every time their feet touched the ground.

After seeing that there was nothing to be scared of, once again I was the fearless hunter, screaming and yelling as loud as I could, "Get him, boy, get him."

I tore out after them. The trails I knew so well were forgotten. I took off straight through the brush. I was tearing my way through some elders when the voices of my dogs stopped.

Holding my breath, I stood still and waited. Then it came, the long-drawn-out bawl of the tree bark. My little hounds had done it. They had treed their first coon.

When I came to them and saw what they had done I was speechless. I groaned and closed my eyes. I didn't want to believe it. There were a lot of big sycamores in the bottoms but the one in which my dogs had treed was the giant of them all.

While prowling the woods, I had seen the big tree many times. I had always stopped and admired it. Like a king in his own domain, it towered far above the smaller trees.

It had taken me quite a while to find a name suitable for the big sycamore. For a while I had called it "the chicken tree." In some ways it had reminded me of a mother hen hovering over her young in a rainstorm. Its huge limbs spread out over the small birch, ash, box elder, and water oak as if it alone were their protector.

Next, I named it "the giant." That name didn't last long. Mama told us children a story about a big giant that lived in the mountains and ate little children that were lost. Right away I started looking for another name.

One day, while lying in the warm sun staring at its magnificent beauty, I found the perfect name. From that day on, it was called "the big tree." I named the bottoms around it "the big tree bottoms."

Walking around it, and using the moon as a light, I started looking for the coon. High up in the top I saw a hollow in the end of a broken limb. I figured that that was the coon's den.

I could climb almost any tree I had ever seen but I knew I could never climb the big sycamore and it would take days to chop it down.

There had been very little hope from the beginning, but on seeing the hollow I gave up. "Come on," I said to my dogs. "There's nothing I can do. We'll go someplace else and find another coon."

I turned to walk away. My hounds made no move to follow. They started whining. Old Dan reared up, placed his front paws on the trunk, and started bawling.

"I know he's there," I said, "but there's nothing I can do. I can't climb it. Why it's sixty feet up to the first limb and it would take me a month to cut it down."

Again I turned and started on my way.

Little Ann came to me. She reared up and started licking my hands. Swallowing the knot in my throat, I said, "I'm sorry, little girl. I want him just as badly as you do, but there's no way I can get him."

She ran back to the tree and started digging in the soft ground close to the roots.

"Come on now," I said in a gruff voice. "You're both acting silly. You know I'd get the coon for you if I could but I can't."

With a whipped-dog look on her face and with her tail between her legs, Little Ann came over. She wouldn't even look at me. Old Dan walked slowly around behind the tree and hid himself. He peeped around the big trunk and looked at me. The message I read in his friendly eyes tore at my heart. He seemed to be saying, "You told us to put one in a tree and you would do the rest."

With tears in my eyes, I looked again at the big sycamore. A wave of anger came over me. Gritting my teeth, I said, "I don't care how big you are, I'm not going to let my dogs down. I told them if they put a coon in a tree I would do the rest and I'm going to. I'm going to cut you down. I don't care if it takes me a whole year."

I walked over and sank my ax as deep as I could in the smooth white bark. My dogs threw a fit. Little Ann started turning in circles. I could hear her pleased whimpering cry. Old Dan bawled and started gnawing on the big tree's trunk.

At first it was easy. My ax was sharp and the chips flew. Two hours later things were different. My arms felt like two dead grapevines, and my back felt like someone had pulled a plug out of one end of it and drained all the sap out.

While taking a breather, I saw I was making more progress than I thought I would. The cut I had started was a foot deep, but I still had a long way to go.

Sitting on their rears, my dogs waited and watched. I smiled at the look on their faces. Every time I stopped chopping they would come over. While Little Ann washed the sweat from my face, Old Dan would inspect my work. He seemed to be pleased with what he saw for he always wagged his tail.

Along about daylight I got my second wind and I really did make the chips fly. This burst of energy cost me dearly. By sunup I was so stiff I could hardly move. My hands and arms were numb. My back screamed with pain. I could go no further. Sitting down, I leaned back against the big tree and fell asleep.

Little Ann woke me up by washing my face. I groaned with the torture of getting to my feet. Every muscle in my body seemed to be tied in a knot. I was thinking of going down to the river to wash my face in the cool water when I heard a loud whoop. I recognized my father's voice. I whooped to let him know where I was.

Papa was riding our red mule. After he rode up, he just sat there and looked me over. He glanced at my dogs and at the big sycamore. I saw the worry leave his face. He straightened his shoulders, pursed his lips, and blew out a little air. He reminded me of someone who had just dropped a heavy load.

In a slow, calm voice, he asked, "Are you all right, Billy?"

"Yes, Papa," I said. "Oh, I'm a little tired and sleepy, otherwise I'm fine."

He slid from the mule's back and came over. "Your mother's worried," he said. "When you didn't come in, we didn't know what had happened. You should've come home."

I didn't know what to say. I bowed my head and looked at the ground. I was trying hard to choke back the tears when I felt his hand on my shoulder.

"I'm not scolding," he said. "We just thought maybe you had an accident or something."

I looked up and saw a smile on his face.

He turned and looked again at the tree. "Say," he said, "this is the sycamore you call "the big tree," isn't it?"

I nodded my head.

"Is there a coon in it?" he asked.

"There sure is, Papa," I said. "He's in that hollow limb. See— that one way up there. That's why I couldn't come home. I was afraid he'd get away."

"Maybe you just think he's there," Papa said. "I believe I'd make sure before I'd cut down a tree that big."

"Oh, he's there all right," I said. "My dogs weren't ten feet behind him when he went up it."

"Why are you so determined to get this coon?" Papa asked. "Couldn't you go somewhere else and tree one? Maybe the tree would be a smaller one."

"I thought about that, Papa," I said, "but I made a bargain with my dogs. I told them that if they would put one in a tree, I'd do the rest. Well, they fulfilled their part of the bargain. Now it's up to me to do my part, and I'm going to, Papa. I'm going to cut it down. I don't care if it takes me a year."

Papa laughed and said, "Oh, I don't think it'll take that long, but it will take a while. I tell you what I'll do. You take the mule and go get some breakfast. I'll chop on it until you get back."

"No, Papa," I said. "I don't want any help. I want to cut it down all by myself. You see, if someone helps me, I wouldn't feel like I kept my part of the agreement."

An astonished look came over my father's face. "Why, Billy," he said, "you can't stay down here without anything to eat and no sleep. Besides, it'll take at least two days to cut that tree down and that's hard work."

"Please, Papa," I begged, "don't make me quit. I just have to get that coon. If I don't, my dogs won't ever believe in me again."

Papa didn't know what to tell me. He scratched his head, looked over to my dogs and back at me. He started walking around. I waited for him to make up his mind. He finally reached a decision.

"Well, all right," he said. "If that's the way you want it, I'm for it even if it is only an agreement between you and your dogs. If a man's word isn't any good, he's no good himself.

"Now I have to get back and tell your mother that you're all right. It's a cinch that you can't do that kind of work on an empty stomach, so I'll send your oldest sister down with a lunch bucket."

With tears in my eyes, I said, "Tell Mama I'm sorry for not coming home last night."

"Don't you worry about your mother," he said, as he climbed on the mule's back. "I'll take care of her. Another thing, I have to make a trip to the store today and I'll talk this over with your grandfather. He may be able to help some way."

After Papa left, things were a little different. The tree didn't look as big, and my ax wasn't as heavy. I even managed to sing a little as I chopped away.

When my sister came with the lunch bucket, I could have kissed her, but I didn't. She took one look at the big tree and her blue eyes got as big as a guinea's egg.

"You're crazy," she gasped, "absolutely crazy. Why, it'll take a month to cut that tree down, and all for an old coon."

I was so busy with the fresh side pork, fried eggs, and hot biscuits, I didn't pay much attention to her. After all, she was a girl, and girls don't think like boys do.

She raved on. "You can't possibly cut it down today, and what are you going to do when it gets dark?"

"I'm going to keep right on chopping," I said. "I stayed with it last night, didn't I? Well, I'll stay till it's cut down. I don't care how long it takes."

My sister got upset. She looked at me, threw back her small head, and looked up to the top of the big sycamore. "You're as crazy as a bedbug," she said. "Why, I never heard of such a thing."

She stepped over in front of me and very seriously asked if she could look in my eyes.

"Look in my eyes?" I said. "What do you want to do that for? I'm not sick."

"Yes, you are, Billy," she said, "very sick. Mama said when Old Man Johnson went crazy, his eyes turned green. I want to see if yours have."

This was too much. "If you don't get out of here," I shouted, "you're going to be red instead of green, and I mean that."

I grabbed up a stick and started toward her. Of course, I wouldn't have hit her for anything.

This scared her and she started for the house. I heard her saying something about an old coon as she disappeared in the under-brush.

Down in the bottom of my lunch bucket I found a neat little package of scraps for my dogs. While they were eating I walked down to a spring and filled the bucket with cool water.

The food did wonders for me. My strength came back. I spit on my hands and, whistling a coon hunter's tune, I started making the chips fly.

The cut grew so big I could have laid down in it. I moved over to another side and started a new one. Once while I was taking a rest, Old Dan came over to inspect my work. He hopped up in the cut and sniffed around.

"You had better get out of there," I said. "If that tree takes a notion to fall, it'll mash you flatter than a tadpole's tail."

With a "no care" look on his friendly face, he gave me a hurry-up signal with a wag of his tail.

Little Ann had dug a bed in a pile of dead leaves. She looked as if she were asleep but I knew she wasn't. Every time I stopped swinging the ax, she would raise her head and look at me.

IX

By LATE EVENING the happy tune I had been whistling was forgotten. My back throbbed like a stone bruise. The muscles in my legs and arms started quivering and jerking. I couldn't gulp enough air to cool the burning heat in my lungs. My strength was gone. I could go no further.

I sat down and called my dogs to me. With tears in my eyes, I told them that I just couldn't cut the big tree down.

I was trying hard to make them understand when I heard someone coming. It was Grandpa in his buggy.

I'm sure no one in the world can understand a young boy like his grandfather can. He drove up with a twinkle in his eyes and a smile on his whiskery old face.

"Hello! How are you gettin' along?" he boomed.

"Not so good, Grandpa," I said. "I don't think I can cut it down. It's just too big. I guess I'll have to give up."

"Give up!" Grandpa barked. "Now I don't want to hear you say that. No, sir, that's the last thing I want to hear. Don't ever start anything you can't finish."

"I don't want to give up, Grandpa," I said, "but it's just too big and my strength's gone. I'm give out."

"Course you are," he said. "You've been going at it wrong. To do work like that a fellow needs plenty of rest and food in his stomach."

"How am I going to get that, Grandpa?" I asked. "I can't leave the tree. If I do, the coon will get away."

"No, he won't," Grandpa said. "That's what I came down here for. I'll show you how to keep that coon in the tree."

He walked around the big sycamore, looking up. He whistled and said, "Boy, this is a big one all right."

"Yes, it is, Grandpa," I said. "It's the biggest one in the river bottoms."

Grandpa started chuckling. "That's all right," he said. "The bigger they are the harder they fall."

"How are you going to make the coon stay in the tree, Grandpa?" I asked.

With a proud look on his face, he said, "That's another one of my coon-hunting tricks; learned it when I was a boy. We'll keep him there all right. Oh, I don't mean we can keep him there for always, but he'll stay for four or five days. That is, until he gets so hungry he just has to come down."

"I don't need that much time," I said. "I'm pretty sure I can have it down by tomorrow night."

Grandpa looked at the cut. "I don't know," he said. "Even though it is halfway down, you must remember you've been cutting on it half of one night and one day. You might make it, but it's going to take a lot of chopping."

"If I can get a good night's sleep," I said, "and a couple of meals under my belt, I can do a lot of chopping."

Grandpa laughed. "Speaking of meals," he said, "your ma is having chicken and dumplings for supper. Now we don't want to miss that, so let's get busy."

"What do you want me to do, Grandpa?" I asked.

"Well, let's see," he said. "First thing we'll need is some sticks about five feet long. Take your ax, go over in that canebrake, and get us six of them."

I hurried to do what Grandpa wanted, all the time wondering what in the world he was going to do. How could he keep the coon in the tree?

When I came back, he was taking some old clothes from the buggy. "Take this stocking cap," he said. "Fill it about half-full of grass and leaves."

While I was doing this, Grandpa walked over and started looking up in the tree. "You're pretty sure he's in that hollow limb, are you?" he asked.

"He's there all right, Grandpa," I said. "There's no other place he could be. I've looked all over it and there's no other hollow anywhere."

"Well, in that case," Grandpa said, "we'd better put our man along about here."

"What man, Grandpa?" I asked in surprise.

"The one we're going to make," he said. "To us it'll be a scarecrow, but to that coon it'll be a man."

Knowing too well how smart coons were, right away I began to lose confidence. "I don't see how anything like that can keep a coon in a tree," I said.

"It'll keep him there all right," Grandpa said. "Like I told you before, they're curious little devils. He'll poke his head out of that hole, see this man standing here, and he won't dare come down. It'll take him four or five days to figure out that it isn't a real honest-to-goodness man. By that time it'll be too late. You'll have his hide tacked on the smokehouse wall."

The more I thought about it, the more I believed it, and then there was that serious look on Grandpa's face. That was all it took. I was firmly convinced.

I started laughing. The more I thought about it, the funnier it got. Great big laughing tears rolled down my cheek.

"What's so funny?" Grandpa asked. "Don't you believe it'll work?"

"Sure it'll work, Grandpa," I said. "I know it will. I was just thinking—those coons aren't half as smart as they think they are, are they?"

We both had a good laugh at this.

With the sticks and some bailing wire, Grandpa made a frame that looked almost like a gingerbread man. On this he put an old pair of pants and a red sweater. We stuffed the loose flabby clothes with grass and leaves. He wired the stocking-cap head in place and stepped back to inspect his work.

"Well, what do you think of it?" he asked.

"If it had a face," I said, "you couldn't tell it from a real man."

"We can fix that," Grandpa chuckled.

He took a stick and dug some black grease from one of the hub caps on the buggy. I stood and watched while he applied his artistic touch. In the stocking-cap head he made two mean-looking eyes, a crooked nose, and the ugliest mouth I had ever seen.

"Well, what do you think of that?" he asked. "Looks pretty good, huh?"

Laughing fit to kill, and talking all at the same time, I told him that I wouldn't blame the coon if he stayed in the tree until Gabriel blew his horn.

"He won't stay that long," Grandpa chuckled, "but he'll stay long enough for you to cut that tree down."

"That's all I want," I said.

"We'd better be going," Grandpa said. "It's getting late and we don't want to miss that supper."

I was so stiff and sore he had to help me to the buggy seat.

I called to my dogs. Little Ann came, but not willingly. Old Dan refused to leave the tree.

"Come on, boy," I coaxed. "Let's go home and get something to eat. We'll come back tomorrow."

He bowed his head and looked the other way.

"Come on," I scolded, "we can't sit here all night."

This hurt his feelings. He walked around behind the big sycamore and hid.

"Well, I'll be darned," Grandpa said as he jumped down from the buggy. "He knows that coon's there and he doesn't want to leave it. You've got a coon hound there and I mean a good one."

He picked Old Dan up in his arms and set him in the buggy.

All the way home I had to hold on to his collar to keep him from jumping out and going back to the tree.

As our buggy wound its way up through the bottoms, Grandpa started talking. "You know, Billy," he said, "about this tree-chopping of yours, I think it's all right. In fact, I think it would be a good thing if all young boys had to cut down a big tree like that once in their life. It does something for them. It gives them determination and will power. That's a good thing for a man to have. It goes a long way in his life. The American people have a lot of it. They have proved that, all down through history, but they could do with a lot more of it."

I couldn't see this determination and will power that Grandpa was talking about very clearly. All I could see was a big sycamore tree, a lot of chopping, and the hide of a ringtail coon that I was determined to have.

As we reached the house, Mama came out. Right away she started checking me over. "Are you all right?" she asked.

"Sure, Mama," I said. "What makes you think something's wrong with me?"

"Well, I didn't know," she said. "The way you acted when you got down from the buggy, I thought maybe you were hurt."

"Aw, he's just a little sore and stiff from all that chopping," Grandpa said, "but he'll be all right. That'll soon go away."

After Mama saw that there were no broken bones, or legs chopped off, she smiled and said, "I never know any more. I guess I'll just have to get used to it."

Papa hollered from the porch, "Come on in. We've been waiting supper on you."

"We're having chicken and dumplings," Mama beamed, "and I cooked them especially for you."

During the meal I told Grandpa I didn't think that the coon in the big tree was the same one my dogs had been trailing at first.

"What makes you think that?" he asked.

I told how the coon had fooled us and how Little Ann had seen or heard this other coon. I figured he had just walked up on my dogs before he realized it.

A smile spread all over Grandpa's face. Chuckling, he said, "It does look that way, but it wasn't. No, Billy, it was the same coon. They're much too smart to ever walk up on a hound like that. He pulled a trick and it was a good one. In fact, it'll fool nine out of ten dogs."

"Well, what did he do, Grandpa?" I asked. "I'm pretty sure he didn't cross the river, so how did he work it?"

Grandpa pushed the dishes back and, using his fork as a pencil, he drew an imaginary line on the tablecloth. "It's called the backtracking trick," he said. "Here's how he worked it. He climbed that water oak but he only went up about fifteen or twenty feet. He then turned around and came down in his same tracks. He backtracked on his original trail for a way. When he heard your dogs coming he leaped far up on the side of the nearest tree and climbed up. He was in that tree all the time your dogs were searching for the lost trail. After everything had quieted down, he figured that they had given up. That's when he came down and that's when Little Ann either heard or saw him."

Pointing the fork at me, Grandpa said very seriously, "You mark my word, Billy, in no time at all that Little Ann will know every trick a coon can pull."

"You know, Grandpa," I said, "she wouldn't bark treed at the water oak like Old Dan did."

"Course she wouldn't," he said. "She knew he wasn't there."

"Why, I never heard of such a thing," Mama said. "I'd no idea coons were that smart. Why, for all anyone knows he may not be in the big tree at all. Maybe he pulled another trick. It'd be a shame if Billy cut it down and found there was no coon in it."

"Oh, he's there, Mama," I hastily replied. "I know he is. They were right on his tail when he went up. Besides, Little Ann was bawling her head off when I came to them."

"Of course he's there," Grandpa said. "They were crowding him too closely. He didn't have time to pull another trick."

Grandpa left soon after supper, saying to me, "I'll be back down in a few days and I want to see that coon hide."

I thanked him for helping me and walked out to the buggy with him.

"Oh, I almost forgot," he said. "I heard there was a fad back in the New England states. Seems like everyone is going crazy over coonskin coats. Now if this is true, I look for the price of coon hides to take a jump."

I was happy to hear this and told my father what Grandpa had said. Papa laughed and said, "Well, if you can keep the coons out of those big sycamores, you might make a little money."

Before I went to bed, Mama made me take a hot bath. Then she rubbed me all over with some liniment that burned like fire and smelled like a civet cat.

It seemed like I had barely closed my eyes when Mama woke me up. "Breakfast is about ready, Billy," she said.

I was so stiff and sore I had trouble putting my clothes on. Mama helped me.

"Maybe you'd better let that coon go," she said. "I don't think he's worth all of this."

"I can't do that, Mama," I said. "I've gone too far now."

Papa came in from the barn. "What's the matter?" he asked. "You a little stiff?"

"A little stiff!" Mama exclaimed. "Why he could hardly put his clothes on."

"Aw, he'll be all right," Papa said. "If I know anything about swinging an ax, it won't be long before he's as limber as a rag."

Mama just shook her head and started putting our breakfast on the table.

While we were eating, Papa said, "You know I woke up several times last night and each time I was sure I heard a hound bawling. It sounded like Old Dan."

I quit the table on the run and headed for my doghouse. I didn't have to go all the way. Little Ann met me on the porch. I asked her where Old Dan was and called his name. He was nowhere around.

Little Ann started acting strangely. She whined and stared toward the river bottoms. She ran out to the gate, came back, and reared up on me.

Mama and Papa came out on the porch.

"He's not here," I said. "I think he has gone back to the tree."

"I don't think he'd do that, would he?" Mama said. "Maybe he's around someplace. Have you looked in the doghouse?"

I ran and looked. He wasn't there.

"Everybody be quiet and listen," I said.

I walked out beyond the gate a little ways and whooped as loud as I could. My voice rang like a bell in the still, frosty morning. Before the echo had died away the deep "Ou-u-u-u" of Old Dan rolled out of the river bottoms.

"He's there," I said. "He wanted to make sure the coon stayed in the tree. You see, Mama, why I have to get that coon. I can't let him down."

"Well, I never in all my life," she said. "I had no idea a dog loved to hunt that much. Yes, Billy, I can see now, and I want you to get him. I don't care if you have to cut down every tree in those bottoms. I want you to get that coon for those dogs."

"I'm going to get him, Mama," I said, "and I'm going to get him today if I possibly can."

Papa laughed and said, "Looks like there wasn't any use in

building that scarecrow. All you had to do was tell Old Dan to stay and watch the tree."

I left the house in a run. Now and then I would stop and whoop. Each time I was answered by the deep voice of Old Dan.

Little Ann ran ahead of me. By the time I reached the big tree, their voices were making the bottoms ring.

When I came tearing out of the underbrush, Old Dan threw a fit. He tried to climb the sycamore. He would back way off, then, bawling and running as fast as he could, he would claw his way far up on its side.

Little Ann, not to be outdone, reared up and placed her small front paws on the smooth white bark. She told the ringtail coon that she knew he was there.

After they had quieted down, I called Old Dan to me. "I'm proud of you, boy," I said. "It takes a good dog to stay with a tree all night, but there wasn't any need in you coming back. The coon wouldn't have gotten away. That's why we built the scarecrow."

Little Ann came over and started rolling in the leaves. The way I was feeling toward her, I couldn't even smile at her playful mood. "Of course you feel good," I said in an irritated voice, "and it's no wonder, you had a good night's sleep in a nice warm doghouse, but Old Dan didn't. He was down here in the cold all by himself, watching the tree. The way you're acting, I don't believe you care if the coon gets away or not."

I would have said more but just then I noticed something. I walked over for a better look. There, scratched deep in the soft leaves were two little beds. One was smaller than the other. Looking at Little Ann, I read the answer in her warm gray eyes.

Old Dan hadn't been alone when he had gone back to the tree. She too had gone along. There was no doubt that in the early morning she had come home to get me.

There was a lump in my throat as I said, "I'm sorry, little girl, I should've known."

The first half-hour was torture. At each swing of the ax my arms felt like they were being torn from their sockets. I gritted my teeth and kept hacking away. My body felt like it did the time my sisters rolled me down the hill in a barrel.

As Papa had said, in a little while the warm heat from the hard work limbered me up. I remembered what my father did when he was swinging an ax. At the completion of each swing, he always said, "Ha!" I tried it. Ker-wham. "Ha!" Ker-wham. "Ha!" I don't know if it helped or not, but I was willing to try anything if it would hurry the job.

Several times before noon I had to stop and rake my chips out of the way. I noticed that they weren't the big, even, solid chips like my father made when he was chopping. They were small and seemed to crumble up and come all to pieces. Neither were the cuts neat and even. They were ragged and looked more like the work of beavers. But I wasn't interested in any beautiful tree-chopping. All I wanted was to hear the big sycamore start popping.

Along in the middle of the afternoon I felt a stinging in one of my hands. When I saw it was a blister I almost cried. At first there was only one. Then two. One after another they rose up on my hands like small white marbles. They filled up and turned a pale pinkish color. When one would burst, it was all I could do to keep from screaming. I tore my handkerchief in half and wrapped my hands. This helped for a while, but when the cloth began to stick to the raw flesh I knew it was the end.

Crying my heart out, I called my dogs to me and showed them my hands. "I can't do it," I said. "I've tried, but I just can't cut it down. I can't hold the ax any longer."

Little Ann whined and started licking my sore hands. Old Dan seemed to understand. He showed his sympathy by nuzzling me with his head.

Brokenhearted, I started for home. As I turned, from the corner of my eye I saw Grandpa's scarecrow. It seemed to be laughing at me. I looked over to the big sycamore. It lacked so little being cut down. A small wedge of solid wood was all that was holding it up. I let my eyes follow the smooth white trunk up to the huge spreading limbs.

Sobbing, I said, "You think you have won, but you haven't. Although I can't get the coon, neither can you live, because I have cut off your breath of life." And then I thought, "Why kill the big tree and not accomplish anything?" I began to feel bad.

Kneeling down between my dogs, I cried and prayed. "Please God, give me the strength to finish the job. I don't want to leave the big tree like that. Please help me finish the job."

I was trying to rewrap my hands so I could go back to work when I heard a low droning sound. I stood up and looked around. I could still hear the noise but couldn't locate it. I looked up. High in the top of the big sycamore a breeze had started the limbs to swaying. A shudder ran through the huge trunk.

I looked over to my right at a big black gum tree. Not one limb was moving. On its branches a few dead leaves hung silent and still. One dropped and floated lazily toward the ground.

Over on my left stood a large hackberry. I looked up to its top. It was as still as a fence post.

Another gust of wind caught in the top of the big tree. It started popping and snapping. I knew it was going to fall. Grabbing my dogs by their collars, I backed off to safety.

I held my breath. The top of the big sycamore rocked and swayed. There was a loud crack that seemed to come from deep inside the heavy trunk. Fascinated, I stood and watched the giant of the bottoms. It seemed to be fighting so hard to keep standing. Several times I thought it would fall, but in a miraculous way it would pull itself back into perfect balance.

The wind itself seemed to be angry at the big tree's stubborn resistance. It growled and moaned as it pushed harder against the wavering top. With one final grinding, creaking sigh, the big sycamore started down. It picked up momentum as the heavy weight of the overbalanced top dove for the ground. A small ash was smothered by its huge bulk. There was a lightning-like crack as its trunk snapped.

In its downward plunge, the huge limbs stripped the branches from the smaller trees. A log-sized one knifed through the top of a water oak. Splintered limbs flew skyward and rained out over the bottoms. With a cyclone roar, the big tree crashed to the ground, and then silence settled over the bottoms.

Out of the broken, twisted, tangled mass streaked a brown furry ball. I turned my dogs loose and started screaming at the top of my voice, "Get him, Dan, get him."

In his eagerness, Old Dan ran head on into a bur oak tree. He sat down and with his deep voice told the river bottoms that he had been hurt.

It was Little Ann who caught the coon. I heard the ringtail

squall when she grabbed him. Scared half to death, I snatched up a club and ran to help her.

The coon was all over her. He climbed up on her head, growling, slashing, ripping, and tearing. Yelping with pain, she shook him off and he streaked for the river. I thought surely he was going to get away. At the very edge of the river's bank, she caught him again.

I was trying hard to get in a lick with my club but couldn't for fear of hitting Little Ann. Through the tears in my eyes I saw the red blurry form of Old Dan sail into the fight. He was a mad hound. His anger at the bur oak tree was taken out on the coon.

They stretched Old Ringy out between them and pinned him to the ground. It was savage and brutal. I could hear the dying squalls of the coon and the deep growls of Old Dan. In a short time it was all over.

With sorrow in my heart, I stood and watched while my dogs worried the lifeless body. Little Ann was satisfied first. I had to scold Old Dan to make him stop.

Carrying the coon by a hind leg, I walked back to the big tree for my ax. Before leaving for home, I stood and looked at the fallen sycamore. I should have felt proud over the job I had done, but for some reason I couldn't. I knew I would miss the giant of the bottoms, for it had played a wonderful part in my life. I thought of the hours I had whiled away staring at its beauty and how hard it had been finding the right name for it.

"I'm sorry," I said. "I didn't want to cut you down, but I had to. I hope you can understand."

I was a proud boy as I walked along in the twilight of the evening. I felt so good even my sore hands had stopped hurting. What boy wouldn't have been proud? Hadn't my little hounds treed and killed their first coon? Along about then I decided I was a full-fledged coon hunter.

Nearing our house, I saw the whole family had come out on the porch. My sisters came running, staring wide-eyed at the dead coon.

Laughing, Papa said, "Well, I see you got him."

"I sure did, Papa," I said. I held the coon up for all to see. Mama took one look at the lifeless body and winced.

"Billy," she said, "when I heard that big tree fall, it scared me half to death. I didn't know but what it had fallen on you."

"Aw, Mama," I said, "I was safe. Why, I backed way off to one side. It couldn't have fallen on me."

Mama just shook her head. "I don't know," she said. "Some times I wonder if all mothers have to go through this."

"Come on," Papa said, "I'll help you skin it."

While we were tacking the hide on the smokehouse wall, I asked Papa if he had noticed any wind blowing that evening.

He thought a bit and said, "No, I don't believe I did. I've been out all day and I'm pretty sure I haven't noticed any wind. Why did you ask?"

"Oh, I don't know, Papa," I said, "but I thought something strange happened down in the bottoms this afternoon."

"I'm afraid I don't understand," said Papa. "What do you mean, 'something strange happened'?"

I told him about how my hands had gotten so sore I couldn't chop any more, and how I had asked for strength to finish the job.

"Well, what's so strange about that?" he asked.

"I don't know," I said, "but I didn't chop the big tree down. The wind blew it over."

"Why that's nothing," Papa said. "I've seen that happen a lot of times."

"It wasn't just the wind," I said. "It was the way it blew. It didn't touch another tree in the bottoms. I know because I looked around. The big tree was the only one touched by the wind. Do you think God heard my prayer? Do you think He helped me?"

Papa looked at the ground and scratched his head. In a sober voice, he said, "I don't know, Billy. I'm afraid I can't answer that. You must remember the big sycamore was the tallest tree in the bottoms. Maybe it was up there high enough to catch the wind where the others couldn't. No, I'm afraid I can't help you there. You'll have to decide for yourself."

It wasn't hard for me to decide. I was firmly convinced that I had been helped.

X

Mama made me a cap out of my first coon hide. I was as proud of it as Papa would've been if someone had given him a dozen Missouri mules. Mama said afterwards that she wished she hadn't made it for me because, in some way, wearing that cap must've affected my mind. I went coon crazy.

I was out after the ringtails every night. About the only time I didn't go hunting was when the weather was bad, and even then Mama all but had to hog-tie me.

What wonderful nights they were, running like a deer through the thick timber of the bottoms, tearing my way through stands of wild cane, climbing over drifts, and jumping logs, running, screaming, and yelling, "Who-e-e-e, get him, boy, get him," following the voices of my little hounds.

It wasn't too hard for a smart old coon to fool Old Dan, but there were none that prowled the riverbanks that could fool my Little Ann.

As Grandpa had predicted, the price of coonskins jumped sky-high. A good-size hide was worth from four to ten dollars, depending on the grade and quality.

I kept the side of our smokehouse plastered with hides. Of course I would spread them out a little to cover more space. I always stretched them on the side facing the road, never on the back side. I wanted everyone in the country to see them.

The money earned from my furs was turned over to my father. I didn't care about it. I had what I wanted—my dogs. I supposed that Papa was saving it for something because I never saw anything new turn up around our home, but, like any young boy, I wasn't bothered by it and I asked no questions.

My whole life was wrapped up in my dogs. Everywhere I went they went along. There was only one place I didn't want them to go with me and that was to Grandpa's store. Other dogs were always there, and it seemed as if they all wanted to jump on Old Dan.

It got so about the only time I went to see my grandfather was when I had a bundle of fur to take to the store. This was always a problem. In every way I could, I would try to slip away from my dogs. Sometimes I swore that they could read my mind. It made no difference what I tried; I couldn't fool them.

One time I was sure I had outsmarted them. The day before I was to make one of my trips I took my furs out to the barn and hid them. The next morning I hung around the house for a while, and then nonchalantly whistled my way out to the barn. I climbed up in the loft and peeked through a crack. I could see them lying in front of their doghouse. They weren't even looking my way.

Taking my furs, I sneaked out through a back door and, walking like a tomcat, I made it to the timber. I climbed a small dogwood tree and looked back. They were still there and didn't seem to know what I'd done.

Feeling just about as smart as Sherlock Holmes, I headed for the store. I was walking along singing my lungs out when they came tearing out of the underbrush, wiggling and twisting, and tickled to death to be with me. At first I was mad but one look at dancing Little Ann and all was forgiven. I sat down on my bundle of fur and laughed till I hurt all over. I could scold them a little, but I could no more have whipped one of them than I could have kissed a girl. After all, a boy just doesn't whip his dogs.

Grandpa always counted my furs carefully and marked something down on a piece of paper. I'd never seen him do this with other hunters and it got the best of my curiosity. One day while he was writing I asked him, "Why do you do that, Grandpa?" He looked at me over his glasses and said kind of sharp, "Never mind. I have my reasons."

When Grandpa talked to me like that I didn't push things any farther. Besides, it didn't make any difference to me if he marked on every piece of paper in the store.

I always managed to make my trips on Saturdays as that was "coon hunters'" day. I didn't have to stand around on the outside of the circle any more and listen to the coon hunters. I'd get right up in the middle and say my piece with the rest of them.

I didn't have to tell any whoppers for some of the things my dogs did were almost unbelievable anyhow. Oh, I guess I did make things a little bigger than they actually were but I never did figure a coon hunter told honest-to-goodness lies. He just kind of stretched things a little.

I could hold those coon hunters spellbound with some of my hunting tales. Grandpa would never say anything while I was telling my stories. He just puttered around the store with a silly little grin on his face. Once in a while when I got too far off the beaten path, he would come around and cram a bar of soap in my pocket. My face would get all red, I'd cut my story short, fly out the door, and head for home.

The coon hunters were always kidding me about my dogs. Some of the remarks I heard made me fighting mad. "I never saw hounds so small, but I guess they are hounds, at least they look like it." "I don't believe Little Ann is half as smart as he says she is. She's so little those old coons think she's a rabbit. I bet she sneaks right up on them before they realize she's a dog." "Some of these nights a big old coon is going to carry her off to his den and raise some little coon puppies."

I always took their kidding with a smile on my face, but it made my blood boil like the water in Mama's teakettle. I had one way of shutting them up. "Let's all go in the store," I'd say, "and see who has the most hides in there."

It was true that my dogs were small, especially Little Ann. She could walk under an ordinary hound; in fact, she was a regular midget. If it had not been for her long ears, no one could have told that she was a hound. Her actions weren't those of a hunting hound. She was constantly playing. She would play with our chickens and young calves, with a piece of paper or a corncob. What my little girl lacked in size, she made up in sweetness. She could make friends with a tomcat.

Old Dan was just the opposite. He strutted around with a

belligerent and tough attitude. Although he wasn't a tall dog, he was heavy. His body was long and his chest broad and thick. His legs were short, big, and solid. The muscles in his body were hard and knotty. When he walked, they would twist and jerk under the skin.

He was a friendly dog. There were no strangers to him. He loved everyone. Yet he was a strange dog. He would not hunt with another hound, other than Little Ann, or another hunter, not even my father. The strangest thing about Old Dan was that he would not hunt, even with me, unless Little Ann was with him. I found this out the first night I tried it.

Little Ann had cut the pad of her right foot on a sharp jagged flint rock. It was a nasty cut. I made a little boot of leather and put it on her wounded foot. To keep her from following me, I locked her in the corncrib.

Two nights later I decided to take Old Dan hunting for a while. He followed me down to the river bottoms and disappeared in the thick timber. I waited and waited for him to strike a trail. Nothing happened. After about two hours, I called to him. He didn't come. I called and called. Disgusted, I gave up and went home.

Coming up through the barn lot, I saw him rolled up in a ball on the ground in front of the corncrib. I immediately understood. I walked over and opened the door. He jumped up in the crib, smelled Little Ann's foot, twisted around in the shucks, and lay down by her side. As he looked up at me, I read this message in his friendly gray eyes, "You could've done this a long time ago."

I never did know if Little Ann would hunt by herself or not. I am sure she would have, for she was a smart and understanding dog, but I never tried to find out.

Little Ann was my sisters' pet. They rubbed and scratched and petted her. They would take her down to the creek and give her baths. She loved it all.

If Mama wanted a chicken caught, she would call Little Ann. She would run the chicken down and hold it with her paws until Mama came. Not one feather would be harmed. Mama tried Old Dan once. Before she got the chicken, there wasn't much left but the feathers.

By some strange twist of nature, Little Ann was destined to go through life without being a mother. Perhaps it was because she was stunted in growth, or maybe because she was the runt in a large litter. That may have had something to do with it.

During the fur season, November through February, I was given complete freedom from work. Many times when I came home, the sun was high in the sky. After each hunt, I always took care of my dogs. The flint rocks and saw briers were hard on their feet. With a bottle of peroxide and a can of salve I would doctor their wounds.

I never knew what to expect from Old Dan. I never saw a coon hound so determined or one that could get into so many predicaments. More than one time, it would have been the death of him if it hadn't been for smart Little Ann.

One night, not long after I had entered the bottoms, my dogs struck the trail of an old boar coon. He was a smart old fellow and had a sackful of tricks. He crossed the river time after time. Finally, swimming to the middle and staying in the swift current, he swam downstream.

Knowing he would have to come out somewhere, my dogs split up. Old Dan took the right side. Little Ann worked the other side. I came out of the bottoms onto a gravel bar and stood and watched them in the moonlight.

Little Ann worked downriver, and then she came up. I saw her when she passed me going up the bank, sniffing and searching for the trail. She came back to me. I patted her head, scratched her ears, and talked to her. She kept staring across the river to where Old Dan was searching for the trail.

She waded in and swam across to help him. I knew that the coon had not come out of the river on her side. If he had, she would have found the trail. I walked up to a riffle, pulled off my shoes, and waded across.

My dogs worked the riverbank, up and down. They circled far out into the bottoms. I could hear the loud snuffing of Old Dan. He was bewildered and mad. I was getting a thrill from it all, as I had never seen them fooled like this.

Old Dan gave up on his side, piled into the river, and swam across to the side Little Ann had worked. I knew that it was useless for him to do that.

I was on the point of giving up, calling them to me, and going elsewhere to hunt, when I heard the bawl of Little Ann. I couldn't believe what I heard. She wasn't bawling on a trail. She was sounding the tree bark. I hurried down the bank.

There was a loud splash. I saw Old Dan swimming back. By this time, Little Ann was really singing a song. In the bright moonlight, I could see Old Dan clearly. His powerful front legs were churning the water.

Then I saw a sight that makes a hunter's heart swell with pride. Still swimming, Old Dan raised his head high out of the water and bawled. He couldn't wait until he reached the bank to tell Little Ann he was coming. From far out in the river he told her.

Reaching the shallows, he plowed out of the river onto a sand bar. Not even taking time to shake the water from his body, again he raised his head and bawled, and tore out down the bank.

In a trot, I followed, whooping to let them know I was coming. Before I reached the tree, Old Dan's deep voice was making the timber shake.

The tree was a large birch, standing right on the bank of the river. The swift current had eaten away at the footing, causing it to lean. The lower branches of the tree dangled in the water.

I saw how the smart old coon had pulled his trick. Coming in toward the bank from midstream, he had caught the dangling limbs and climbed up. Exhausted from the long swim, he stayed there in the birch thinking he had outsmarted my dogs. I couldn't understand how Little Ann had found him.

It was impossible to fall the tree toward the bottoms. It was too much off balance. I did the next best thing. I cut a long elder switch. Unbuckling one of my suspenders, I tied it to the end and climbed the tree.

The coon was sitting in a fork of a limb. Taking my switch, I whopped him a good one and out he came. He sailed out over the river. With a loud splash, he hit the water and swam for the other side. My dogs jumped off the bank after him. They were no match against his expert swimming. On reaching the other bank, he ran downriver.

Climbing down out of the tree, I picked up my ax and lantern, and trotted down to another riffle and waded across. I could tell by the bawling of my dogs, they were close to the coon. He would have to climb a tree, or be caught on the ground.

All at once their voices stopped. I stood still and waited for them to bawl treed. Nothing happened. Thinking the coon had taken to the river again, I waited to give them time to reach the opposite bank. I waited and waited. I could hear nothing. By then I knew he had not crossed over. I thought perhaps they had caught him on the ground. I hurried on.

I came to a point where a slough of crystal-clear water ran into the river. On the other side was a bluff. I could hear one of my dogs over there. As I watched and waited, I heard a dog jump in the water. It was Little Ann. She swam across and came up to me. Staying with me for just a second, she jumped in the slough and swam back to the other side.

I could hear her sniffing and whining. I couldn't figure out where Old Dan was. By squatting down and holding the lantern high over my head, I could dimly see the opposite bank. Little Ann was running up and down. I noticed she always stayed in one place of about twenty-five yards, never leaving that small area.

She ran down to the water's edge and stared out into the slough. The horrible thought came that Old Dan had drowned. I knew a big coon was capable of drowning a dog in water by climbing on his head and forcing him under.

As fast as I could run, I circled the slough, climbed up over the bluff, and came down to where Little Ann was. She was hysterical, running up and down the bank and whining.

I tied my lantern on a long pole, held it out over the water, and looked for Old Dan's body. I could see clearly in the clear spring waters, but I couldn't see my dog anywhere. I sat down on the bank, buried my face in my hands, and cried. I was sure he was gone.

Several minutes passed, and all that time Little Ann had never stopped. Running here and there along the bank, she kept sniffing and whining.

I heard when she started digging. I looked around. She was ten feet from the water's edge. I got up and went over to her. She was digging in a small hole about the size of a big apple. It was the air hole for a muskrat den.

I pulled Little Ann away from the hole, knelt down, and put my ear to it. I could hear something, and feel a vibration in the ground. It was an eerie sound and seemed to be coming from far away. I listened. Finally I understood what the noise was.

It was the voice of Old Dan. Little Ann had opened the hole up enough with her digging so his voice could be heard faintly. In some way he had gotten into that old muskrat den.

I knew that down under the bank, in the water, the entrance to the den could be found. Rolling up my sleeve, I tried to find it with my hand. I had no luck. It was too far down.

There was only one thing to do. Leaving my ax and lantern, I ran for home. Picking up a long-handled shovel, I hurried back.

The sun was high in the sky before I had dug Old Dan out. He was a sight to see, nothing but mud from the tip of his nose to the end of his tail. I held on to his collar and led him down to the river to wash him off. The water there was much warmer than the cold spring water of the slough.

After washing him, I turned him loose. Right back to the hole he ran. Little Ann was already digging. I knew the coon was still there. Working together, we dug him out.

After the coon was killed, I saw what had made him so smart. His right front foot was twisted and shriveled. At one time he must have been caught in a trap and had pulled himself free. He was an old coon. His face was almost white. He was big and heavy and had beautiful fur.

Tired, muddy, wet, and hungry, I started for home.

I've often wondered how Old Dan got into that old muskrat den. Perhaps there was another entrance I had overlooked. I'll never know.

One night, far back in the mountains, in a place called "The Cyclone Timber," Old Dan really pulled a good one.

Many years before my time, a terrible cyclone had ripped its way through the mountains, leaving its scar in the form of fallen timber, twisted and snarled. The path of the cyclone was several miles wide and several miles long. It was a wonderful place to hunt as it abounded with game.

My dogs had struck the trail of a coon about an hour before. They had really been warming him up. I knew it was about time for him to take up a tree, and sure enough, I heard the deep voice of Old Dan telling the world he had a coon up a tree.

I was trotting along, going to them, when his voice stopped. I could hear Little Ann, but not Old Dan. I wondered why, and was a little scared, for I just knew something had happened. Then I heard his voice. It seemed louder than it had been before. I felt much better.

When I came up to the tree I thought Little Ann had treed Old Dan. She was sitting on her haunches staring up and bawling the tree bark. There, a good fifteen feet from the ground, with his hind legs planted firmly in the center of a big limb, and his front feet against the trunk of the tree, stood Old Dan, bawling for all he was worth.

Above him some eight or nine feet was a baby coon. I was glad it was a young one, for if it had been an old one, he would have jumped out. Old Dan would have followed, and he surely would have broken all of his legs.

From where I was standing, I could see it was impossible for Old Dan to have climbed the tree. It was dead and more of an old snag than a tree, with limbs that were crooked and twisted. The bark had rotted away and fallen off, leaving the trunk bare and slick as glass. It was a good ten feet up to the first limb. I couldn't figure out how Old Dan had climbed that tree. There had to be a solution somewhere.

Walking around to the other side, I saw how he had accomplished his feat. There in the bottom was a large hole. The old tree was hollow. Stepping back, I looked up and could see another hole, which had been hidden from me because of Old Dan's body.

He had simply crawled into the hole at the bottom, climbed up the hollow of the tree, and worked his way out on the limb. In some way he had turned around and reared up, placing his front feet against the trunk.

There he was. I didn't know what to do. I couldn't cut the tree down and I was afraid to climb it for fear I would scare the coon into jumping out. If he did, Old Dan would jump, too, and break his legs.

I ran plan after plan around in my mind. None would work. I finally came to the conclusion that I had to climb the tree and get ahold of that crazy dog. I blew out my lantern, pulled off my shoes and socks, and started shinnying up the tree. I prayed that the coon wouldn't jump out.

Inching along, being as quiet as I could, I made it up to Old Dan and grabbed his collar. I sat down on the limb, and held him tight. He would bawl now and then, and all but burst my eardrums. I couldn't drop him to the ground, and I couldn't climb down with him. I couldn't sit there on that limb and hold him all night. I would be no better off when daylight came.

Glancing at the hole by my side gave me the solution to my problem. I thought, "If he came out of this hole, he can go back in it."

That was the way I got my dog down from the tree. This had its problems, too. In the first place, Old Dan didn't want to be put in the hole head first. By scolding, pushing, shoving, and squeezing, I finally got him started on his way.

Like a fool, I sat there on the limb, waiting to see him come out at the bottom, and come out he did. Turning around, bawling as he did, right back in the hole he went. There was nothing I could do but sit and wait. I understood why his voice had stopped for a while. He just took time out to climb a tree.

Putting my ear to the hole, I could hear him coming. Grunting and clawing, up he came. I helped him out of the hole, turned him around, and crammed him back in. That time I wasn't too gentle with my work. I was tired of sitting on the limb, and my bare feet were getting cold.

I started down the same time he did. He beat me down. Looking over my shoulder, I saw him turn around and head back for the hole. I wasn't far from the ground so I let go. The flint rocks didn't feel too good to my feet when I landed.

I jumped to the hole just in time to see the tip end of his long tail disappearing. I grabbed it. Holding on with one hand, I worked his legs down with my other, and pulled him out. I stopped his tree-climbing by cramming rocks and chunks into the hole.

How the coon stayed in the tree, I'll never know, but stay he did. With a well-aimed rock, I scared him out. Old Dan satisfied his lust to kill.

I started for home. I'd had all the hunting I wanted for that night.

XI

I HAD OFTEN WONDERED what Old Dan would do if Little Ann got into some kind of a predicament. One night I got my answer.

For several days a northern blizzard had been blowing. It was a bad one. The temperature dropped down to ten below. The storm started with a slow cold drizzle and then sleet. When the wind started blowing, everything froze, leaving the ground as slick as glass.

Trapped indoors, I was as nervous as a fish out of water. I told Mama I guessed it was just going to storm all winter.

She laughed and said, "I don't think it will, but it does look like it will last for a while."

She ruffled up my hair and kissed me between the eyes. This did rile me up. I didn't like to be kissed like that. It seemed that I could practically rub my skin off and still feel it, all wet and sticky, and kind of burning.

Sometime on the fifth night, the storm blew itself out and it snowed about three inches. The next morning I went out to my doghouse. Scraping the snow away from the two-way door, I stuck my head in. It was as warm as an oven. I got my face washed all over by Little Ann. Old Dan's tail thumped out a tune on the wall.

I told them to be ready because we were going hunting that night. I knew the old ringtails would be hungry and stirring for they had been denned up during the storm.

That evening as I was leaving the house, Papa said, "Billy, be careful tonight. It's slick down under the snow, and it would be easy to twist an ankle or break a leg."

I told him I would and that I wasn't going far, just down back of our fields in the bottoms.

"Well, anyway," he said, "be careful. There'll be no moon tonight and you're going to see some fog next to the river."

Walking through our fields I saw my father was right about it being slick and dark. Several times I slipped and sat down. I couldn't see anything beyond the glow of my lantern, but I wasn't worried. My light was a good one, and Mama had insisted that I make two little leather pouches to cover the blades of my ax.

Just before I reached the timber, Old Dan shook the snow from the underbrush with his deep voice. I stopped and listened. He bawled again. The deep bass tones rolled around under the tall sycamores, tore their way out of the thick timber, traveled out over the fields, and slammed up against the foothills. There they seemed to break up and die away in the mountains.

Old Dan was working the trail slowly and I knew why. He would never line out until Little Ann was running by his side. I thought she would never get there. When she did, her beautiful voice made the blood pound in my temples. I felt the excitement of the hunt as it ate its way into my body. Taking a deep breath, I reared back and whooped as loud as I could.

The coon ran upriver for a way and then, cutting out of the bottoms, he headed for the mountains. I stood and listened until their voices went out of hearing. Slipping and sliding, I started in the direction I had last heard them. About halfway to the foothills I heard them coming back.

Somewhere in the rugged mountains, the coon had turned and headed toward the river. It was about time for him to play out a few tricks and I was wondering what he would do. I knew it would be hard for him to hide his trail with snow on the ground, and I realized later that the smart old coon knew this, too.

As the voices of my dogs grew louder, I could tell that they were coming straight toward me. Once I started to blow out my lantern, thinking that maybe I could see them when they crossed our field, but I realized I didn't stand a chance of seeing the race in the skunk-black night.

Down out of the mountains they brought him, singing a hound-dog song on his heels. The coon must have scented me, or seen my lantern. He cut to my right and ran between our house and me. I heard screaming and yelling from my sisters. My father started whooping.

I knew my whole family was out on the porch listening to the beautiful voices of my little red hounds. I felt as tall as the tallest sycamore on the riverbank. I yelled as loud as I could. Again I heard the squealing of my sisters and the shouts of my father.

The deep "Ou-ou-ou's" of Old Dan and the sharp "Aw-aw-aw-aw's" of Little Ann bored a hole in the inky-black night. The vibrations rolled and quivered in the icy silence.

The coon was heading for the river. I could tell my dogs were crowding him, and wondered if he'd make it to the water. I was hoping he wouldn't, for I didn't want to wade the cold water unless I had to do it.

I figured the smart old coon had a reason for turning and coming back to the river and wondered what trick he had in mind. I remembered something my grandfather had told me. He said, "Never underestimate the cunning of an old river coon. When the nights are dark and the ground is frozen and slick, they can pull some mean tricks on a hound. Sometimes the tricks can be fatal."

I was halfway through the fog-covered bottoms when the voices of my dogs stopped. I stood still, waited, and listened. A cold silence settled over the bottoms. I could hear the snap and crack of sap-frozen limbs. From far back in the flinty hills, the long, lonesome howl of a timber wolf floated down in the silent night. Across the river I heard a cow moo. I knew the sound was coming from the Lowery place.

Not being able to hear the voices of my dogs gave me an uncomfortable feeling. I whooped and waited for one of them to bawl. As I stood waiting I realized something was different in the bottoms. Something was missing.

I wasn't worried about my dogs. I figured that the coon had pulled some trick and sooner or later they would unravel the trail. But the feeling that something was just not right had me worried.

I whooped several times but still could get no answer. Stumbling, slipping, and sliding, I started on. Reaching the river, I saw it was frozen over. I realized what my strange uneasy feeling was. I had not been able to hear the sound of the water.

As I stood listening I heard a gurgling out in the middle of the stream. The river wasn't frozen all the way across. The still eddy waters next to the banks had frozen, but out in the middle, where the current was swift, the water was running, leaving a trough in the ice pack. The gurgling sound I had heard was the swift current as it sucked its way through the channel.

The last time I had heard my dogs they were downstream from me. I walked on, listening.

I hadn't gone far when I heard Old Dan. What I heard froze the blood in my veins. He wasn't bawling on a trail or giving the tree bark. It was one, long, continuous cry. In his deep voice there seemed to be a pleading cry for help. Scared, worried, and with my heart beating like a churn dasher, I started toward the sound.

I almost passed him but with another cry he let me know where he was. He was out on the ice pack. I couldn't see him for the fog. I called to him and he answered with a low whine. Again I called his name. This time he came to me.

He wasn't the same dog. His tail was between his legs and his head was bowed down. He stopped about seven feet from me. Sitting down on the ice, he raised his head and howled the most mournful cry I had ever heard. Turning around, he trotted back out on the ice and disappeared in the fog.

I knew something had happened to Little Ann. I called her name. She answered with a pleading cry. Although I couldn't see her, I guessed what had happened. The coon had led them to the river. Running out on the ice, he had leaped across the trough. My dogs, hot on the trail, had followed. Old Dan, a more powerful dog than Little Ann, had made his leap. Little Ann had not made it. Her small feet had probably slipped on the slick ice and she had fallen into the icy waters. Old Dan, seeing the fate of his little friend, had quit the chase and come back to help her. The smart old coon had pulled his trick, and a deadly one it was.

I had to do something. She would never be able to get out by herself. It was only a matter of time until her body would be paralyzed by the freezing water.

Laying my ax down, I held my lantern out in front of me and stepped out on the ice. It started cracking and popping. I jumped back to the bank. Although it was thick enough to hold the light weight of my dogs, it would never hold me.

Little Ann started whining and begging for help. I went all to pieces and started crying. Something had to be done and done quickly or my little dog was lost. I thought of running home for a rope or for my father, but I knew she couldn't last until I got back. I was desperate. It was impossible for me to swim in the freezing water. I wouldn't last for a minute. She cried again, begging for the one thing I couldn't give her, help.

I thought, "If only I could see her maybe I could figure out some way I could help."

Looking at my lantern gave me an idea. I ran up the bank about thirty feet, turned, and looked back. I could see the light, not well, but enough for what I had in mind. I grabbed my lantern and ax and ran for the bottoms.

I was looking for a stand of wild cane. After what seemed like ages, I found it. With the longest one I could find, I hurried back. After it was trimmed and the limber end cut off, I hung the lantern by the handle on the end of it and started easing it out on the ice.

I saw Old Dan first. He was sitting close to the edge of the trough, looking down. Then I saw her. I groaned at her plight. All I could see was her head and her small front paws. Her claws were spread out and digging into the ice. She knew if she ever lost that hold she was gone.

Old Dan raised his head and howled. Hound though he was, he knew it was the end of the trail for his little pal.

I wanted to get my light as close to Little Ann as I could, but my pole was a good eight feet short. Setting the lantern down, I eased the pole from under the handle. I thought, "I'm no better off than I was before. In fact I'm worse off. Now I can see when the end comes."

Little Ann cried again. I saw her claws slip on the ice. Her body settled lower in the water. Old Dan howled and started fidgeting. He knew the end was close.

I didn't exactly know when I started out toward my dog. I had taken only two steps when the ice broke. I twisted my body and fell toward the bank. Just as my hand closed on a root I thought my feet touched bottom, but I wasn't sure. As I pulled myself out I felt the numbing cold creep over my legs.

It looked so hopeless. There didn't seem to be any way I could save her.

At the edge of the water stood a large sycamore. I got behind it, anything to blot out that heartbreaking scene. Little Ann, thinking I had deserted her, started crying. I couldn't stand it.

I opened my mouth to call Old Dan. I wanted to tell him to come on and we'd go home as there was nothing we could do. The words just wouldn't come out. I couldn't utter a sound. I lay my face against the icy cold bark of the sycamore. I thought of the prayer I had said when I had asked God to help me get two hound pups. I knelt down and sobbed out a prayer. I asked for a miracle which would save the life of my little dog. I promised all the things that a young boy could if only He would help me.

Still saying my prayer and making promises, I heard a sharp metallic sound. I jumped up and stepped away from the tree. I was sure the noise I heard was made by a rattling chain on the front end of a boat.

I shouted as loud as I could. "Over here. I need help. My dog is drowning."

I waited for an answer. All I could hear were the cries of Little Ann.

Again I hollered. "Over here. Over on the bank. Can you see my light? I need help. Please hurry."

I held my breath waiting for an answering shout. I shivered from the freezing cold of my wet shoes and overalls. A straining silence settled over the river. A feathery rustle swished by in the blackness. A flock of low-flying ducks had been disturbed by my loud shouts. I strained my ears for some sound. Now and then I could hear the lapping slap of the ice-cold water as it swirled its way through the trough.

I glanced to Little Ann. She was still holding on but I saw her paws were almost at the edge. I knew her time was short.

I couldn't figure out what I had heard. The sound was made by metal striking metal, but what was it? What could have caused it?

I looked at my ax. It couldn't have made the sound as it was too close to me. The noise had come from out in the river.

When I looked at my lantern I knew that it had made the strange sound. I had left the handle standing straight up when I had taken the pole away. Now it was down. For some unknown reason the stiff wire handle had twisted in the sockets and dropped. As it had fallen it had struck the metal frame, making the sharp metallic sound I had heard.

As I stared at the yellow glow of my light, the last bit of hope faded away. I closed my eyes, intending to pray again for the help I so desperately needed. Then like a blinding red flash the message of the lantern bored its way into my brain. There was my miracle. There was the way to save my little dog. In the metallic sound I had heard were my instructions. They were so plain I couldn't help but understand them. The bright yellow flame started flickering and dancing. It seemed to be saying, "Hurry. You know what to do."

Faster than I had ever moved in my life I went to work. With a stick I measured the water in the hole where my feet had broken through the ice. I was right. My foot had touched bottom. Eighteen inches down I felt the soft mud.

With my pole I fished the lantern back to the bank. I took the handle off, straightened it out, and bent a hook in one end. With one of my shoelaces I tied the wire to the end of the cane pole. I left the hook sticking out about six inches beyond the end of it.

I started shouting encouragement to Little Ann. I told her to hang on and not to give up for I was going to save her. She answered with a low cry.

With the hook stuck in one of the ventilating holes in the top of my light, I lifted it back out on the ice and set it down. After a little wiggling and pushing, I worked the hook loose and laid the pole down.

I took off my clothes, picked up my ax, and stepped down into the hole in the icy water. It came to my knees. Step by step, breaking the ice with my ax, I waded out.

The water came up to my hips, and then to my waist. The cold bite of it took my breath away. I felt my body grow numb. I couldn't feel my feet at all but I knew they were moving. When the water reached my armpits I stopped and worked my pole toward Little Ann. Stretching my arms as far out as I could, I saw I was still a foot short. Closing my eyes and gritting my teeth, I moved on. The water reached my chin.

I was close enough. I started hooking at the collar of Little Ann.
Time after time I felt the hook almost catch. I saw I was fishing on
a wrong angle. She had settled so low in the water I couldn't reach
her collar. Raising my arms above my head so the pole would be
on a slant I kept hooking and praying. The seconds ticked by. I
strained for one more inch. The muscles in my arms grew numb
from the weight of the pole.

Little Ann's claws slipped again. I thought she was gone. At
the very edge of the ice, she caught again. All I could see now
were her small red paws and her nose and eyes.

By Old Dan's actions I could tell he understood and wanted to
help. He ran over close to my pole and started digging at the
ice. I whopped him with the cane. That was the only time in my
life I ever hit my dog. I had to get him out of the way so I could
see what I was doing.

Just when I thought my task was impossible, I felt the hook
slide under the tough leather. It was none too soon.

As gently as I could I dragged her over the rim of the ice.
At first I thought she was dead. She didn't move. Old Dan
started whining and licking her face and ears. She moved her
head. I started talking to her. She made an effort to stand but
couldn't. Her muscles were paralyzed and the blood had long
since ceased to flow.

At the movement of Little Ann, Old Dan threw a fit. He
started barking and jumping. His long red tail fanned the air.

Still holding onto my pole, I tried to take a step backward. My
feet wouldn't move. A cold gripping fear came over me. I
thought my legs were frozen. I made another effort to lift my
leg. It moved. I realized that my feet were stuck in the soft muddy
bottom.

I started backing out, dragging the body of my little dog. I
couldn't feel the pole in my hands. When my feet touched the icy
bank, I couldn't feel that either. All the feeling in my body was
gone.

I wrapped Little Ann in my coat and hurried into my clothes.
With the pole I fished my light back.

Close by was a large drift. I climbed up on top of it and dug
a hole down through the ice and snow until I reached the dry

limbs. I poured half of the oil in my lantern down into the hole and dropped in a match. In no time I had a roaring fire.

I laid Little Ann close to the warm heat and went to work. Old Dan washed her head with his warm red tongue while I massaged and rubbed her body.

I could tell by her cries when the blood started circulating. Little by little her strength came back. I stood her on her feet and started walking her. She was weak and wobbly but I knew she would live. I felt much better and breathed a sigh of relief.

After drying myself out the best I could, I took the lantern handle from the pole, bent it back to its original position, and put it back on the lantern. Holding the light out in front of me, I looked at it. The bright metal gleamed in the firelight glow.

I started talking to it. I said, "Thanks, old lantern, more than you'll ever know. I'll always take care of you. Your globe will always be clean and there'll never be any rust or dirt on your frame."

I knew if it had not been for the miracle of the lantern, my little dog would have met her death on that night. Her grave would have been the cold icy waters of the Illinois River.

Out in the river I could hear the cold water gurgling in the icy trough. It seemed to be angry. It hissed and growled as it tore its way through the channel. I shuddered to think of what could have happened.

Before I left for home, I walked back to the sycamore tree. Once again I said a prayer, but this time the words were different. I didn't ask for a miracle. In every way a young boy could, I said "thanks." My second prayer wasn't said with just words. All of my heart and soul was in it.

On my way home I decided not to say anything to my mother and father about Little Ann's accident. I knew it would scare Mama and she might stop my hunting.

Reaching our house, I didn't hang the lantern in its usual place. I took it to my room and set it in a corner with the handle standing up.

The next morning I started sneezing and came down with a terrible cold. I told Mama I had gotten my feet wet. She scolded me a little and started doctoring me.

For three days and nights I stayed home. All this time I kept checking the handle of the lantern. My sisters shook the house from the roof to the floor with their playing and romping, but the handle never did fall.

I went to my mother and asked her if God answered prayers every time one was said. She smiled and said, "No, Billy, not every time. He only answers the ones that are said from the heart. You have to be sincere and believe in Him."

She wanted to know why I had asked.

I said, "Oh, I just wondered, and wanted to know."

She came over and straightened my suspenders, saying, "That was a very nice question for my little Daniel Boone to ask."

Bending over, she started kissing me. I finally squirmed away from her, feeling as wet as a dirt dauber's nest. My mother never could kiss me like a fellow should be kissed. Before she was done I was kissed all over. It always made me feel silly and baby-like. I tried to tell her that a coon hunter wasn't supposed to be kissed that way, but Mama never could understand things like that.

I stomped out of the house to see how my dogs were.

XII

THE FAME OF MY DOGS spread all over our part of the Ozarks. They were the best in the country. No coon hunter came into my grandfather's store with as many pelts as I did. Grandpa never overlooked an opportunity to brag. He told everyone the story of my dogs, and the part he had played in getting them.

Many was the time some farmer, coming to our home, would say, "Your Grandpa was telling me you got three big coons over in Pea Vine Hollow the other night." I would listen, knowing I only got one, or maybe none, but Grandpa was my pal. If he said I caught ten in one tree, it was just that way.

Because of my grandfather's bragging, and his firm belief in my dogs and me, a terrible thing happened.

One morning, while having breakfast, Mama said to Papa, "I'm almost out of corn meal. Do you think you can go to the mill today?"

Papa said, "I intended to butcher a hog. We're about out of meat." Looking at me, he said, "Shell a sack of corn. Take one of the mules and go to the mill for your mother."

With the help of my sisters, we shelled the corn. Throwing it over our mule's back, I started for the store.

On arriving at the millhouse, I tied my mule to the hitching post, took my corn, and set it by the door. I walked over to the store and told Grandpa I wanted to get some corn ground.

He said, "I'll be with you in just a minute."

As I was waiting, I heard a horse coming. Looking out, I saw who it was and I didn't like what I saw. It was the two youngest

Pritchard boys. I had run into them on several occasions during pie suppers and dances.

The Pritchards were a large family that lived upriver about five miles. As in most small country communities, there is one family that no one likes. The Pritchards were it. Tales were told that they were bootleggers, thieves, and just all-round "no-accounts." The story had gone round that Old Man Pritchard had killed a man somewhere in Missouri before moving to our part of the country.

Rubin was two years older than I, big and husky for his age. He never had much to say. He had mean-looking eyes that were set far back in his rugged face. They were smoky-hued and unblinking, as if the eyelids were paralyzed. I had heard that once he had cut a boy with a knife in a fight over at the sawmill.

Rainie was the youngest, about my age. He had the meanest disposition of any boy I had ever known. Because of this he was disliked by young and old. Wherever Rainie went, trouble seemed to follow. He was always wanting to bet, and would bet on anything. He was nervous, and could never seem to stand still.

Once at my grandfather's store, I had given him a piece of candy. Snatching it out of my hand, he ate it and then sneered at me and said it wasn't any good. During a pie supper one night, he wanted to bet a dime that he could whip me.

My mother told me always to be kind to Rainie, that he couldn't help being the way he was. I asked, "Why?" She said it was because his brothers were always picking on him and beating him.

On entering the store, they stopped and glared at me. Rubin walked over to the counter. Rainie came over to me.

Leering at me, he said, "I'd like to make a bet with you."

I told him I didn't want to bet.

He asked if I was scared.

"No. I just don't want to bet," I said.

His neck and ears looked as though they hadn't been washed in months. His ferret-like eyes kept darting here and there. Glancing down to his hands, I saw the back of his right sleeve was stiff and starchy from the constant wiping of his nose.

He saw I was looking him over, and asked if I liked what I saw.

I started to say, "No," but didn't, turned, and walked away a few steps.

Rubin ordered some chewing tobacco.

"Aren't you a little young to be chewing?" Grandpa asked.

"Ain't for me. It's for my dad," Rubin growled.

Grandpa handed two plugs to him. He paid for it, turned around, and handed one plug to Rainie. Holding the other up in front of him, he looked it over. Looking at Grandpa, he gnawed at one corner of it.

Grandpa mumbled something about how kids were brought up these days. He came from behind the counter, saying to me, "Let's go grind that corn."

The Pritchard boys made no move to follow us out of the store.

"Come on," Grandpa said. "I'm going to lock up till I get this corn ground."

"We'll just stay here. I want to look at some of the shirts," said Rubin.

"No, you won't," said Grandpa. "Come on, I'm going to lock up."

Begrudgingly, they walked out.

I helped Grandpa start the mill and we proceeded to grind the corn. The Pritchard boys had followed us and were standing looking on.

Rainie walked over to me. "I hear you have some good hounds," he said.

I told him I had the best in the country. If he didn't believe me, he could just ask my grandfather.

He just leered at me. "I don't think they're half as good as you say they are," he said. "Bet our old blue tick hound can out-hunt both of them."

I laughed, "Ask Grandpa who brings in the most hides."

"I wouldn't believe him. He's crooked," he said.

I let him know right quick that my grandfather wasn't crooked.

"He's a storekeeper, ain't he?" he said.

I glanced over at Grandpa. He had heard the remark made by Rainie. His friendly old face was as red as a turkey gobbler's wattle.

The last of my corn was just going through the grinding stones. Grandpa pushed a lever to one side, shutting off the power. He came over and said to Rainie, "What do you do? Just go around looking for trouble. What do you want, a fight?"

Rubin sidled over. "This ain't none of your business," he said. "Besides, Rainie's not looking for a fight. We just want to make a bet with him."

Grandpa glared at Rubin. "Any bet you would make sure would be a good one all right. What kind of a bet?"

Rubin spat a mouthful of tobacco juice on the clean floor. He said, "Well, we've heard so much about them hounds of his, we just think it's a lot of talk and lies. We'd like to make a little bet; say about two dollars."

I had never seen my old grandfather so mad. The red had left his face. In its place was a sickly, paste-gray color. The kind old eyes behind the glasses burned with a fire I had never seen.

In a loud voice, he asked, "Bet on what?"

Rubin spat again. Grandpa's eyes followed the brown stain in its arch until it landed on the clean floor and splattered.

With a leering grin on his ugly, dirty face, Rubin said, "Well, we got an old coon up in our part of the country that's been there a long time. Ain't no dog yet ever been smart enough to tree him, and I—"

Rainie broke into the conversation, "He ain't just an ordinary coon. He's an old-timer. Folks call him the 'ghost coon.' Believe me, he is a ghost. He just runs hounds long enough to get them all warmed up, then climbs a tree and disappears. Our old blue hound has treed him more times than—"

Rubin told Rainie to shut up and let him do the talking. Looking over at me, he said, "What do you say? Want to bet two dollars your hounds can tree him?"

I looked at my grandfather, but he didn't help me.

I told Rubin I didn't want to bet, but I was pretty sure my dogs could tree the ghost coon.

Rainie butted in again, "What's the matter? You 'yellow'?"

I felt the hot blood rush into my face. My stomach felt like something alive was crawling in it. I doubled up my right fist and was on the point of hitting Rainie in one of his eyes when I felt my grandfather's hand on my shoulder.

I looked up. His eyes flashed as he looked at me. A strange little smile was tugging at the corner of his mouth. The big artery in his neck was pounding out and in. It reminded me of a young bird that had fallen out of a nest and lay dying on the ground.

Still looking at me, he reached back and took his billfold from his pocket, saying, "Let's call that bet." Turning to Rubin, he said, "I'm going to let him call your bet, but now you listen. If you boys take him up there to hunt the ghost coon, and jump on him and beat him up, you're sure going to hear from me. I don't mean maybe. I'll have both of you taken to Tahlequah and put in jail. You had better believe that."

Rubin saw he had pushed my grandfather far enough. Backing up a couple of steps, he said, "We're not going to jump on him. All we want to do is make a bet."

Grandpa handed me two one-dollar bills, saying to Rubin, "You hold your money and he can hold his. If you lose, you had better pay off." Looking back to me, he said, "Son, if you lose, pay off."

I nodded my head.

I asked Rubin when he wanted me to come up for the hunt.

He thought a minute. "You know where that old log slide comes out from the hills onto the road?" he asked.

I nodded.

"We'll meet you there tomorrow night about dark," he said.

It was fine with me, I said, but I told him not to bring his hounds because mine wouldn't hunt with other dogs.

He said he wouldn't.

I agreed to bring my ax and lantern.

As they turned to leave, Rainie smirked. "Sucker!" he said.

I made no reply.

After the Pritchard boys had gone, my grandfather looked at me and said, "Son, I have never asked another man for much, but I sure want you to catch the ghost coon."

I told him if the ghost coon made one track in the river bottoms, my dogs would get him.

Grandpa laughed.

"You'd better be getting home. It's getting late and your mother is waiting for the corn meal," he said.

I could hear him chuckling as he walked toward his store. I thought to myself, "There goes the best grandpa a boy ever had."

Lifting the sack of meal to the back of my old mule, I started for home. All the way, I kept thinking of Old Dan, Little Ann, ghost coons, and the two ugly, dirty Pritchard boys. I decided not to tell my mother and father anything about the hunt for I knew Mama wouldn't approve of anything I had to do with the Pritchards.

The following evening I arrived at the designated spot early. I sat down by a red oak tree to wait. I called Little Ann over to me and had a good talk with her. I told her how much I loved her, scratched her back, and looked at the pads of her feet.

"Sweetheart," I said, "you must do something for me tonight. I want you to tree the ghost coon for it means so much to Grandpa and me."

She seemed to understand and answered by washing my face and hands.

I tried to talk to Old Dan, but I may as well have talked to a stump for all the attention he paid to me. He kept walking around sniffing here and there. He couldn't understand why we were waiting. He was wanting to hunt.

Rubin and Rainie showed up just at dark. Both had sneers on their faces.

"Are you ready?" Rubin asked.

"Yes," I said, and asked him which way was the best to go.

"Let's go downriver a way and work up," he said. "We're sure to strike him coming upriver, and that way we've got the wind in our favor."

"Are these the hounds that we've been hearing so much about?" Rainie asked.

I nodded.

"They look too little to be any good," he said.

I told him dynamite came in little packages.

He asked me if I had my two dollars.

"Yes," I said.

He wanted to see my money. I showed it to him. Rubin, not to be outdone, showed me his.

We crossed an old field and entered the river bottoms. By this time it was quite dark. I lit my lantern and asked which one wanted to carry my ax.

"It's yours," Rainie said. "You carry it."

Not wanting to argue, I carried both the lantern and the ax.

Rainie started telling me how stingy and crooked my grandfather was. I told him I hadn't come to have any trouble or to fight. All I wanted to do was to hunt the ghost coon. If there was going to be any trouble, I would just call my dogs and go home.

Rubin had a nickel's worth of sense, but Rainie had none at all. Rubin told him if he didn't shut up, he was going to bloody his nose. That shut Rainie up.

Old Dan opened up first. It was a beautiful thing to hear. The deep tones of his voice rolled in the silent night.

A bird in a canebrake on our right started chirping. A big swamp rabbit came running down the riverbank as if all hell was close to his heels. A bunch of mallards, feeding in the shallows across the river, took flight with frightened quacks. A feeling that only a hunter knows slowly crept over my body. I whooped to my dogs, urging them on.

Little Ann came in. Her bell-like tones blended with Old Dan's, in perfect rhythm. We stood and listened to the beautiful music, the deep-throated notes of hunting hounds on the hot-scented trail of a river coon.

Rubin said, "If he crosses the river up at the Buck Ford, it's the ghost coon, as that's the way he always runs."

We stood and listened. Sure enough, the voices of my dogs were silent for a few minutes. Old Dan, a more powerful swimmer than Little Ann, was the first to open up after crossing over. She was close behind him.

Rubin said, "That's him, all right. That's the ghost coon."

They crossed the river again.

We waited.

Rainie said, "You may as well get your money out now."

I told him just to wait a while, and I'd show him the ghost coon's hide.

This brought a loud laugh from Rainie, which sounded like someone had dropped an empty bucket on a gravel bar and then had kicked it.

The wily old coon crossed the river several times, but couldn't shake my dogs from his trail. He cut out from the bottoms, walked a rail fence, and jumped from it into a thick canebrake. He piled into an old slough. Where it emptied into the river, he swam to the middle. Doing opposite to what most coons do, which is swim downstream, he swam upstream. He stopped at an old drift in the middle of it.

Little Ann found him. When she jumped him from the drift,

Old Dan was far downriver searching for the trail. If he could have gotten there in time, it would have been the last of the ghost coon, but Little Ann couldn't do much by herself in the water. He fought his way free from her, swam to our side, and ran upstream.

I could hear Old Dan coming through the bottoms on the other side, bawling at every jump. I could feel the driving power in his voice. We heard him when he hit the water to cross over. It sounded like a cow had jumped in.

Little Ann was warming up the ghost coon. I could tell by her voice that she was close to him.

Reaching our side, Old Dan tore out after her. He was a mad hound. His deep voice was telling her he was coming.

We were trotting along, following my dogs, when I heard Little Ann's bawling stop.

"Wait a minute," I said. "I think she has treed him. Let's give her time to circle the tree to make sure he's there."

Old Dan opened up bawling treed. Rubin started on.

"Something's wrong," I said. "I can't hear Little Ann."

Rainie spoke up, "Maybe the ghost coon ate her up."

I glared at him.

Hurrying on, we came to my dogs. Old Dan was bawling at a hole in a large sycamore that had fallen into the river.

At that spot, the bank was a good ten feet above the water level. As the big tree had fallen, the roots had been torn and twisted from the ground. The jagged roots, acting as a drag, had stopped it from falling all the way into the stream. The trunk lay on a steep slant from the top of the bank to the water. Looking down, I could see the broken tangled mass of the top. Debris from floods had caught in the limbs, forming a drift.

Old Dan was trying to dig and gnaw his way into the log. Pulling him from the hole, I held my lantern up and looked down into the dark hollow. I knew that somewhere down below the surface there had to be another hole in the trunk, as water had filled the hollow to the river level.

Rubin, looking over my shoulder, said, "That coon couldn't be in there. If he was, he'd be drowned."

I agreed.

Rainie spoke up. "You ready to pay off?" he asked. "I told you them hounds couldn't tree the ghost coon."

I told him the show wasn't over.

Little Ann had never bawled treed, and I knew she wouldn't until she knew exactly where the coon was. Working the bank up and down, and not finding the trail, she swam across the river and worked the other side. For a good half-hour she searched that side before she came back across to where Old Dan was. She sniffed around the hollow log.

"We might as well get away from here," Rainie said. "They ain't going to find the ghost coon."

"It sure looks that way," Rubin said.

I told them I wasn't giving up until my dogs did.

"You just want to be stubborn," Rubin said. "I'm ready for my money now."

I asked him to wait a few minutes.

"Ain't no use," he said. "No hound yet ever treed that ghost coon."

Hearing a whine, I turned around. Little Ann had crawled up on the log and was inching her way down the slick trunk toward the water. I held my lantern up so I could see better. Spraddle-legged, claws digging into the bark, she was easing her way down.

"You'd better get her out of there," Rubin said. "If she gets down in that old tree top, she'll drown."

Rubin didn't know my Little Ann.

Once her feet slipped. I saw her hind quarters fall off to one side. She didn't get scared. Slowly she eased her legs back up on the log.

Again Rubin said, "You'd better get her out of there."

I made no reply. I just watched and waited.

Little Ann eased herself into the water. Swimming to the drift, she started sniffing around. In places it was thin and her legs would break through. Climbing, clawing, and swimming, she searched the drift over, looking for the lost trail.

I saw when she stopped searching. With her body half in the water, and her front feet curved over a piece of driftwood, she turned her head and looked toward the shore. I could see her head twisting from side to side. I could tell by her actions that she had gotten the scent. With a low whine, she started back.

I told Rubin, "I think she smells something."

Slowly and carefully she worked her way through the tangled mass. I lost sight of her when she came close to the undermined bank. She wormed her way under the overhang. I could hear her clawing and wallowing around, and then all hell broke loose. Out from under the bank came the biggest coon I had ever seen, the ghost coon.

He came out right over Little Ann. She caught him in the old treetop. I knew she was no match for him in that tangled mass of limbs and logs. He fought his way free and swam for the opposite bank. She was right behind him.

Old Dan didn't wait, look, or listen. He piled off the ten-foot bank and disappeared from sight. I looked for him. I knew he was tangled in the debris under the surface. I started to take off my overalls, but stopped when I saw his red head shoot up out of the water. Bawling and clawing his way free of the limbs and logs, he was on his way.

On reaching midstream, the ghost coon headed downriver with Little Ann still on his tail.

We ran down the riverbank. I could see my dogs clearly in the moonlight. The ghost coon was about fifteen feet ahead of Little Ann. About twenty-five yards behind them came Old Dan, trying so hard to catch up. I whooped to them.

Rubin grabbed a pole, saying, "He may come out on this side."

Knowing the ghost coon was desperate, I wondered what he would do. Reaching a gravel bar below the high bank, we ran out on it to the water's edge. Then the ghost coon did something that I never expected. Coming even with us, he turned from midstream and came straight for us.

I heard Rubin yell, "Here he comes!"

He churned his way through the shallows and ran right between us. Rubin swung his pole, missed the coon, and almost hit Little Ann. The coon headed for the river bottoms with her right on his heels.

The bawling of Little Ann and our screaming and hollering made so much noise, I didn't hear Old Dan coming. He tore out of the river, plowed into me, and knocked me down.

We ran through the bottoms, following my dogs. I thought the ghost coon was going back to the sycamore log but he didn't. He ran upriver.

While hurrying after them, I looked over at Rainie. For once in his life, I think he was excited. He was whooping and screaming, and falling over logs and limbs.

I felt good all over.

Glancing over at me, Rainie said, "They ain't got him yet."

The ghost coon crossed the river time after time. Seeing that he couldn't shake Old Dan and Little Ann from his trail, he cut through the river bottoms and ran out into an old field.

At this maneuver, Rubin said to Rainie, "He's heading for that tree."

"What tree?" I asked.

"You'll see," Rainie said. "When he gets tired, he always heads for that tree. That's where he gets his name, the ghost coon. He just disappears."

"If he disappears, my dogs will disappear with him," I said. Rainie laughed.

I had to admit one thing. The Pritchard boys knew the habits of the ghost coon. I knew he couldn't run all night. He had already far surpassed any coon I had ever chased.

"They're just about there," Rubin said.

Just then I heard Old Dan bark treed. I waited for Little Ann's voice. I didn't hear her. I wondered what it could be this time.

"He's there all right," Rubin said. "He's in that tree."

"Well, come on," I said. "I want to see that tree."

"You might as well get your money out," Rainie said.

I told him he had said that once before, back on the riverbank.

XIII

COMING UP TO THE TREE, I could see it was a huge bur oak. It wasn't tall. It was just the opposite, rather low and squatty. The top was a thick mass of large limbs, and it hadn't shed all of its leaves yet.

It stood by itself in an old field. There were no other trees within fifty yards of it. About fifteen feet to the left were the remains of a barbed-wire fence. An old gate hung by one rusty hinge from a large corner post. I could tell that at one time a house had stood close by.

Rubin saw me looking around. "A long time ago some Indians lived here and farmed these fields," he said.

I walked around the tree looking for the coon, but could see very little in the dark shadows.

"Ain't no use to look," Rubin said. "He won't be there."

Rainie spoke up. "This ain't the first time we've been to this tree," he said.

Rubin told Rainie to shut up. "You talk too much," he said.

In a whining voice, Rainie said, "Rubin, you know the coon ain't in that tree. Make him pay off and let's go home. I'm getting tired."

I told Rubin I was going to climb the tree.

"Go ahead," he said. "It won't do you any good."

The tree was easy to climb. I looked all over it, on each limb, and in every dark place. I looked for a hollow. The ghost coon wasn't there. I climbed back down, scolded Old Dan to stop his loud bawling, and looked for Little Ann.

I saw her far up the old fence row, sniffing and running here and there. I knew the ghost coon had pulled a real trick, but I couldn't figure out what it was. Little Ann had never yet barked treed. I knew if the coon was in the tree she wouldn't still be searching for a trail.

Old Dan started working again.

My dogs covered the field. They circled and circled. They ran up and down the barbed-wire fence on both sides.

I knew the coon hadn't walked the barbed wire. Ghost or no ghost, he couldn't do that. I walked over to the old gate and looked around. I sat down and stared up into the tree. Little Ann came to me.

Old Dan, giving up his search, came back to the tree and bawled a couple of times. I scolded him again.

Rubin came over. Leering at me, he said, "You give up?"

I didn't answer.

Little Ann once again started searching for the lost trail. Old Dan went to help her.

Rainie said, "I told you that you couldn't tree the ghost coon. Why don't you pay off so we can go home?"

I told him I hadn't given up. My dogs were still hunting. When they gave up, I would, too.

Rubin said, "Well, we're not going to stay here all night."

Looking back to the tree, I thought perhaps I had overlooked something. I told Rubin I was going to climb it again.

He laughed, "Go ahead. Won't do any good. You climbed it once. Ain't you satisfied?"

"No, I'm not satisfied," I said. "I just don't believe in ghost coons."

Rubin said, "I don't believe in ghosts either, but facts are facts. To tell you the truth, I've climbed that tree a dozen times and there just ain't no place in it for a coon to hide."

Rainie spoke up. "Our old blue hound has treed the ghost coon in this tree more times than one. Maybe you two don't believe in ghosts, but I do. Why don't you pay off so we can get away from here."

"I'll climb it one more time," I said. "If I can't find him, I'll pay off."

Climbing up again, I searched and searched. When I got through, I knew the ghost coon wasn't in that tree. When I came down, I saw my dogs had given up. That took the last resistance out of me. I knew if they couldn't find the ghost coon, I couldn't.

Digging the two one-dollar bills out of my pocket, I walked over to Rubin. Little Ann was by my side. I handed my money over, saying, "Well, you won it fair and square."

With a grin on his face, Rubin took my money. He said, "I bet this will break your old grandpa's heart."

I didn't reply.

Reaching down, I caught Little Ann's head in my hands. Looking into her warm friendly eyes, I said, "It's all right, little girl, we haven't given up yet. We'll come back. We may never catch the ghost coon, but we'll run him until he leaves the country.

She licked my hands and whined.

A small breeze began to stir. Glancing up into the tree, I saw some leaves shaking. I said to Rubin, "Looks like the wind is coming up. It may blow up a storm. We'd better be heading for home."

Just as I turned, I saw Little Ann throw up her head and whine. Her body grew stiff and taut. I watched her. She was testing the wind. I knew she had scented something in the breeze. Stiff-legged, head high in the air, she started walking toward the tree. Almost there, she turned back and stopped. I knew she had caught the scent but could only catch it when a breeze came.

Looking at Rubin, I said, "I haven't lost that two dollars yet."

Another breeze drifted out of the river bottoms. Little Ann caught the scent again. Slowly she walked straight to the large gatepost, reared up on it with her front feet, and bawled the most beautiful tree bark I ever heard in my life.

Old Dan, not understanding why Little Ann was bawling, stood and looked. He walked over to the post, reared up on it, and sniffed. Then, raising his head, he shook the dead leaves in the bur oak tree with his deep voice.

I looked at Rainie. Laughing, I said, "There's your ghost coon. Now what do you think of my dogs?"

For once he made no reply.

Going over to the post, I saw it was a large black locust put there many years ago to hang the gate. Looking up at the tree, I saw how the ghost coon had pulled his trick. One large long limb ran out and hung directly over the gate. It was a drop of a good twelve feet from the branch to the top of the gatepost, but I knew we weren't after an ordinary coon. This was the ghost coon.

I said to Rubin, "Boost me up and I'll see if the post is hollow."

After breaking off a long Jimpson weed to use as a prod, I got up on Rubin's shoulder, and he raised me up. The post was hollow. Not knowing how far down the hole went, I started the switch down. About halfway, I felt something soft. I gave it a hard jab.

I heard him coming. He boiled out right in my face. I let go of everything. Hitting the ground, I rolled over on my back and looked up.

For a split second, the ghost coon stayed on top of the post, and then he jumped. My dogs were on him the instant he hit the ground. The fight was on.

I knew the coon didn't have a chance as he wasn't in the waters of the river. He didn't give up easily even though he was on dry land. He was fighting for his life and a good account he gave. He fought his way to freedom, and made it back to the bur oak tree. He was a good six feet up the side when Old Dan, leaping high in the air, caught him and pulled him back down.

At the foot of the tree, the fight went on. Again the ghost coon fought his way free. This time he made it and disappeared in the dark shadows of the tree. Old Dan was furious. Never before had I seen a coon get away from him.

I told Rubin I would climb up and run him out. As I started climbing, I saw Little Ann go to one side and Old Dan to the other. My dogs would never stay together when they had treed a coon, so that any way he left a tree, he was met by one of them.

About halfway up, far out on a limb, I found the ghost coon. As I started toward him, my dogs stopped bawling. I heard something I had heard many times. The sound was like the cry of a small baby. It was the cry of a ringtail coon when he knows it is the end of the trail. I never liked to hear this cry, but it was all in the game, the hunter and the hunted.

As I sat there on the limb, looking at the old fellow, he cried again. Something came over me. I didn't want to kill him.

I hollered down and told Rubin I didn't want to kill the ghost coon.

He hollered back, "Are you crazy?"

I told him I wasn't crazy. I just didn't want to kill him.

I climbed down.

Rubin was mad. He said, "What's the matter with you?"

"Nothing," I told him. "I just don't have the heart to kill the coon."

I told him there were plenty more; why kill him? He had lived here a long time, and more than one hunter had listened to the voices of his hounds bawling on his trail.

Rainie said, "He's chicken-livered, that's what it is."

I didn't like that but, not wanting to argue, I didn't say anything.

Rubin said, "I'll go up and run him out."

"I won't let my dogs kill him," I said.

Rubin glared at me. "I'm going up and run that coon out," he said. "If you stop your dogs, I'm going to beat you half to death."

"Do it anyway, Rubin," Rainie said.

"I've a good mind to," said Rubin.

Just as Rubin started to climb the tree, Old Dan growled. He was staring into the darkness. Something was coming.

"What's that?" I asked.

"I don't know," Rubin said. "Don't sound like anything I ever heard."

"It's ghosts," Rainie said. "Let's get away from here."

An animal was coming out of the darkness. It was walking slowly in an odd way, as if it were walking sideways. The hair on the back of my neck stood straight out.

As the animal came closer, Rainie said, "Why, it's Old Blue. How did he get loose?"

It was a big blue tick hound. Around his neck was a piece of rope about three feet long. One could see that the rope had been gnawed in two. The frayed end had become entangled in a fair-sized dead limb. Dragging the limb was what made the dog look so odd. I felt much better when I found out what it was.

The blue tick hound was like the Pritchards, mean and ugly. He was a big dog, tall and heavy. His chest was thick and solid. He came up growling. The hair on his back was standing straight up. He walked stiff-legged around Old Dan, showing his teeth.

I told Rainie he had better get hold of his dog, or there was sure to be a fight.

"You better get hold of your dog," he said. "I'm not worried about Old Blue. He can take care of himself."

I said no more.

"Don't make no difference now whether you kill the ghost coon or not," Rubin said. "Old Blue will take care of him."

I knew the killing of the coon was out of my control, but I didn't want to see him die. I said to Rubin, "Just give back my two dollars and I'll go home. I can't keep you from killing him, but I don't have to stay and see it."

"Rubin, don't give him the money," Rainie said. "He ain't killed the ghost coon."

"That's right," Rubin said. "You ain't, and I wouldn't let you now, even if you wanted to."

I told them my dogs had treed the ghost coon and that was the bet, to tree the ghost coon.

"No, it wasn't," Rubin said. "You said you would kill him."

"It was no such thing," I said. "I've done all I said I would."

Rubin walked up in front of me. He said, "I ain't going to give you the money. You didn't win it fair. Now what are you going to do about it?"

I looked into his mean eyes. I started to make some reply, but decided against it.

He saw my hesitation, and said, "You better get your dogs and get out of here before you get whipped."

In a loud voice, Rainie said, "Bloody his nose, Rubin."

I was scared. I couldn't whip Rubin. He was too big for me. I started to turn and leave when I thought of what my grandfather had told them.

"You had better remember what my grandpa said," I reminded them. "He'll do just what he said he would."

Rubin didn't hit me. He just grabbed me and with his brute strength threw me down on the ground. He had me on my back with my arms outspread. He had a knee on each arm. I made no effort to fight back. I was scared.

"If you say one word to your grandpa about this," Rubin said, "I'll catch you hunting some night and take my knife to you."

Looking up into his ugly face, I knew he would do just what he said. I told him to let me up and I would go and not say anything to anyone.

"Don't let him up, Rubin," Rainie said. "Beat the hell out of him, or hold him and let me do it."

Just then I heard growling, and a commotion off to one side. The blue hound had finally gotten a fight out of Old Dan. Turning my head sideways, I could see them standing on their hind legs, tearing and slashing at each other. The weight of the big hound pushed Old Dan over.

I told Rubin to let me up so we could stop the fight.

He laughed, "While my dog is whipping yours, I think I'll just work you over a little." So saying, he jerked my cap off, and started whipping me in the face with it.

I heard Rainie yell, "Rubin, they're killing Old Blue."

Rubin jumped up off me.

I clambered up and looked over to the fight. What I saw thrilled me. Faithful Little Ann, bitch though she was, had gone to the assistance of Old Dan.

I knew my dogs were very close to each other. Everything they did was done as a combination, but I never expected this. It is a very rare occasion for a bitch dog to fight another dog, but fight she did.

I could see that Little Ann's jaws were glued to the throat of the big hound. She would never loosen that deadly hold until the last breath of life was gone.

Old Dan was tearing and slashing at the soft belly. I knew the destruction his long sharp teeth were causing.

Again Rainie yelled, "Rubin, they're killing him. They're killing Old Blue. Do something quick."

Rubin darted over to one side, grabbed my ax from the ground, and said in a loud voice, "I'll kill them damn hounds."

At the thought of what he was going to do with the ax, I screamed and ran for my dogs. Rubin was about ten feet ahead of me, bent over, running with the ax held out in front of him. I knew I could never get to them in time.

I was screaming, "No, Rubin, no!"

I saw the small stick when it whipped up from the ground. As if it were alive, it caught between Rubin's legs. I saw him fall. I ran on by.

Reaching the dogfight, I saw the big hound was almost gone. He had long since ceased fighting. His body lay stretched full-length on the ground. I grabbed Old Dan's collar and pulled him back. It was different with Little Ann. Pull as I might, she wouldn't let go of the hound's throat. Her jaws were locked.

I turned Old Dan loose and, getting astraddle of Little Ann, I pried her jaws apart with my hands. Old Dan had darted back in. Grabbing his collar again, I pulled them off to one side.

The blue hound lay where he was. I thought perhaps he was already dead, and then I saw him move a little.

Still holding my dogs by their collars, I looked back. I couldn't understand what I saw. Rubin was laying where he had fallen. His back was toward me, and his body was bent in a "U" shape. Rainie was standing on the other side of him, staring down.

I hollered and asked Rainie, "What's the matter?"

He didn't answer. He just stood as though in a trance, staring down at Rubin.

I hollered again. He still didn't answer. I didn't know what to do. I couldn't turn my dogs loose. They would go for the hound again.

Again I hollered at Rainie, asking him to come and help me. He neither moved nor answered. I had to do something.

Looking around, my glance fell on the old barbed-wire fence. I led my dogs to it. Holding onto their collars with one hand, I worked a rusty barbed wire backwards and forwards against a staple until it broke. Running the end of it under their collars, I tied them up. They made two or three lunges toward the hound, but the wire held.

I walked over and stopped at Rainie's side. I again asked, "What's the matter?"

He said not a word.

I could see that Rainie was paralyzed with fright. His mouth and eyes were opened wide, and his face was as white as chalk. I laid my hand on his shoulder. At the touch of my hand, he jumped and screamed. Still screaming, he turned and started running. I watched him until he disappeared in the darkness.

Looking down at Rubin, I saw what had paralyzed Rainie. When Rubin had tripped, he had fallen on the ax. As it entered his stomach, the sharp blade had sunk to the eye of the double-bitted ax.

Turning my back to the horrible sight, I closed my eyes. The muscles in my stomach knotted and jerked. A nauseating sickness spread over my body. I couldn't look at him.

I heard Rubin whisper. Turning around, I knelt down by his side with my back to the ax. I couldn't understand what he was whispering. Kneeling down closer, I heard and understood. In a faint voice, he said, "Take it out of me."

I hesitated.

Again he pleaded, "Please, take it out of me."

Turning around, I saw his hands were curled around the protruding blade as if he himself had tried to pull it from his stomach.

How I did it, I'll never know. Putting my hands over his and pressing down, I pulled the ax from the wound. The blood gushed. I felt the warm heat as it spread over my hands. Again the sickness came over me. I stumbled to my feet and stepped back a few paces.

Seeing a movement from Rubin, I thought he was going to get up. With his hands, he pushed himself halfway up. His eyes were wide open, staring straight at me. Stopping in his effort of getting up, still staring at me, his mouth opened as if to say something. Words never came. Instead, a large red bubble slowly worked its way out of his mouth and burst. He fell back to the ground. I knew he was dead.

Scared, not knowing what to do, I called for Rainie. I got no answer. I called his name again and again. I could get no reply. My voice echoed in the darkness of the silent night. A cold chill ran over my body.

I suppose it is natural at a time like that for a boy to think of his mother. I thought of mine. I wanted to get home.

Going over to my dogs, I glanced to where the blue hound was. He was trying to get up. I was glad he wasn't dead.

Picking up my lantern, I thought of my ax. I left it. I didn't care if I never saw it again.

Knowing I couldn't turn my dogs loose, I broke off enough of the wire to lead them. As I passed under the branches of the bur oak tree, I looked up into the dark foliage. I could see the bright eyes of the ghost coon. Everything that had happened on this terrible night was because of his very existence, but it wasn't his fault.

I also knew he was a silent witness to the horrible scene. Behind me lay the still body of a young boy. On my left a blue tick hound lay torn and bleeding. Even after all that had happened, I could feel no hatred for the ghost coon and was not sorry I had let him live.

Arriving home, I awakened my mother and father. Starting at my grandfather's mill, I told everything that had happened. I left nothing out. My mother had started crying long before I had completed my story. Papa said nothing, just sat and listened. When I had finished, he kept staring down at the floor in deep thought. I could hear the sobbing of my mother in the silence. I walked over to her. She put her arms around me and said, "My poor little boy."

Getting to his feet, Papa reached for his coat and hat. Mama asked him where he was going.

"Well, I'll have to go up there," he said. "I'm going to get Grandpa, for he is the only man in the country that has authority to move the body."

Looking at me, he said, "You go across the river and get Old Man Lowery, and you may as well go on up and tell the Bufords, too. Tell them to meet us at your grandfather's place."

I hurried to carry the sad message.

The following day was a nasty one. A slow, cold drizzle had set in. Feeling trapped indoors, I prowled from room to room. I couldn't understand why my father hadn't come back from the Pritchards'. I sat by the window and watched the road.

Understanding my feelings, Mama said, "Billy, I wouldn't worry. He'll be back before long. It takes time for things like that."

"I know," I said, "but you would think he would've been back by now."

Time dragged slowly by. Late in the afternoon, I saw Papa coming. Our old mule was jogging along. Water was shooting out from under his feet in small squirts at every step.

Papa had tied the halter rope around the mule's neck. He was sitting humped over, with his hands jammed deep in the pockets of his patched and worn mackinaw. I felt sorry for him. He was soaking wet, tired, sleepy, and hungry.

Telling Mama, "Here he is," I grabbed my jumper and cap, and ran out to the gate and waited.

I was going to ask him what had happened at the Pritchards'

but on seeing his tired face and wet clothes, I said, "Papa, you had better go in to the fire. I'll take care of the mule, and do the feeding and milking."

"That would be fine," he said.

After doing the chores, I hurried to the house. I couldn't wait any longer. I had to find out what had happened.

Walking into the front room, I saw my father had changed clothes. He was standing in front of the fireplace, drinking coffee.

"Boy, that's bad weather, isn't it?" he said.

I said it was, and asked him about Rubin.

"We went to the old tree and got Rubin's body," Papa said. "We were on our way back to the Pritchards' when we met them. They were just this side of their place. They had started to look for him. Rainie had been so dazed when he got home, they couldn't make out what he was trying to tell them, but they knew it must have been something bad. They wanted to know what had happened. I did my best to explain the accident. It hit Old Man Pritchard pretty hard. I felt sorry for him."

Mama asked how Mrs. Pritchard was taking it.

Papa said he didn't know as he never did get to see any of the womenfolks. He said they were the funniest bunch he had ever seen. He couldn't understand them. There wasn't one tear shed that he could see. All of the men had stayed out at the barn. They never had been invited in for a cup of coffee or anything.

Mama asked when they were to have the funeral.

"They have their own graveyard right there on the place," Papa said. "Old Man Pritchard said they would take care of everything, and didn't want to bother people. He said it was too far for anyone to come, and it was bad weather, too."

Mama said she couldn't help feeling sorry for Mrs. Pritchard, and wished they were more friendly.

I asked Papa about Rainie.

Papa said, "According to what Old Man Pritchard said, Rainie just couldn't seem to get over the shock. They were figuring on taking him into town to see the doctor."

In a stern voice, Papa said, "Billy, I don't want you fooling around with the Pritchards any more. You have plenty of country around here so you don't have to go there to hunt."

I said I wouldn't.

I felt bad about the death of Rubin. I didn't feel like hunting and kept having bad dreams. I couldn't forget the way he had looked at me just before he died. I moped and wandered around in a daze. I wanted to do something but didn't know what it was.

I explained my feelings to my mother. She said, "Billy, I feel the same way and would like to do something to help, but I guess there's nothing we can do. There are people like the Pritchards all through the hills. They live in little worlds of their own and are all alone. They don't like to have outsiders interfere."

I told my mother I had been thinking about how dangerous it was to carry an ax while hunting, and I had decided I'd save a few coon hides and get a good gun. Boy, I just shouldn't have mentioned getting a gun. My mother got "sitting-hen" mad.

"You're not getting a gun," she said. "I won't have that at all. I told you a long time ago you could have one when you are twenty-one years old, and I mean just that. I worry enough with you out there in the hills all hours of the night, running and jumping, but I couldn't stand it if I knew you had a gun with you. No, sir. You can just forget about a gun."

"Yes, Mama," I said, and sulked off to my room.

Lying on my bed, still trying to figure out what I could do to help, I glanced over to the wall. There, tied in a small bundle, was just what I needed.

Some time back my sisters had made some flowers for Decoration Day. They had given me a small bouquet for my room. Taking them down, I could see they had faded a little, and looked rather old, but they were still pretty. I blew the dust off and straightened the crinkled petals. Putting them inside my shirt, I left the house.

I hadn't gone far when I heard something behind me. It was my dogs. I tried to tell them I wasn't going hunting. I just had a little business to attend to, and if they would go back, I'd take them out that night. It was no use. They couldn't understand.

Circling around through the flats, I came to the hollow above the Pritchards' place. Down below me, I could see the graveyard, and the fresh mound of dirt. As quietly as I could, I started easing myself down the mountainside.

Old Dan loosened a rock. The further it bounced, the louder it got. It slammed up against a post oak tree and sounded like a gunshot. I held my breath and watched the house. No one came out.

I glared at Old Dan. He wagged his tail, and just to show off, he sat down on his rear and started digging at a flea with his hind leg. The way his leg was thumping in the leaves, anyone could have heard it for a mile. I waited until he quit thumping before starting on.

Reaching the bottom, I had about twenty yards of clearing to cross, but the grass and bushes were pretty thick. Laying down on my stomach, with my heart beating like a trip hammer, I wiggled my way to Rubin's grave. I laid the flowers on the fresh mound of earth, and then turned around and scooted for the timber.

Just as we reached the mountaintop, my foot slipped and I kicked loose a large rock. Down the side of the mountain it rolled. This time the blue tick hound heard the noise. He came out from under the house bawling. I heard a door slam and Mrs. Pritchard came out. She stood looking this way and that way.

The hound ran up to the graveyard and started sniffing and bawling. Mrs. Pritchard followed him. Seeing the flowers on Rubin's grave, she picked them up and looked at them. She scolded the hound, and then looked up at the hillside. I knew she couldn't see me because the timber was too thick, but I felt uncomfortable anyway.

Scolding the hound again, she knelt down and arranged the flowers on the grave. Taking one more look at the hillside, she started back. Halfway to the house, I saw her reach down and gather the long cotton skirt in her hand and dab at her eyes.

I felt much better after paying my respects to Rubin. Everything looked brighter, and I didn't have that funny feeling any more.

All the way home my dogs kept running out in front of me. They would stop, turn around, and look at me. I had to smile, for I knew what they wanted. I stopped and petted them a little and told them that as soon as I got home and had my supper, we would go hunting.

XIV

A FEW DAYS LATER, on his way back from the mill, one of the Hatfield boys stopped at our place. He told me my grandfather wanted to see me. It was unusual for Grandpa to send for me and it had me worried. I figured that he wanted to talk to me about the death of Rubin Pritchard. I always enjoyed talking to my grandpa but I didn't want to talk about Rubin's death. Every time I thought of him, I lived the horrible tragedy all over again.

After a practically sleepless night, the next morning I started for the store. I was walking along deep in thought when Little Ann zipped by me. She was as happy as a young gray squirrel. She wiggled and twisted and once she barked at me. I looked behind me. There was Old Dan trotting along. He stopped when I turned around. Little Ann came up to me. I scolded them and tried to explain that I wasn't going hunting. I was just going up to the store to see what my grandpa wanted. They couldn't, or didn't, want to understand.

I picked up a small stick and slapped my leg with it. In a deep voice I said, "Now you go home, or I'm going to wear you out."

This hurt their feelings. With their tails between their legs and trotting side by side, they started back. Every little way they would stop and look back at me. It was too much. I couldn't stand it. I began to feel bad all over.

"Well, all right," I said. "Come on, you can go, but, Dan, if there are any dogs around the store, and you get in a fight, I won't take you hunting for a whole year, and I mean that," although I knew I didn't.

They came running, tickled to death. Little Ann took one of

her silly spells. She started nipping at the long red tail of Old Dan. Not getting any reaction from him, she jumped over him. She barked at him. He wouldn't even look at her. She ran around in front of him and laid down in the trail, acting like a cat ready to spring. Stiff-legged, he walked up close to her, stopped, and showed his teeth. I laughed out loud. I knew he wouldn't bite her any more than he would bite me. He was just acting tough because he was a boy dog.

After several attempts to get him to play, Little Ann gave up. Together they started sniffing around in the underbrush.

As I walked up in front of the store, Grandpa hollered at me from the barn. I went over to him. Right away he wanted to know all about Rubin's accident. He listened while I told the story over again.

After I had had my say, Grandpa stood looking down at the ground. There was a deep frown on his face, and a hurt look in his eyes. His quietness made me feel uneasy. He finally raised his head and looked at me. What I could see in his friendly old face tore at my heart. It seemed that there were more wrinkles than I had ever seen before. His uncombed, iron-gray hair looked almost white. I noticed that his wrinkled old hand trembled as he rubbed the wire-stiff stubble on his chin.

In a low voice that quivered as he talked, he said, "Billy, I'm sorry about all this. Truly sorry. I can't help but feel that in a way it was my fault."

"No, Grandpa," I said, "it wasn't your fault. It wasn't anyone's fault. It just happened and no one could help it."

"I know," he said, "but if I hadn't called Rubin's bet, nothing would have happened. I guess when a man gets old he doesn't think straight. I shouldn't have let those boys get under my skin."

"Grandpa," I said, "Rubin and Rainie could get under anybody's skin. You couldn't help that. Why, they get under everyone's skin that gets close to them."

"Yes, I know," he said, "but still I acted like a fool. Billy, I had no idea things were going to turn out like they did, or I wouldn't have called that bet."

Wanting to change the conversation, I said, "Grandpa, we won that bet fair and square, but they took my money anyway."

I saw the fire come back to his eyes. This made me feel better. He was more like the Grandpa I loved.

"That's all right," he said. "We'll just forget the whole thing." He stepped over and laid his hand on my shoulder. In a solemn voice, he said, "We won't talk about this again. Now, I want you to forget it ever happened because it wasn't your fault. Oh, I know it's hard for a boy to ever completely forget something like that. All through your life you'll think of it now and then, but try not to let it bother you, and don't ever feel guilty about it. It's not good for a young boy to feel that way."

I nodded my head, thinking if people would just stop questioning me about Rubin's death, maybe I could forget.

Grandpa said, "Well, the accident wasn't the only thing I wanted to talk to you about. I've got something else—something I think will help us both forget a lot of things."

The twinkle in Grandpa's eyes reminded me of what my father had said: "Seems like that old man can cook up more deals than anyone in the country."

I didn't care how many deals my grandpa cooked up. He was still the best grandpa in the whole wide world.

"What have you got?" I asked.

"Come over to the store," he said, "and I'll show you."

On our way over, I heard him mutter, "I hope this doesn't turn out like the ghost-coon hunt."

On entering the store, Grandpa walked to the post office department, and came back with a newspaper in his hand. He spread it out on the counter.

Pointing with his finger, he said in a loud voice, "Look, there!"

I looked. The large black letters read: CHAMPIONSHIP COON HUNT TO BE HELD. My eyes popped open. Again I read the words. Grandpa was chuckling.

I said, "Boy, if that isn't something. A championship coon hunt." Wide-eyed, I asked, "Where are they having this hunt, and what does it have to do with us?"

Grandpa was getting excited. Off came his glasses and out came the old red handkerchief. He blew his breath on the lens and polished them. He snorted a time or two, reared back, and almost shouted, "Do with us? Why it has everything to do with us. All my life I've wanted to go to one of these big coon hunts.

Why I've even dreamed about it. And now the opportunity has come. Yes, sir, now I can go." He paused. "That is, if it's all right with you."

I was dumbfounded. I said, "All right with me? Why, Grandpa, you know it's all right with me, but what have I got to do with it?"

Grandpa was so excited I thought he was going to burst a blood vessel.

Talking excitedly, he said, "I've got it all fixed, Billy. We can enter Old Dan and Little Ann in this championship hunt."

I was so surprised at what Grandpa had said I couldn't utter a word. At first I was scared and then a wonderful feeling came over me. I felt the excitement of the big hunt as it burned its way into my body. I started breathing like I had been running for a hundred miles. After several attempts, I croaked, "Can just any dog be in this hunt?"

Grandpa almost jumped as he answered, "No, sir, not just any hound can be entered. They have to be the best, and they have to be registered, too."

He started talking with his hands. Pointing to a chair, he said, "Sit down and I'll tell you all about it."

Grandpa calmed down a little and started talking in a serious voice. "Billy," he said, "it takes some doing to have a set of dogs entered in this hunt. I've been working on this for months. I've written letters on top of letters. I've even had several good friends in town helping me. You see, I've kept a record of all the coons your dogs have caught, and believe me, their catch is up there with the best of them. Now, I have already paid the entry fee and everything is fixed. All we have to do is go."

"Entry fee? How much did it cost?" I asked.

"You let me worry about that," he said. "Now what do you say? Want to give it a whirl? I understand the winner receives a gold cup, and you never can tell, we might come home with it. We have as good a chance as anyone else."

Grandpa had me so worked up by this time, I didn't think anyone else had any good hounds but me.

I reared back and blurted, "It's all right with me, Grandpa. Just tell me what to do."

Grandpa flew out of gear like a Model-T Ford. He slapped the counter with his hand. In a pent-up voice, he said, "That's the boy! That's the way I like to hear a coon hunter talk."

With a questioning look on his face, he asked, "Didn't I see your dogs with you when you came up?"

"Yes, they followed me," I said. "They're outside."

"Well, call them in," he said. "I've got something for them."

I called to them. Little Ann came in the store, walking like she was scared. Old Dan came to the door and stopped. I tried to coax him in. It was no use. My dogs, never being allowed in the house, were scared to come in.

Grandpa walked over to a hoop of cheese and cut off two chunks about the size of my fist. He walked to the door, talking to Old Dan. "What's the matter, boy?" he said. "You scared to come in? Well, that shows you're a good dog."

He handed him a piece of the cheese. I heard it rattle in his throat as he gulped it down.

Grandpa came back and set Little Ann up on the counter. He chuckled as he broke the cheese up in small pieces and fed her.

"Yes, sir," he said, "I think we have the best darn coon hounds in these Ozark Mountains, and just as sure as shootin', we're going to win that gold cup."

Grandpa didn't have to say that. The way I was feeling, I already had the cup. All I had to do was go and get it.

Finished with his feeding of Little Ann, Grandpa said, "Now, let's see. The hunt starts on the twenty-third. That's about—well, let's see—this is the seventeenth." Counting on his fingers he finally figured it out. "That's six days from now," he said in a jubilant voice.

I nodded my head.

"We can leave here early on the morning of the twenty-second," he said, "and barring accidents, we should make the camp ground in plenty of time for the grand opening."

I asked how we were going.

"We'll go in my buggy," he said. "I'll load the tent and everything the night before."

I asked him what he wanted me to bring.

"Nothing," he said, "but these two little hounds, and you be here early; and I believe I'd let these dogs rest, 'cause we want them in tiptop shape when we get there."

I saw the thinking wrinkles bunch up on Grandpa's forehead.

"You reckon your daddy would like to go?" he asked. "As late in the fall as it is, I don't think he's too busy, is he?"

"No, our crops are all gathered," I said. "We've been clearing some of the bottom land, but that's almost done now."

"Well, ask him," he said. "Tell him I'd like to have him go."

"I'll ask him," I said, "but you know how Papa is. The farm comes first with him."

"I know," Grandpa said, "but you ask him anyway, and tell him what I said. Now it's getting late and you had better be heading for home."

I was almost to the door when Grandpa said, "Wait a minute."

He walked over behind the candy counter and shook out one of the quarter sacks. He filled it up to the brim, bounced it on the counter a few times, and dropped in a few more gumdrops.

With a twinkle in his eye, and a smile on his face, he handed it to me saying, "Save some for your sisters."

I was so choked up I couldn't say anything. I took it and flew out the door, calling to my dogs.

On my way home I didn't walk on the ground. I was way up in the clouds just skipping along. With a song, I told the sycamore trees and the popeyed gray squirrels how happy I was.

Little Ann sensed my happiness. She pranced along on the trail. With a doggish grin on her face, she begged for a piece of candy, which I so gladly gave.

Even Old Dan felt the pleasant atmosphere. His long red tail fanned the air. Once he raised his head and bawled. I stood still and listened to the droning tones of his deep voice. The sound seemed to be trapped for an instant in the thick timber. It rolled around under the tall white sycamores, beat its way through the wild cane, and found freedom out over the clear blue waters of the river. The sound, following the river's course, rolled like the beat of a jungle drum.

As the echo died away in the distance, silence settled over the bottoms. The gray squirrels stopped their chattering. The wild birds quit their singing. I stood still. No sound could be heard. It seemed that all the creatures of the wild were holding their breath. I gazed up to the towering heights of the tall trees. No leaf was stirring. The silence seemed strained and expectant, like a young boy waiting for a firecracker to explode.

I looked at Old Dan. He was standing perfectly still, with his right front foot raised and his long ears fanned open. He seemed to be listening, and challenging any living creature to make a noise.

The silence was broken by the "Whee-e-e-e" of a red-tailed hawk. This seemed to be a signal. All around me the happy atmosphere resumed its natural state.

I heard the "Bam, bam, bam" of a woodpecker high in the top of a box elder snag. The cry of a kingfisher and the scream of a bluejay blended perfectly with the drumlike beat. A barking red squirrel, glued to the side of a hackberry tree, kept time to the music with the beat of his tail.

Each noise I heard and each sight I saw was very familiar to me but I never grew tired of listening and watching. They were a God-sent gift and I enjoyed them all.

As I skipped along, it was hard for me to realize all the wonderful things that had happened to me in such a few short years. I had two of the finest little hounds that ever bawled on the trail of a ringtail coon. I had a wonderful mother and father and three little sisters. I had the best grandpa a boy ever had, and to top it all, I was going on a championship coon hunt. It was no wonder that my heart was bursting with happiness. Wasn't I the luckiest boy in the world?

Everyone was just sitting down to supper when I got home. My sisters quit the table for the candy. I told them to divide it equally. The oldest one asked if I wanted any of it.

"No," I said. "I brought it all for you." Of course, I didn't tell them about the four pieces I had in my pocket.

They thanked me with their clear blue eyes.

I guess it's pretty hard for a young boy to fool his mama. She took one look at me and called me over. She ruffled up my hair, kissed me, and said, "If my little boy's eyes get any bigger they're going to pop right out of his head. Now tell me, what are you so happy about?"

Before I could say anything, Papa chuckled and asked, "What's going on between you and your grandpa? What are you and that old man cooking up now?"

As fast as I could talk I started telling about the big coon hunt. I told how hard Grandpa had been working to have my dogs entered, and how he had already paid my entry fee.

Catching my breath and looking at Papa, I said, "We're going in his buggy and he wants you to go."

I waited in silence for his reply. Papa sat there staring off into space, sipping his coffee and saying nothing. I knew he was thinking.

In the silence I was sure I could hear my heart thumping.

I said, "Papa, please go. We'll have a lot of fun and besides the winner receives a big golden cup."

He scratched his head and said, "Billy, I'd sure like to go, but I don't see how I can with all this work around here."

I was beginning to think that Papa wasn't going to go. Then Mama started talking.

"Work?" she said. "Why, all the work is practically done. I don't know of one thing you couldn't put off for a few days. Why don't you go? You haven't been anywhere since I don't know when."

"It's not only the work I'm thinking of," Papa said. "It's you and the girls."

"Why, don't worry about the girls and me," Mama said. "We'll be all right. Besides, it'll be several months yet before I need any help."

When Mama said this, it dawned on me. I had been so busy with my coon hunting I hadn't noticed anything unusual. Mama's tummy was all swelled up. She was going to have a baby. I felt guilty for not having noticed. I went over and put my arms around her and kissed her.

Papa spoke up. "It's sure going to be a big hunt," he said. "I heard something about it up at the store one day."

"Grandpa said there would be hunters there from everywhere," I said, "and some of the best coon hounds in the country."

"Do you think you have a chance to win the cup?" Papa asked.

I started to answer him when the little one piped up. "They can't beat Old Dan and Little Ann," she said. "I just bet they can't."

Everyone laughed at her serious remark. I would have kissed her but she had candy, corn bread, and molasses all over her face.

I told Papa I didn't know how good those dogs were, but there was one thing I did know. If they beat mine, they would have to hunt harder than they ever had before.

After I had had my say about the dogs, a silence settled over the dining room. Everyone was looking at Papa and waiting for his answer.

I saw a pleased smile spread over his face. He stood up. "All right, I'll go," he said, "and, by golly, we'll bring that gold cup back, too."

My sisters started clapping their hands and squealing with delight. A satisfied smile spread over my mother's face.

At that moment I'm sure no boy in the world could have been happier than I. Tears of happiness rolled down my cheeks. Mama wiped them away with her apron.

In the midst of all the excitement, my little sister, saying not a word, climbed down from her chair. No one said anything. We just watched her.

Still clutching a spoon in her small hand, she came around the table and walked up to me. Looking down at the floor, in a bashful voice, she asked, "Can I have the gold cup?"

Putting my finger under her sticky little chin, I tilted her head up. I smiled as I looked into her clear blue eyes. I said, "Honey, if I win it, I'll give it to no one but you."

I had to cross my heart and hope to die several times before she was satisfied.

Back in her chair she gloated over the others. "You just wait and see," she said. "It'll be all mine, nobody's but mine, and I'll put my banty eggs in it."

"Silly, you don't put banty eggs in a gold cup," the oldest one said. "They're just made to look at."

That night I dreamed about gold cups, little red hounds, and coons as big as rain barrels. Once I woke myself up whooping to my dogs.

The next few days were busy ones for me. Knowing that Papa and I would be gone for several days, I did everything I could to make things convenient for Mama. I chopped a large pile of wood and stacked it close to the kitchen door. To make it easy for her to feed our stock, I cut some poles from the hillside and boxed up one of the stalls in the barn. I filled it full of hay so she wouldn't have to climb the ladder to the loft.

Papa laid down the law to my sisters about being good and helping Mama while we were gone.

The day before we were to leave, I was as nervous as a June bug in a henhouse. The day seemed endless. A few of the miserable hours were spent talking to my dogs. I told them all about the big hunt and how important it was.

"Now if you don't win the golden cup," I said, "I won't be mad because I know you will do your best."

Old Dan wouldn't even look at me, and paid no attention to what I said. He was sulking because I hadn't been taking him hunting. When I talked to Little Ann, it was different. She listened and seemed to understand everything I said.

I dreaded to go to bed that night. I thought sleep would be impossible. I must have been more tired than I thought I was. I fell asleep almost immediately. Old Red, our rooster, woke me at daybreak, crowing his fool head off.

It was a beautiful morning, clear and frosty.

After a good breakfast, we kissed Mama good-bye and started for the store.

I'm sure there were a lot of coon hunters in the Ozarks, but on that morning none could have felt as big and important as I. Walking along by the side of my father, I threw out my chest and tried hard to keep pace with his long strides. He noticed and laughed.

"You'll have to grow a little bit," he said, "before you can take steps that long."

I didn't say anything. I just smiled.

Hearing a noise overhead, I looked up. The gray ones were winging their way southward. I listened to their talking and wondered what they were saying.

Looking to the mountains around us, I saw that the mysterious artist who comes at night had paid us a visit. I wondered how he could paint so many different colors in one night; red, wine, yellow, and rust.

My dogs were trotting along in front of us. I smiled at the way their hind quarters shifted to the right. Little Ann would jump and bounce and try to get Old Dan to play, but the solemn old boy just jogged along, heedless of everything.

"You know," Papa said, "she doesn't even act like a hound. She is bouncing and playing all the time. Why, she acts more like a little pup than a hound."

"Yes, I know," I said. "I've noticed that myself, but you know one thing, Papa, she's the smartest dog I've ever seen. Why, some of the things she does are almost unbelievable."

"Yes, I know," said Papa, "but still it's strange, very strange."

"There's only one thing wrong with her, Papa," I said.

"Yea, what's that," he asked.

"You won't believe it," I said, "but she's gun-shy."

"Gun-shy? How do you know she's gun-shy?" Papa asked.

"I didn't know for a long time," I said, "until one day when I was hoeing corn down in the field by the old slough. She and Old Dan were digging in a bank after a ground hog. Across the river some fishermen started shooting a gun. It scared Little Ann, and she came running to me, shaking all over."

"Aw," Papa said, "maybe you just thought she was scared."

"No, I didn't, Papa," I said. "It happened again up at the store one day. Grandpa shot a chicken hawk. When the gun went off, it scared her half to death. No, she's gun-shy all right."

"Aw, well," Papa said, "that doesn't mean anything. A lot of dogs are afraid of guns."

"I know," I said, "but you wouldn't think she would be that way. I believe if I had a gun of my own I could break her of being gun-shy."

Papa looked at me. He said, "From what your mother says, you won't be getting a gun for some time yet."

"Yes, I know," I said.

When we reached the store we saw the team was already hitched to the buggy and was standing in front of the store. Grandpa had loaded the tent and several boxes of groceries.

I had never seen him in such high spirits. He slapped Papa on the back, saying, "I'm sure glad you could go with us. It'll do you good to get out once in a while."

Papa laughed and said, "It looked like I had to go or have everyone in the family mad at me."

Looking in the buggy I saw my ax. I didn't think I ever wanted to see it again, but for some reason it didn't look like I thought it would. There was no blood on it and it looked harmless enough laying there all clean and bright.

Grandpa saw me looking at it. He came over.

"I kept it a few days," he said, "just in case the marshal wanted to ask some questions. Everything seems to be all right now, and we may need a good ax on this hunt."

Grandpa sensed how I felt about the ax. He waited in silence for my answer.

The excitement of the hunt was so strong in me, even the sight of the ax brought back only a fleeting remembrance of Rubin's accident.

I said, "Yes, we will need one. Besides, it's a good one and there's no use in throwing it away."

Grandpa laughed, reached over, and screwed my cap around on my head, saying, "That's the boy, that's what I wanted you to say. Now, you better go to the barn and get some hay and make a bed in the buggy box for your dogs."

"Aw, Grandpa," I said, "they can walk. They don't ever get tired; besides, they're used to walking."

"Walk!" Grandpa almost shouted. "They're not going to walk. No, sir, not if I can help it. You want them to be footsore when we get there?"

Papa chuckled and said, "We can't win a gold cup with two sore-footed hounds, can we?"

"Of course not," Grandpa said. "Now, you go and get that hay like I said."

As I turned to go to the barn I couldn't help but smile. It made me feel good to have my papa and grandpa so concerned about my dogs.

I had taken only a few steps when Grandpa said, "Oh, wait a minute."

I stopped and turned around.

Walking up to me and glancing toward the house as he did, he whispered, "In that empty kraut barrel in the harness room, there's a jug of corn liquor. Cover it up in the hay so your grandma won't see it, and bring it back with you."

With a twinkle in his eye, he said, "You never can tell when we'll need some medicine."

I knew my father wouldn't drink any of the liquor, but if Grandpa wanted to take along a whole barrel, it was all right with me.

Just when I thought we were ready to leave, Grandma came bustling out.

Grandpa got nervous. He whispered and asked, "Did you hide the jug good?"

I nodded my head.

Grandma handed Grandpa a pair of long-handle underwear and a scarf, saying, "I knew you'd forget something."

Grandpa snorted but knew there was no use arguing with her. She started picking around in the groceries, asking about salt, pepper, and matches.

"Nannie, we've got everything," he said. "You must think I'm a baby and don't know how to pack a grub box."

"A baby," Grandma snorted. "Why, you're worse than a baby. At least they have a little sense. You don't have any at all. An old codger like you out chasing a coon all over the hills."

At her biting remark, I thought Grandpa was going to blow up. He snorted like Daisy, our milk cow, when she had seen a booger.

I crawled up in the buggy box with my dogs and hung my feet out.

Grandma came over and asked me about warm clothes. I told her I had plenty.

She kissed me good-bye and we were on our way.

XV

OVER A DIM ROCKY ROAD, in a northeasterly direction, our buggy moved on.

I noticed that the road stayed at the edge of the foothills, but always in sight of the river.

About the middle of the afternoon we stopped at a small stream to water the team. Papa asked Grandpa if he intended to go all the way to the campground before stopping.

"No," he said, "I figure to put up for the night when we reach Bluebird Creek. With a good early start in the morning we can make the campgrounds in plenty of time to pitch our tent and set up camp."

Late that evening we reached Bluebird Creek. We didn't set up our tent. With a tarp we made a lean-to and built a large fire out in front of it.

While Grandpa fed and watered the team, Papa and I carried our bedding to the shelter and made down our beds.

Grandpa said, "While we're cooking supper, you see to your dogs. Feed them and fix them a warm bed."

"I figure to cook them some corn-meal mush," I said. "That's what they're used to eating."

"Mush!" Grandpa growled. "They're not going to have mush, not if I can help it."

He walked over to a grocery box, mumbling as he did, "Mush! A hound can't hunt on a bellyful of that stuff."

He came back and handed me two large cans of corned-beef hash, saying, "Here. Reckon they'll eat this."

I wanted to hug my old grandpa's neck. "Sure, Grandpa," I said, "they'll love that."

Opening one of the cans, I dumped it out on a piece of bark in front of Old Dan. He sniffed at it and refused to eat. I laughed, for I knew why. While I was opening the other can, Grandpa came over.

"What's the matter," he asked. "Won't he eat it?"

"Sure, Grandpa," I said, "he'll eat, but not before Little Ann gets her share."

With the second can opened, I fed her on another piece of bark. Both of them started eating at the same time.

With an astonished look on his face, Grandpa exclaimed, "Well, I'll be darned. I never saw anything like that. Why, I never saw a hound that wouldn't eat. Did you train them to do that?"

"No, Grandpa," I said. "They've always been that way. They won't take anything away from each other, and everything they do, they do it as one."

Papa had overheard our conversation. He said, "You think that's strange. You should have seen what I saw one day.

"One of the girls threw two cold biscuits out in the back yard to Old Dan. He stood and looked at them for a bit, then, picking both of them up in his mouth, he trotted around the house. I followed just to see what he was going to do. He walked up in front of the doghouse, laid them down, and growled; not like he was mad. It was a strange kind of a growl. Little Ann came out of the doghouse and each of them ate a biscuit. Now, I saw this with my own eyes. Believe me, those dogs are close to each other—real close."

After Papa had stopped talking, silence settled over the camp.

Grandpa stood staring at my dogs. In a slow voice, as if he were picking his words, he said, "You know, I've always felt like there was something strange about those dogs. I don't know just what it is, and I can't exactly put my finger on it, yet I can feel it. Maybe it's just my imagination. I don't rightly know."

Turning to my father, he said, "Did you ever notice the way they watch this boy? They see every move he makes."

Papa said, "Yes, I've noticed a lot of things they have done. In fact, I could tell you of a few that you would never believe, but right now here's something you had better believe. Supper is ready."

While I was helping myself to hot dutch-oven corn bread, fried potatoes, and fresh side meat, Grandpa poured the coffee. Instead of the two cups I expected to see, he set out three and filled them to the brim with the strong black liquid.

I had never been allowed to drink coffee at home and didn't exactly know what to do. I glanced at Papa. He seemed too busy with his eating to pay any attention to me. Taking the bull by the horns, I reached over and ran my finger through the cup's handle. I held my breath as I walked over and sat down by a post oak stump. Nothing was said. Grandpa and Papa paid no attention to what I did. My head swelled up as big as a number-four washtub. I thought, "I'm not only big enough to help Papa with the farm. Now I'm big enough to drink coffee."

With supper over and the dishes washed, Grandpa said, "Well, we had better turn in as I want to get an early start in the morning."

Long after Grandpa and Papa had fallen asleep, I lay thinking of the big hunt. My thoughts were interrupted when the wonders of night life began to stir in the silence around us.

From a ridge on our right a red fox started barking. He was curious and, in his small way, challenging the intruders that had dared to stop in his wild domain. From far back in the flinty hills, the monotonous call of a hoot owl floated down in the silent night. It was the mating call and was answered from a distant mountain.

I could hear the stamping feet of our horses, and the grinding, crunching noise made by their strong teeth as they ate the hard, yellow kernels of corn in their feed boxes. A night hawk screamed as he winged his way through the starlit night. An eerie screech from a tree close by made shivers run up and down my spine. It was a screech owl.

I didn't like to hear the small owl, for there was a superstition in the mountains concerning them. It was said that if you heard one owl it meant nothing at all, but if you heard more than one, it meant bad luck.

I lay and listened to the eerie twittering sound. It was coming from the left of our camp. The creepy noise stopped, and for several moments there was silence. When next I heard the cry, it was coming from the right. I sat up in alarm. Had I heard two owls?

My movement had awakened Grandpa. In a sleepy voice, he asked, "What's the matter? Can't you sleep? What are you sitting up like that for?"

"Grandpa, I heard two screech owls," I said.

Grunting and mumbling, he sat up. Rubbing the sleep from his eyes, he said, "You heard two screech owls. Why, that's nothing. I've heard two—oh, I see. You're thinking of the bad-luck superstition. There's nothing to that; nothing at all. Now you lie down and go to sleep. Tomorrow is going to be a big day."

I tried hard to fall asleep, but couldn't. I couldn't get the owls out of my mind. Had I really heard two? Were we going to have bad luck? Surely nothing bad could happen. Not on such a wonderful hunt.

I found peace in my mind by telling myself that the owl had changed trees. Yes, that was it. He had simply flown out of one tree to another.

The next morning, while having breakfast, Grandpa started kidding me about the screech owls.

"I wish you could have caught one of those owls last night," he said. "We could have boiled him in our coffee pot. I've heard there is nothing like strong hoot-owl coffee."

"It wasn't a hoot owl, Grandpa," I said. "It was a screech owl. I don't know for sure if I heard one or two. It could have been just one." Pointing to a small red oak, I said, "I think the first time I heard him, he was over there. The next time, it was over in that direction. Maybe he changed trees. I sure hope so."

Grandpa saw I was bothered. "You don't believe that hogwash superstition, do you? Bad luck! Baw, there's nothing to it."

Papa laughed, and said, "These mountains are full of that jinx stuff. If a man believed it all, he'd go crazy."

The encouraging words from Papa and Grandpa helped some, but there was still some doubt. It's hard for a young boy to completely forget things like that.

Breakfast over, and our gear stowed back in the buggy, we left Bluebird Creek.

On that day Grandpa drove a little faster than he had on the previous one. I was glad of this, for I was anxious to reach the campground.

About noon he stopped the team. I heard him ask Papa, "Is this Black Fox Hollow?"

"No," Papa said. "This is Waterfall. Black Fox is the next one over. Why?"

"Well," Grandpa said, "there's supposed to be a white flag in the mouth of Black Fox. That's where we leave the road. The camp is in the river bottoms."

By this time I was so excited, I stood up in the buggy box so I could get a better view.

"Maybe you ought to step them up a little, Grandpa," I said. "It's getting pretty late."

Papa joined in with his loud laughter. "You just take it easy," he said. "We'll get there in plenty of time. Besides, these mares can't fly."

I saw the flag first. "There it is, Grandpa," I shouted.

"Where?" he asked.

"Over there. See, tied on that grapevine."

As we left the main road, I heard Papa say, "Boy, look at all those tracks. Sure has been a lot of traveling on this road."

"That smoke over there must be coming from the camps," Grandpa said.

When we came in sight of the camp, I couldn't believe what I saw. I stared in amazement. I had never seen so many people at one gathering. Tents were spread out over an acre and a half of ground; all colors, shapes, and sizes. There were odd-looking cars, buggies, wagons, and saddle horses.

I heard Grandpa say almost in a whisper, "I knew there would be a lot of people here but I never expected so many."

I saw the astonished look on my father's face.

Off to one side of the camp, under a large black gum tree, we set up our tent. I tied my dogs to the buggy, and fixed a nice bed for them under it. After everything was taken care of, I asked if I could look around the camp.

"Sure," Grandpa said. "Go any place you want to go, only don't get in anyone's way."

I started walking through the large camp. Everyone was friendly.

Once I heard a voice say, "That's the boy who owns the two little red hounds. I've heard they're pretty good."

If my head had gotten any bigger, I know it would have burst. I walked on, as straight as a canebrake cane.

I looked at the hounds. They were tied in pairs here and there. I had seen many coon hounds but none that could equal these. There were redbones, blue ticks, walkers, and blood hounds. I marveled at their beauty. All were spotlessly clean with slick and glossy coats. I saw the beautiful leather leashes and brass-studded collars.

I thought of my dogs. They were tied with small cotton ropes, and had collars made from old check-line leather.

As I passed from one set of dogs to another, I couldn't help but wonder if I had a chance to win. I knew that in the veins of these hounds flowed the purest of breeded blood. No finer coon hounds could be found anywhere. They came from the Smoky Mountains of Tennessee, the bayou country of Louisiana, the Red River bottoms of Texas, and the flinty hills of the Ozarks.

Walking back through the camp, I could feel the cold fingers of doubt squeezing my heart. One look at my dogs drove all doubt away. In the eyes of Little Ann it seemed I could read this message: "Don't worry. Just wait. We'll show them."

That night, Grandpa said, "Tomorrow they'll have a contest for the best-looking hound. Which one are you going to enter?"

I told him I didn't think I'd enter either one of my dogs. They were so little. I didn't think they had a chance.

Grandpa got all huffed up. He said, "It doesn't make any difference how little they are. They're coon hounds, aren't they?"

I asked him if he had seen any of the other hounds.

He said, "Yes, I've seen them all. Sure they're big, and good dogs, too, but it makes no difference. I don't care if your dogs are no bigger than a snuff can. They still have a chance. Now, which one are you going to enter?"

I couldn't decide. I said, "I'll think it over tonight and let you know tomorrow."

The next morning when I stepped outside the tent I saw men everywhere. They were combing and brushing their dogs, and getting them pruned for the beauty contest. Beautiful combs and brushes were used to brush expensive oils into their glossy hair.

Going over to my dogs, I stood and looked at them. I started to untie Old Dan but, taking a closer look at him, I could see he could never win a beauty contest. His face and ears were a mass of old scars, caused from the many fights with tough old coons and bobcats. I held his head in my hands and felt sorry for him, but loved him that much more.

I looked Little Ann over and couldn't see any scars. I laughed because I knew why. She was too smart to walk right up in the face of a fight. She would wait until Old Dan took hold and then dart in.

I untied her rope and walked her over to our tent.

My father and grandfather were gone. No doubt they were over in some tent visiting old friends and making new ones.

Looking around to find something I could use to groom my dog, I saw Grandpa's open suitcase. There, right on top, was the very thing I needed, his beautiful bone-handled hairbrush and his ivory comb. Picking them up, I turned them over and over in my hand.

Little Ann stood looking at me. Impulsively I reached down and raked her from shoulder to hip with the brush. She seemed to like it. I knew I shouldn't do it, but I decided to use them.

Knowing I had no oils, I got some butter from our grocery box. With the homemade butter and Grandpa's hair set, I brushed her until she shone. All the time I was grooming her, she tried to lick the butter from my hands.

The job completed, I stepped back and inspected her. I was surprised at the change. Her short red hair glistened and every one was in perfect place.

Shaking my finger at her, I said, "If you lay down and roll, I'll wear you out," although I knew I wouldn't.

Hearing a lot of movement outside, I looked out. Men were setting their dogs on a long table which had been built in the center of the camp ground. Leading Little Ann to it, I picked her up and set her on the table, too.

I told her to act like a lady. She wagged her tail as though she understood. I untied the rope and stepped back.

After the dogs were all lined up, the judging started. Four judges walked around and around the table, looking at them from all angles. When one of them would point at a hound, he was taken down and eliminated from the contest. Dog after dog was disqualified. Little Ann was still on the table.

My eyes were wide, my throat dry, and my heart thumping. One judge stopped in front of Little Ann. My heart stopped, too. Reaching over, he patted her on the head.

Turning to me, he asked, "Is this your dog?"

I couldn't speak. I just nodded my head.

He said, "She's a beautiful hound."

He walked on down the line. My heart started beating again.

There were eight dogs left. Little Ann was still holding her own. Then there were four. I was ready to cry. Two more were taken down. Little Ann and a big walker hound owned by a Mr. Kyle were the only ones left. The judges couldn't seem to make up their minds.

Everyone started shouting, "Walk them! Walk them!"

I didn't know what they meant.

Mr. Kyle and I were told to go to one end of the table. Our dogs were placed at the other end. Mr. Kyle snapped his fingers and called to his dog.

The big hound started walking toward his master. What a beautiful sight it was. He walked like a king. His body was stiff and straight, his head high in the air, his large muscles quivered and jerked under his glossy coat, but something went wrong. Just before he reached the end, he broke his stride, turned, and jumped down from the table.

A low murmur ran through the crowd.

It was my turn. Three times I tried to call to Little Ann. Words just wouldn't come out. My throat was too dry. The vocal cords refused to work, but I could snap my fingers. That was all I needed. She started toward me. I held my breath. There was silence all around me.

As graceful as any queen, with her head high in the air, and her long red tail arched in a perfect rainbow, my little dog walked down the table. With her warm gray eyes staring straight at me, on she came. Walking up to me, she laid her head on my shoulder. As I put my arms around her, the crowd exploded.

During the commotion I felt hands slapping me on the back, and heard the word "congratulations" time after time. The head judge came over and made a speech. Handing me a small silver cup, he said, "Congratulations, son. It was justly won."

The tears came rolling. I gathered my dog up in my arms and walked to our tent. Grandpa followed, proudly carrying the cup.

That evening the head judge stepped up on the table. He had a small box in his hand. He shouted, "Over here, men! I have some announcements to make."

We all gathered around.

In a loud voice, he said, "Gentlemen, the contest will start tonight. I'm sure most of you men have been in these hunts before. For those of you who haven't, I will explain the rules. Each night five sets of dogs will be taken out to hunt. A judge will go along with each pair of hounds. Every morning, the judges will turn in that night's catch. The two hounds that tree the most coons will qualify for the championship runoff. The other four sets will be eliminated from the hunt. Of course, if there is a tie, both sets will qualify. On the following nights, only those hounds tying the first night's score, or getting more, will be in the runoff.

"Now, gentlemen, this hunt must be carried out in a sportsman-like way. If the coon is treed where he can't be caught, such as in a bluff, it will not be counted. You must catch the coon, skin it, and turn the hide over to your judge.

"You are allowed to take an ax, a lantern, and a gun with bird shot, which you can use to get a coon out of a tree.

"Twenty-five sets of hounds have been entered in the hunt. In this box, I have twenty-five cards. Everyone in the contest will now line up for the drawing. The card you draw will tell you what night your hounds are to hunt."

Walking along in the line, I noticed the beautiful red coats, the caps, and the soft leather boots worn by the other hunters. I felt out of place in my faded blue overalls, old sheepskin coat, and scuffed and worn shoes, but to the wonderful men it made no difference. They treated me like a man, and even talked to me like a man.

When it came my time to draw, my hand was shaking so hard I could hardly get it in the box. Pulling the card out, I saw I had drawn the fourth night.

After the hunters had left, we stood around our campfires

sipping strong black coffee and listening to the baying of the hounds. Time after time, we heard the tree bark.

Once two hounds came close to the camp, hot on a trail. We listened to their steady bawling. All at once they stopped.

After several minutes of waiting, a hunter said, "You know what? That old coon took to the river and in some way has fooled those dogs."

Another one said, "Yes, sir, he sure has."

A friendly hunter looked at me and asked, "Do you think he could have fooled your dogs?"

Thinking his question over, I said, "You know, sometimes when I am hunting, away back in the mountains or down on the river, I sing a little song I made up myself. One of the verses goes like this:

> You can swim the river, Old Mister Ringtail,
> And play your tricks out one by one.
> It won't do any good, Old Mister Ringtail,
> My Little Ann knows every one.

The hunters roared with laughter. Some slapped me on the back.

Tired and sleepy, but with a smile on my face, I went off to bed.

The next morning two blue tick hounds, from the Smoky Mountains of Tennessee, came out in the lead with three big coons to their credit. The other four sets were eliminated.

The following morning all five sets of dogs were eliminated. None had even tied the blue ticks, although two sets had gotten two coons, and one of these had treed a third one in a bluff.

That day, while eating dinner, my grandfather asked me if my dogs had ever treed three coons in one night.

I said, "Yes, four different times, but that's all."

"Where do you think we should hunt on our night?" Papa asked.

I told him if we could get our judge to go with us in the buggy, we would be better off if we could go far downriver and get out of the range where other dogs had hunted.

He said, "That's a good idea. I'll go to see the judges about it."

While I was washing the dishes, Grandpa said, "I think I'll shave."

I should've left the tent then, but I wasn't done with my dish-washing.

With a pin, Grandpa hung a small mirror on the tent wall. After much snorting, mumbling, and screwing of his face this way and that, the job was completed. Dabbing a little water on his iron-gray hair, he reached for his brush and comb.

From the corner of my eye I watched him. I had tried to clean the beautiful brush but hadn't been able to get all the short red hair from it.

With two fingers, Grandpa pulled some of the hair from the bristles. Holding it in front of him, he looked it over carefully. Then, bending over close to the mirror, peeking over his glasses, he inspected his head. Straightening up, he looked at the brush again. Turning around quickly, he looked straight at me and said, "Say, young—"

Not waiting for anything more, I scooted for the door. Crawling under the buggy, I lay down between my dogs. I knew he wouldn't be mad at me, but it would be best to stay away for a while.

The third night, the blue ticks were tied by two black and tan hounds from the bayou country of Louisiana.

All that day I was restless. I prowled through the camp. Every little while I would go and see how Old Dan and Little Ann were. Once I took two weenies from our groceries. I heated them and gave them to my dogs for a treat. Old Dan swallowed his down in one gulp, and looked at me as if to say, "Is that all?" Little Ann ate hers in a ladylike way. I could have sworn I saw a small grin on her face.

Grandpa was hopping around like a grasshopper, going here and there. Once, passing a tent, I heard his voice. I knew he was bragging about my dogs. I smiled to myself.

Another hunter stopped me and asked, "Is it true that your hounds have treed six coons in one night, three up in one tree, or is that old man just blowing off steam?"

I told him my grandfather had a little steam, but he was the best grandpa a boy ever had.

He patted me on the head, turned, and walked away laughing.

XVI

IN THE AFTERNOON our judge came over and introduced himself. He told us he'd be going with us that night.

About sundown we piled in our buggy and drove a few miles downriver. I noticed other hunters doing the same thing. Everyone was trying to get away from the already-hunted territory.

It was dark by the time Grandpa stopped. I untied the ropes from my dogs. Little Ann reared up on me and whined. Old Dan walked off a few yards, stretched his body, and dragged his claws through the soft bottom soil. Opening his mouth, he let out one loud bawl, and then disappeared in the thick timber. Little Ann was right on his heels.

We took off after them.

Grandpa got nervous. He said to me, "Don't you think you ought to whoop to them?"

I told him to wait a little while. There would be plenty of time for whooping.

He snorted and said he thought a hunter always whooped to his dogs.

"I do, Grandpa," I said, "but not before they strike a trail."

We walked on. Every now and then we would stop and listen. I could hear the loud snuffing of Old Dan. Once we caught a glimpse of Little Ann as she darted across an opening that was bathed in moonlight. She was as silent as a ghost and as quick as a flitting shadow.

Papa said, "It sure is a beautiful night for hunting."

The judge said, "You can't beat these Ozark Mountain nights for beauty. I don't care where you go."

Grandpa started to say something. His voice was drowned out by the bell-like cry of Little Ann.

In a whisper, I said, "Come on, Dan. Hurry and help her."

As if in answer to my words, his deep voice hammered its way up through the river bottoms. I felt the blood tingling in my veins. That wonderful feeling that only a hunter knows crept over my body.

Looking over at Grandpa, I said, "Now you can whoop."

Jerking off his hat and throwing back his head, he let out a yell. It wasn't a whoop, or a screech, it was about halfway in between. Everyone laughed.

The coon was running upriver toward our campground. We turned and followed. I could tell by the dogs' voices that they were running side by side, and were hot on the trail. Closing my eyes, I could almost see them running, bodies stretched to their fullest length, legs pounding up and down, white steam rolling from their hot breath in the frosty night.

Grandpa got tangled up in some underbrush, and lost his hat and spectacles. It took us a while to find the glasses. Papa said something about getting them wired on with bailing wire. Grandpa snorted. The judge laughed.

The coon crossed the river and ran on upstream. Soon my dogs were out of hearing distance. I told Papa we had better stay on our side of the river and keep going until we could hear them again.

Twenty minutes later we heard them coming back. We stopped.

"I think they have crossed back to our side," I said.

All at once the voices of my dogs were drowned out by a loud roar.

"What in the world was that?" Grandpa said.

"I don't know," the judge said. "Reckon it was wind or thunder?"

About that time we heard it again.

The judge started laughing. "I know now what it is," he said. "Those hounds have run that coon right back by our camp. The noise we heard was the other hunters whooping to them."

Everyone laughed.

A few minutes later I heard my dogs bawling treed. On reaching the tree, Papa ran his hand back under his coat. He pulled out Grandpa's gun.

"That's a funny-looking gun," the judge said. "It's a 410-gauge pistol, isn't it?"

"It's the very thing for this kind of work," Papa said. "You couldn't kill a coon with it if you tried, especially if you're using bird shot. All it will do is sting his hide a little."

At the crack of the gun, the coon gave a loud squall and jumped. My dogs lost no time in killing him.

We skinned the coon, and soon were on our way again.

The next time my dogs treed, they were across the river from us. Finding a riffle, we pulled off our shoes and started across.

Grandpa very gingerly started picking his way. His tender old feet moved from one smooth rock to another. Everything was fine until we reached midstream, where the current was much swifter. He stepped on a loose round rock. It rolled and down he went.

As the cold river water touched his body, he let out a yell that could have been heard for miles. He looked so funny we couldn't keep from laughing.

Papa and the judge helped him to his feet. Laughing every step of the way, we finally reached the other side. Grandpa kept going in his wet clothes until we reached the tree where the dogs were.

After killing the coon, we built a large fire so Grandpa could dry his clothes. He'd get up as close to the fire as he could, and turn this way and that. He looked so funny standing there with his long underwear steaming. I started rolling with laughter.

He looked over at me and snapped, "What's so funny?"

I said, "Nothing."

"Well, why are you laughing?" he said.

At this remark, Papa and the judge laughed until their eyes watered.

Mumbling and grumbling, Grandpa said, "If you fellows were as cold as I am, you wouldn't be laughing."

We knew we shouldn't be laughing, but we couldn't help ourselves.

The judge looked at his watch. "It's after three o'clock," he said. "Do you think they'll tree another one?"

As if to throw the words back in the judge's face, Old Dan

opened up. I stood up and whooped. "Whoo-e-e! Get him, Dan! Get him! Put him up a little tree."

There was a mad scramble. Grandpa tried to put his britches on backwards. The judge and Papa ran over to help him with his shoes. Each one tried to put a shoe on the wrong foot. I was laughing so hard I could do nothing.

A hundred yards from the fire, I realized we had forgotten the coonskins. I ran back for them.

My dogs had jumped the coon in swampland. He tore out for the river bottoms. I could tell they were close to him by their fast bawling. All at once their baying stopped. We stood still and listened. Old Dan bawled treed a few more times and then stopped.

Grandpa asked, "What's happened?"

I told him the coon had probably pulled some kind of trick.

Coming up to my dogs, we saw they were working up and down an old rail fence. We stood and watched. Every now and then, Old Dan would rear up on a large hackberry tree that was standing about seven feet from the fence and bawl treed.

As yet Little Ann had not bawled the tree bark. We watched her. She was working everywhere. She climbed up on the rail fence and followed its zigzag course until she disappeared in the darkness.

I told Papa I was sure the coon had walked the rail fence and in some way had fooled my dogs.

Old Dan would keep coming back to the hackberry tree. He would rear up on it and bawl treed. We walked up to him. Looking the tree over, we could see that the coon wasn't in it.

The judge said, "It looks like he has them fooled."

"Maybe you had better call them off," Grandpa said. "We can go someplace else and hunt. We've got to get one more coon, even if I have to tree it myself."

For some reason, no one laughed at his remark.

"It's almost daylight," Papa said.

"Yes, that's what has me worried," I said. "We don't have time to do any more hunting. If we lose this one, we're beat."

Hearing the word beat, Grandpa began to fidget. He asked me, "What do you think happened? How did that coon fool them?"

"I don't know for sure," I said. "He walked that rail fence.

The hackberry tree has something to do with his trick, but I don't know what."

"Son," the judge said, "I wouldn't feel too badly if I were you. I've seen some of the very best hounds fooled by a smart old coon."

Regardless of all the discouraging talk, the love and belief I had in my little red hounds never faltered. I could see them now and then, leaping over old logs, tearing through the underbrush, sniffing and searching for the lost trail. My heart swelled with pride. I whooped, urging them on.

In a low voice, the judge said, "I'll say one thing. They don't give up easily."

Birds began to chirp all around us. The sky took on a light gray color. Tiny dim stars were blinking the night away.

"It looks like we're beat," Papa said. "It's getting daylight."

At that moment, the loud clear voice of a redbone hound, bawling treed, rang through the river bottoms. It was the voice of Little Ann.

Sucking in a mouthful of air, I held it. I could feel my heart pounding against my ribs. I closed my eyes tight and gritted my teeth to keep the tears from coming.

"Let's go to them," Grandpa said.

"No, wait a minute," I said.

"Why?" he asked.

"Wait till Old Dan gets there," I said. "It's daylight now, and if we walk up to the tree, the coon will jump out. It's hard to keep a coon in a tree after daylight. Let's wait until Old Dan gets there. Then if he jumps, he won't have a chance to get away."

"The boy's right," the judge said. "It's hard to keep a coon in a tree after daybreak."

Just then we heard Old Dan. His deep voice shattered the morning silence. Searching for the lost trail, he had crossed the fence and worked his way out into an old field. Turning around, we saw him coming. He was a red blur in the gray morning shadows. Coming to the rail fence, and without breaking his stride, he raised his body into the air. About halfway over and while still in the air he bawled.

Hitting the ground with a loud grunt, he ran past us. Everyone whooped to him. Ahead was a deep washout about ten feet wide.

On the other side was a canebrake. His long red body, stretched to its fullest length, seemed to float in the air as he sailed over it. We could hear the tall stalks rattling as he plowed his way through them. A bunch of sleepy snow birds rose from the thick cane, flitted over, and settled in a row on the old rail fence.

Nearing the tree, we could see it was a tall sycamore, and there high in the top was the coon.

Grandpa threw a fit. He hopped around whooping and hollering. He threw his old hat down on the ground and jumped up and down on it. Then he ran over and kissed Little Ann right on the head.

After we killed and skinned the coon, the judge said, "Let's walk back to that old fence. I think I know how the old fellow pulled his trick."

Back at the fence, the judge stood and looked around for a few minutes. Smiling, he said, "Yes, that's how he did it."

"How?" Grandpa asked.

Still smiling, the judge said, "That old coon walked this rail fence. Coming even with the hackberry tree, he leaped up on its side, and climbed up. Notice how thick the timber is around here. See that limb way up there in the top, the one that runs over and almost touches the sycamore?"

We saw what he meant.

"The coon walked out on that limb," he said, "leaped over, and caught the sycamore limb. Repeating this over and over, from tree to tree, he worked his way far out into the river bottoms. What I can't figure out is how that hound found him."

Gazing at Little Ann, he shook his head and said, "I've been hunting coons and judging coon hunts for forty years, but I've never seen anything like that."

He looked at me. "Well, son," he said, "you have tied the leading teams. There's only one more night of eliminations. Even if some of them get more than three coons, you will still be in the runoff, and from what I've seen here tonight, you have a good chance of winning the cup."

I knew that Little Ann had scented the coon in the air, the same as she had the ghost coon. I walked over and knelt down by her side. The things I wanted to say to her I couldn't, for the knot in my throat, but I'm sure she understood.

As we came into the campground, the hunters came out of their tents and gathered around us. The judge held up the three big coon hides. There was a roar from the crowd.

One man said, "That was the most beautiful sight I've ever seen."

"What was a beautiful sight?" Grandpa asked.

"Last night those little red hounds brought that coon right through camp."

The judge said, "We figured they did when we heard the noise."

Laughing, the man said, "We heard them when they ran up the other side of the river. Way up above here they crossed over. We could tell they were coming back so we doused all the fires and, sure enough, they came right through camp. Those two little hounds weren't fifty yards behind the coon, running side by side. Boy, they were picking them up and laying them down, and bawling every time their feet touched the ground. I'll tell you, it was the prettiest sight I ever saw."

When the judge started telling about the last coon Little Ann had treed I took my dogs over to our tent and fed and watered them. After they had had their fill, I gave them a good rubdown with a piece of gunny sack. Taking them out to the buggy, I tied them up. I stood and watched while they twisted around in the hay making their bed.

That day I tried to get some sleep in our tent, but the soaking Grandpa had taken in the river had given him a cold, causing him to snore. I never heard such a racket in all my life. I'd have sworn he rattled the paper sacks in our grocery boxes. Taking a blanket, I went out to my dogs. Little Ann had wiggled up as close to Old Dan as she could. Prying them apart, I lay down between them and fell asleep.

The last night of the eliminations turned out like the second night. None of the judges turned in more than two hides.

That day, about noon, the owners of the other winning teams and I were called for a conference with the head judge. He said, "Gentlemen, the eliminations are over. Only three sets of hounds are left for the runoff. The winner of tonight's hunt will receive the gold cup. If there is a tie for the championship, naturally there will be another runoff."

He shook hands with each of us and wished us good luck.

Tension began to build up in the camp. Here and there hunters were standing in small groups, talking. Others could be seen going in and out of tents with rolls of money in their hands. Grandpa was the busiest one of all. His voice could be heard all over the camp. Men were looking at me, and talking in low tones. I strutted like a turkey gobbler.

That evening, while we were having supper, a hunter dropped by. He had a small box in his hand. Smiling, he said, "Everyone has agreed that we should have a jackpot for the winner. I've been picked to do the collecting."

Grandpa said, "You may as well leave it here now."

Looking at me, the hunter said, "Son, I think almost every man in this camp is hoping you win it, but it's not going to be easy. You're going up against four of the finest hounds there are." Turning to my father, he said, "Did you know the two big walker hounds have won four gold cups?"

Very seriously, Papa said, "You know I have two mules down on my place. One is almost as big as a barn. The other one isn't much bigger than a jack rabbit, but that little mule can outpull the big one every time."

Smiling, the hunter turned to leave. He said, "You could be right."

Papa asked me again where I thought we should start hunting.

I had been thinking about this all day. I said, "You remember where we jumped the last coon in the swamp?"

Papa said, "Yes."

"Well, the way I figure, more than one coon lives in that swamp," I said. "It's a good place for them as there are lots of crawfish and minnows in those potholes. If a hound jumps one there, he has a good chance to tree him."

Papa asked, "Why?"

"It's a long way back to the river, and about the same distance to the mountains," I said. "Either way he runs, a dog can get pretty close to him, and so he would have to take to a tree."

That evening we climbed into Grandpa's buggy and headed for the swamp. It was dark by the time we reached it.

Grandpa handed Papa his gun, saying, "You're getting to be a pretty good shot with this thing."

"I hope I get to shoot it a lot tonight," Papa said.

Under my breath, I said, "I do, too."

After untying the ropes from my dogs, I held onto their collars for a minute. Pulling them up close, I knelt down and whispered, "This is the last night. I know you'll do your best."

They seemed to understand and tugged at their collars. When I turned them loose, they started for the timber. Just as they reached the dark shadows, they stopped, turned around, and stared straight at me for an instant.

The judge saw their strange actions. Laying a hand on my shoulder, he asked, "What did they say, son?"

I said, "Nothing that anyone could understand, but I can feel that they know this hunt is important. They know it just as well as you or I."

It was Little Ann who found the trail. Before the echo of her sharp cry had died away, Old Dan's deep voice floated out of the swamp.

"Well, let's go," Papa said eagerly.

"No, let's wait a minute," I said.

"Wait? Why?" Grandpa asked.

"To see which way he's going to run," I said.

The coon broke out of the swamp and headed for the river. Listening to my dogs, I could tell they were close to him. I said to Papa, "I don't think he'll ever make it to the river. They're right on his heels now."

By the time we had circled the swamp, they were bawling treed. The judge said, "Boy, that was fast."

I felt my father's hand on my shoulder. Looking at me, he smiled and nodded his head. Papa and I knew I had judged the coon perfectly. He didn't have time to reach the river or the mountains.

My dogs had treed the coon in a tall ash which stood about fifty yards from the river. I knew the fifty yards had saved us a good hour, because he could have pulled trick after trick if he had gotten in the water.

We spied the coon in the topmost branches. At the crack of the gun, he ran far out on a limb and jumped. He landed in an old fallen treetop. He scooted through it. Coming out on the other side, he ran for the river. The tangled mass of limbs slowed my dogs and they all but tore the treetop apart getting out of it. The coon was just one step ahead of them as they reached the river. We heard them hit the water.

Running over, we stood and watched the fight. The coon was at home in the river. He crawled up on Old Dan's head, trying to force him under. Before he could do it, Little Ann reached up and pulled him off.

In a scared voice, Papa said, "That water looks deep to me."

"Maybe you had better call them off," said the judge. "That's a big coon and he could drown one of them easily in that deep water."

"Call them off?" I said. "Why, you couldn't whip them off with a stick. There's no use for anyone to get scared. They know exactly what they're doing. I've seen this more times than one."

Grandpa was scared and excited. He was jumping up and down, whooping and hollering.

Papa raised the gun to aim.

I jumped and grabbed his arm. "Don't do that," I yelled. "You're sure to hit one of my dogs."

Round and round in the deep water the fight went on. The coon climbed up on Old Dan's head and sank his teeth in one of his long tender ears. Old Dan bawled with pain. Little Ann swam in and caught one of the coon's hind legs in her mouth. She tried hard to pull him off. All three disappeared under the water.

I held my breath.

The water churned and boiled. All three came to the top about the same time. The coon was between the bank we were standing on and my dogs. He swam toward us. They caught him again just as he reached shore. He fought his way free and ran for a large sycamore. Old Dan caught him just as he started up. I knew that was the end of the fight.

After it was all over and the coon had been skinned, Grandpa said, "I hope we don't have to go through that again tonight. For a while I sure thought your dogs were goners."

The judge said, "Well, have you ever seen that? Look over there!"

Old Dan was standing perfectly still, with eyes closed and head hanging down. Little Ann was licking at his cut and bleeding ears.

"She always does that," I said. "If you'll watch, when she gets done with him, he'll do the same for her."

We stood and watched until they had finished doctoring each other. Then, trotting side by side, they disappeared in the darkness.

We followed along, stopping now and then to listen.

XVII

LOOKING UP AT THE SKY, Papa said, "That doesn't look good up there. I think we are in for a storm."

The sky had turned a dark gray. Fast-moving clouds were rolling through the heavens.

Grandpa said, "Looks like we're going to get some wind, too."

Scared and thinking everyone might want to stop hunting because of a few clouds, I said, "If a storm is brewing, it's a good night to hunt. All game stirs just before a storm."

Thirty minutes later, Papa said, "Listen."

We stood still. A low moaning sound could be heard in the tops of the tall sycamores.

Grandpa said, "I was afraid of that. We're going to get some wind."

We heard a rattling in the leaves and underbrush. It was beginning to sleet. The air turned cold and chilly.

From far downriver, we heard the deep baying of a hound on a trail. It was Old Dan. Seconds later, the rhythmic crying of Little Ann could be heard. Swallowing the lump that had jumped up in my throat, I whooped as loud as I could.

The ground was turning white with sleet. The storm had really set in. We hurried along.

I said to Papa, "If this keeps up that old coon won't run long. He'll head for his den."

"If it gets much worse," Grandpa said, "I know some coon hunters that won't be running very long. They'll be frozen too stiff to run."

The judge asked if there was any danger of getting lost.

"I don't know," Papa said. "It's all strange country to me."

My dogs' voices sounded far away. I knew they were much closer than they sounded as they were downwind from us. Finding three large sycamores growing close together, we stopped on the leeward side.

Papa shouted above the wind, "I don't know if we can take much more of this."

"It is bad," Grandpa replied, "and it looks like it's going to get worse."

"You can't see over fifteen feet now," the judge said. "Do you think we can find the buggy?"

"I think we can find the buggy all right," Papa said.

I could no longer hear the voices of my dogs. This had me worried. I didn't want to leave them out in the storm.

"Can anyone hear the hounds?" Grandpa asked.

"I can't," Papa said.

The judge spoke up. "Fellows, I think we'd better go in," he said. "There's no telling where they are. They may have crossed the river."

Scared and knowing I had to do something, I said, "They're closer than you think, probably treed by now. You can't hear them for this wind." I begged, "Let's go a little further."

There was no reply and no one made a move to leave the shelter of the trees.

Taking a few steps, I said, "I'll take the lead. Just follow me."

"Billy, we couldn't find them," Papa said. "You can't see or hear a thing. We had better start back for camp."

"I think so, too," the judge said.

At this remark, I cried, "I've been out in storms like this before, all by myself. I've never left my dogs in the woods, and I'm not going to now, even if I have to look for them by myself."

No one answered.

"Please go just a little further," I begged. "I just know we'll hear them."

Still no one spoke or made a move to go on.

Stepping over to my father, I buried my face in his old mackinaw coat. Sobbing, I pleaded with him not to turn back.

He patted my head. "Billy," he said, "a man could freeze to

death in this storm, and besides, your dogs will give up and come in."

"That's what has me worried," I cried. "They won't come in. They won't, Papa. Little Ann might, but not Old Dan. He'd die before he'd leave a coon in a tree."

Papa was undecided. Making up his mind, he stepped away from the tree and said to the others, "I'm going on with him. You fellows coming, or going back?"

He turned and followed me. Grandpa and the judge fell in behind him.

By this time the ground was covered with a thin white layer of sleet. We kept slipping and falling. I could hear Grandpa mumbling and grumbling. The wind-driven sleet stung our skin like thousands of pricking needles. Strong gusts of wind growled and moaned through the tops of the tall timber.

Once during a momentary lull of the storm, I thought I heard the baying of a hound. I told my father I thought I had heard Old Dan.

"From which direction?" he asked.

"From that way," I said, pointing to our left.

We started on. A few minutes later Papa stopped. He shouted to my grandfather, "Did you hear anything?"

"No," Grandpa shouted back. "I can't hear anything in this storm."

"I thought I did, but I'm not sure," the judge said.

"Where was it coming from?" Papa asked.

"Over that way," the judge said, pointing to our right.

"That's the way it sounded to me," Papa said.

At that moment, all of us heard the deep voice of Old Dan.

"It sounds as if they're close," Grandpa said.

"Let's split up," said the judge. "Maybe one of us can find them."

"No," Papa said, "it'd be easy to get lost in this storm."

"I think they're more to the right of us," I said.

"I do, too," Papa said.

We trudged on. Old Dan bawled again. The sound of his voice seemed to be all around us.

"The way that wind is whipping the sound through this timber," the judge said, "we'd be lucky if we ever found them."

Papa shouted over the roar of the wind, "We can't take much more of this. We'll freeze to death."

The men were giving up. I felt the knot again as it crawled up in my throat. Salt water froze on my eyelashes. Kneeling down, I put my ear close to the icy ground in hopes I could hear my dogs, but I couldn't hear anything above the roar of the blizzard.

Standing up, I peered this way and that. All I could see was a white wall of whirling sleet. I closed my eyes and said a silent prayer and hoped for a miracle.

We heard a sharp crack and a loud crashing noise. A large limb, torn from a tree by the strong wind, fell to the ground. The sharp crack of the limb gave me the idea. Shouting to my father, I said, "Shoot the gun. If my dogs are close enough to hear it, maybe Little Ann will come to us."

Papa didn't hesitate. Pointing the gun high over his head, he pulled the trigger. The sharp crack rang out into the teeth of the storm.

We waited.

Just when I had given up all hope and had sunk to the lowest depth of despair, out of the white wall of driving sleet, my little dog came to me. I knelt down and gathered her in my arms.

Taking one of the lead ropes from my pocket, I tied it to her collar. I said, "Find him, little girl. Please find Old Dan."

Right then I didn't care about coons, gold cups, or anything. All I wanted was my dogs.

I don't know how she did it. Straight into the face of the storm she led us. Time after time she would stop and turn her head this way and that. I knew she couldn't scent or see anything. Instinct alone was guiding her. Over a winding and twisting trail, we followed.

Coming out of the bottoms, she led us into a thick canebrake. The tall stalks sheltered us from the storm. The roaring of the wind didn't seem as loud. Like ghostly figures, large trees loomed out of the almost solid mass. Falling and stumbling, we kept pushing on.

Grandpa shouted, "Hold up a minute. I'm just about all in."

We stopped.

"Do you think that hound knows what she's doing?" the judge asked. "Maybe we're just running around in circles."

Looking at me, Papa said, "I hope she does. Some of these canebrakes cover miles. If we get lost in here, we'll be in bad shape."

Grandpa said, "I think we've gone too far. The last time I heard Old Dan, he sounded quite close."

"That was because the wind carried the sound," I said.

The judge spoke up, "Fellows, no dog is worth the lives of three men. Now let's do the smart thing and get out of here while we can. Our clothes are wet. If we keep on wandering around in this jungle, we'll freeze to death. It doesn't look like this blizzard is ever going to let up."

I could hear the roar of the blizzard back in the thick timber of the bottoms. Two large limbs being rubbed together by the strong wind made a grinding creaking sound. The tall slender cane around us rattled and swayed.

I could feel the silence closing in. I knew the judge's cold logic had had its effect on my father and grandfather. The men had given up. There was no hope left for me.

Kneeling down, I put my arms around Little Ann. I felt the warm heat from her moist tongue caressing my ear. Closing my eyes, I said, "Please, Dan, bawl one more time, just one more time."

I waited for my plea to be answered.

With its loud roaring, the north wind seemed to be laughing at us. All around, tall stalks of cane were weaving and dancing to the rattling rhythm of their knife-edged blades.

My father tried to talk above the wind, but his words were lost in the storm. Just before another blast, clear as a foghorn on a stormy sea, Old Dan's voice rang loud and clear. It seemed louder than the roar of the wind or the skeleton-like rustling of the tall swaying cane.

I jumped to my feet. My heart did a complete flip-flop. The knot in my throat felt as big as an apple. I tried to whoop, but it was no use. Little Ann bawled and tugged on the rope.

There was no mistaking the direction. We knew that Little Ann had been right all along. Straight as an arrow, she had led us to him.

Old Dan was treed down in a deep gully. I slid off the bank and ran to him. His back was covered with a layer of frozen sleet. His frost-covered whiskers stood out straight as porcupine quills.

I worked the wedges of ice from between his toes, and scraped the sleet from his body with my hands. Little Ann came over and tried to wash his face. He didn't like it. Jerking loose from me, he ran over to the tree, reared up on it, and started bawling.

Hearing shouting from the bank above me, I looked up. I could dimly see Papa and the judge through the driving sleet. At first I thought they were shouting to me, but on peering closer I could see that they had their backs to me. Catching hold of some long stalks of cane that were hanging down from the steep bank, I pulled myself up.

Papa shouted in my ear, "Something has happened to your grandfather."

Turning to the judge, he said, "He was behind you. When was the last time you saw him?"

"I don't know for sure," the judge said. "I guess it was back there when we heard the hound bawl."

"Didn't you hear anything?" Papa asked.

"Hear anything?" the judge exclaimed. "How could I hear anything in all that noise? I thought he was behind me all the time, and didn't miss him until we got here."

I couldn't hold back the tears. My grandfather was lost and wandering in that white jungle of cane. Screaming for him, I started back.

Papa caught me. He shouted, "Don't do that."

I tried to tear away from him but his grip on my arm was firm.

"Shoot the gun," the judge said.

Papa shot time after time. It was useless. We got no answer.

Little Ann came up out of the washout. She stood and stared at me. Turning, she disappeared quickly in the thick cane. Minutes later we heard her. It was a long, mournful cry.

The only times I had ever heard my little dog bawl like that were when she was baying at a bright Ozark moon, or when someone played a French harp or a fiddle close to her ear. She didn't stop until we reached her.

Grandpa lay as he had fallen, face down in the icy sleet. His right foot was wedged in the fork of a broken box elder limb.

When the ankle had twisted, the searing pain must have made him unconscious.

Papa worked Grandpa's foot free and turned him over. I sat down and placed his head in my lap. While Papa and the judge massaged his arms and legs, I wiped the frozen sleet from his eyes and face.

Burying my face in the iron-gray hair, I cried and begged God not to let my grandfather die.

"I think he's gone," the judge said.

"I don't think so," Papa said. "He took a bad fall when that limb tripped him, but he hasn't been lying here long enough to be frozen. I think he's just unconscious."

Papa lifted him to a sitting position and told the judge to start slapping his face. Grandpa moaned and moved his head.

"He's coming around," Papa said.

I asked Papa if we could get him back to the gully where Old Dan was. I had noticed there was very little wind there and we could build a fire.

"That's the very place," he said. "We'll build a good fire and one of us can go for help."

Papa and the judge made a seat by catching each other's wrists. They eased Grandpa between them.

By the time we reached the washout, Grandpa was fully conscious again, and was mumbling and grumbling. He couldn't see why they had to carry him like a baby.

After easing him over the bank and down into the gully, we built a large fire. Papa took his knife and cut the boot from Grandpa's swollen foot. Grandpa grunted and groaned from the pain. I felt sorry for him but there was nothing I could do but look on.

Papa examined the foot. Shaking his head, he said, "Boy, that's a bad one. It's either broken or badly sprained. I'll go for some help."

Grandpa said, "Now wait just a minute. I'm not going to let you go out in that blizzard by yourself. What if something happens to you? No one would know."

"What time is it?" he asked.

The judge looked at his watch. "It's almost five o'clock," he said.

"It's not long till daylight," Grandpa said. "Then if you want to go, you can see where you're going. Now help me get propped up against this bank. I'll be all right. It doesn't hurt any more. It's numb now."

"He's right," the judge said.

"Think you can stand it?" Papa asked.

Grandpa roared like a bear. "Sure I can stand it. It's nothing but a sprained ankle. I'm not going to die. Build that fire up a little more."

While Papa and the judge made Grandpa comfortable, I carried wood for the fire.

"There's no use standing around gawking at me," Grandpa said. "I'm all right. Get the coon out of that tree. That's what we came for, isn't it?"

Up until then, the coon-hunting had practically been forgotten. The tree was about thirty feet from our fire. We walked over and took a good look at it for the first time. My dogs, seeing we were finally going to pay some attention to them, started bawling and running around the tree.

Papa said, "It's not much of a tree, just an old box elder snag. There's not a limb on it."

"I can't see any coon," said the judge. "It must be hollow."

Papa beat on its side with the ax. It gave forth a loud booming sound. He said, "It's hollow all right."

He stepped back a few steps, scraped his feet on the slick ground for a good footing, and said, "Stand back, and hold those hounds. I'm going to cut it down. We need some wood for our fire anyway."

Squatting down between my dogs, I held onto their collars.

Papa notched the old snag so it would fall away from our fire. As the heavy ax chewed its way into the tree, it began to lean and crack. Papa stopped chopping. He said to the judge, "Come on and help me. I think we can push it over now."

After much grunting and pushing, snapping and popping, it fell. I turned my dogs loose.

On hitting the ground, the snag split and broke up. Goggle-eyed, I stood rooted in my tracks and watched three big coons roll out of the busted old trunk.

One started up the washout, running between us and the fire.

Old Dan caught him and the fight was on. The second coon headed down the washout. Little Ann caught him.

Hearing a loud yell from Grandpa, I looked that way. Old Dan and the coon were fighting close to his feet. He was yelling and beating at them with his hat. The judge and Papa ran to help.

The third coon started climbing up the steep bank close to me. Just before reaching the top, his claws slipped in the icy mud. Tumbling end over end, down he came. I grabbed up a stick and threw it at him. Growling and showing his teeth, he started for me. I threw the fight to him then and there. Some ten yards away I looked back. He was climbing the bank. That time he made it and disappeared in the thick cane.

Hearing a squall of pain from Little Ann, I turned. The coon was really working her over. He had climbed up on her back and was tearing and slashing. She couldn't shake him off. Grabbing a club from the ground, I ran to help her.

Before we had killed our coon, Old Dan came tearing in. We stood and watched the fight. When the coon was dead, Papa picked it up and we walked back to the fire.

"How many coons were in that old snag?" Papa asked.

"I saw three," I said. "The one that got away climbed out over there." I pointed in the direction the coon had taken.

I never should have pointed. My dogs turned as one, and started bawling and clawing their way up the steep bank. I shouted and scolded, but to no avail. They disappeared in the rattling cane.

We stood still, listening to their voices. The sound died away in the roaring storm. Sitting down close to the fire, I buried my face in my arms and cried.

I heard the judge say to my father, "This beats anything I have ever seen. Why, those dogs can read that boy's mind. He just pointed at that bank and away they went. I never saw anything like it. I can't understand some of the things they have done tonight. Hounds usually aren't that smart. If they were collies, or some other breed of dog, it would be different, but they're just redbone hounds, hunting dogs."

Papa said, "Yes, I know what you mean. I've seen them do things that I couldn't understand. I'd never heard of hounds that ever had any affection for anyone, but these dogs are different.

Did you know they won't hunt with anyone but him, not even me?"

Hearing my grandfather call my name, I went over and sat down by his side. Putting his arm around me, he said, "Now, I wouldn't worry about those dogs. They'll be all right. It's not long till daylight. Then you can go to them."

I said, "Yes, but what if the coon crosses the river? My dogs will follow him. If they get wet they could freeze to death."

"We'll just have to wait and hope for the best," he said. "Now straighten up and quit that sniffling. Act like a coon hunter. You don't see me bawling, and this old foot is paining me something awful."

I felt better after my talk with Grandpa.

"Come on, let's skin these coons," Papa said.

I got up to help him.

After the skins were peeled from the carcasses, I had an idea. Holding one up close to the fire until it was warm, I took it over and wrapped it around Grandpa's foot. Chuckling, he said, "Boy, that feels good. Heat another skin the same way."

I kept it up for the rest of the night.

XVIII

JUST BEFORE DAWN, the storm blew itself out with one last angry roar. It started snowing. A frozen silence settled over the canebrake.

Back in the thick timber of the river bottoms, the sharp snapping of frozen limbs could be heard. The tall stalks of wild cane looked exhausted from the hellish night. They were drooping and bending from the weight of the frozen sleet.

I climbed out of the deep gully and listened for my dogs. I couldn't hear them. Just as I started back down the bank, I heard something. I listened. Again I heard the sound.

Papa was watching me. "Can you hear the dogs?" he asked.

"No, not the dogs," I said, "but I can hear something else."

"What does it sound like?" he asked.

"Like someone whooping," I said.

Papa and the judge hurried up the bank. We heard the sound again. It was coming from a different direction.

"The first time I heard it," I said, "it was over that way."

"It's the men from camp," the judge said. "They're searching for us."

We started whooping. The searchers answered. Their voices came from all directions. The first one to reach us was Mr. Kyle. He looked haggard and tired. He asked if everything was all right.

"Yes, we're all right," Papa said, "but the old man has a bad ankle. It looks like we'll have to carry him out."

"Your team broke loose and came back to camp about midnight," Mr. Kyle said. "This really spooked us. We were sure some-

thing bad had happened. Twenty-five of us have been searching
since then."

Several men climbed down the bank and went over to Grandpa.
They looked at his ankle. One said, "I don't think it's broken,
but it sure is a bad sprain."

"You're in luck," another one said. "We have one of the best
doctors in the state of Texas in our camp, Dr. Charley Lathman.
He'll have you fixed up in no time."

"Yes," another said, "and if I know Charley, he's probably got
a small hospital with him."

Back in the crowd, I heard another man say, "You mean that
Lathman fellow, who owns those black and tan hounds, is a
doctor?"

"Sure is," another said. "One of the best."

Mr. Kyle asked where my dogs were. I told him that they were
treed somewhere.

"What do you mean, treed somewhere?" he asked.

Papa explained what had happened.

With a wide-eyed look on his face, he said, "Do you mean to
tell me those hounds stayed with the tree in that blizzard?"

I nodded.

Looking at me, he said, "Son, I hope they have that coon treed,
because you need that one to win the cup. Those two walker
hounds caught three before the storm came up. When it got bad,
all the hunters came in.

The judge spoke up. "I'll always believe that those hounds knew
that boy needed another coon to win," he said. "If you fellows had
seen some of the things those dogs have done, you'd believe it,
too."

One hunter walked over to the broken snag. "Three out of
one tree," he said. "No wonder, look here! That old snag was half-
full of leaves and grass. Why, it was a regular old den tree."

Several of the men walked over. I heard one say, "I've seen this
happen before. Remember that big hunt in the Red River bottoms,
when the two little beagle hounds treed four coons in an old hollow snag? They won the championship, too."

"I wasn't there but I remember reading about it," one said.

"Say, I don't see Benson," Mr. Kyle said.

The men started looking at each other.

"He was searching farther downriver than the rest of us," one fellow said. "Maybe he didn't hear us shouting."

Some of the men climbed out of the gully. They started whooping. From a distance we heard an answering shout.

"He hears us," someone said. "He's coming."

Everyone looked relieved.

Mr. Benson struck the washout a little way above us. He was breathing hard, as if he'd been running. He started talking as soon as he was within hearing distance.

"It scared me when I first saw them," he said. "I didn't know what they were. They looked like white ghosts. I'd never seen anything like it."

A hunter grabbed Mr. Benson by the shoulder, shaking him. "Get ahold of yourself, man," he said. "What are you talking about?"

Mr. Benson took a deep breath to control himself, and started again in a much calmer voice. "Those two hounds," he said. "I found them. They're frozen solid. They're nothing but white ice from the tips of their noses to the ends of their tails."

Hearing Mr. Benson's words, I screamed and ran to my father. Everything started whirling around and around. I felt light as a feather. My knees buckled. I knew no more.

Regaining consciousness, I opened my eyes and could dimly see the blurry images of the men around me. A hand was shaking me. I could hear my father's voice but I couldn't understand his words. Little by little the blackness faded away. My throat was dry and I was terribly thirsty. I asked for some water.

Mr. Benson came over. He said, "Son, I'm sorry, truly sorry. I didn't mean it that way. Your dogs are alive. I guess I was excited. I'm very sorry."

I heard a deep voice say, "That's a hell of a thing to do. Come running in here saying the dogs are frozen solid."

Mr. Benson said, "I didn't mean it to sound that way. I said I'm sorry. What more do you want me to do?"

The deep voice growled again. "I still think it was a hell of a thing for a man to do."

Mr. Kyle took over. "Now let's not have any more of this," he said. "We have work to do. We've been standing here acting like a bunch of schoolkids. All this time that old man has been lying there suffering. A couple of you men cut two poles and make a stretcher to carry him."

While the men were getting the poles, Papa heated the coonskins again and rewrapped Grandpa's foot.

With belts and long leather laces from their boots, the hunters made a stretcher. Very gently they put Grandpa on it.

Again Mr. Kyle took command. "Part of us will start for camp with him," he said. "The others will go after the dogs."

"Here, take this gun," Papa said. "I'll go with him."

Looking at me, Mr. Kyle said, "Come on, son. I want to see your hounds."

Mr. Benson led the way. "As soon as we get out of this cane," he said, "we may be able to hear them. They have the coon treed in a big black gum tree. You're going to see a sight. Now I mean a sight. They've walked a ring around that tree clear down through the ice and snow. You can see the bare ground."

"Wonder why they did that?" someone asked.

"I don't know," Mr. Benson replied, "unless they ran in that circle to keep from freezing to death, or to keep the coon in the tree."

I figured I knew why my dogs were covered with ice. The coon had probably crossed the river, maybe several times. Old Dan and Little Ann would have followed him. They had come out of the river with their coats dripping wet, and the freezing blast of the blizzard had done the rest.

Nearing the tree, we stopped and stared.

"Did you ever see anything like that?" Mr. Benson asked. "When I first saw them, I thought they were white wolves."

My dogs hadn't seen us when we came up. They were trotting round and round. Just as Mr. Benson had said, we could see the path they had worn down through the ice and snow till the bare black earth was visible. Like ghostly white shadows, around and around they trotted.

In a low voice, someone said, "They know that if they stop they'll freeze to death."

"It's unbelievable," said Mr. Kyle. "Come on. We must do something quick."

With a choking sob, I ran for my dogs.

On hearing our approach, they sat down and started bawling

treed. I noticed their voices didn't have that solid ring. Their ice-covered tails made a rattling sound as they switched this way and that on the icy ground.

A large fire was built. Standing my dogs close to the warm heat, the gentle hands of the hunters went to work. With handkerchiefs and scarves heated steaming hot, little by little the ice was thawed from their bodies.

"If they had ever lain down," someone said, "they would've frozen to death."

"They knew it," another said. "That's why they kept running in that circle."

"What I can't understand is why they stayed with the tree," Mr. Benson said. "I've seen hounds stay with a tree for a while, but not in a northern blizzard."

"Men," said Mr. Kyle, "people have been trying to understand dogs ever since the beginning of time. One never knows what they'll do. You can read every day where a dog saved the life of a drowning child, or lay down his life for his master. Some people call this loyalty. I don't. I may be wrong, but I call it love—the deepest kind of love."

After these words were spoken, a thoughtful silence settled over the men. The mood was broken by the deep growling voice I had heard back in the washout.

"It's a shame that people all over the world can't have that kind of love in their hearts," he said. "There would be no wars, slaughter, or murder; no greed or selfishness. It would be the kind of world that God wants us to have—a wonderful world."

After all the ice was thawed from my dogs and their coats were dried out, I could see they were all right. I was happy again and felt good all over.

One of the hunters said, "Do you think those hounds are thawed out enough to fight a coon?"

"Sure, just run him out of that tree," I said.

At the crack of the gun, the coon ran far out on a big limb and stopped. Again the hunter sprinkled him with bird shot. This time he jumped. Hitting the ground, he crouched down.

Old Dan made a lunge. Just as he reached him, the coon sprang straight up and came down on his head. Holding on with his claws, the coon sank his teeth in a long tender ear. Old Dan was furious. He started turning in a circle, bawling with pain.

Little Ann was trying hard to get ahold of the coon but she couldn't. Because of his fast circling, Old Dan's feet flew out from under him and he fell. This gave Little Ann a chance. Darting in, her jaws closed on the back of the coon's neck. I knew the fight was over.

Arriving back at camp, I saw that all the tents had been taken down but ours. A hunter said, "Everyone was in a hurry to get out before another blizzard sets in."

Papa told me to take my dogs into the tent as Grandpa wanted to see them.

I saw tears in my grandfather's eyes as he talked to them. His ankle was wrapped in bandages. His foot and toes were swollen to twice their normal size. They had turned a greenish-yellow color. Placing my hand on his foot, I could feel the feverish heat.

Dr. Lathman came over. "Are you ready to go now?" he asked.

Snorting and growling, Grandpa said, "I told you I wasn't going anywhere till I see the gold cup handed to this boy."

Turning to face the crowd, Dr. Lathman said, "Men, let's get this over. I want to get this man to town. That's one of the meanest sprains I've ever seen and it should be in a cast, but I don't have any plaster of Paris with me."

The hunter who had come by our tent collecting the jackpot money came up to me. Handing me the box, he said, "Here you are, son. There's over three hundred dollars in this box. It's all yours."

Turning to the crowd, he said, "Fellows, I can always say this. On this hunt I've seen two of the finest little coon hounds I ever hope to see."

There was a roar of approval from the crowd.

Looking down, I saw the box was almost full of money. I was shaking all over. I tried to say "Thanks," but it was only a whisper. Turning, I handed the box to my father. As his rough old hands closed around it, I saw a strange look come over his face. He turned and looked at my dogs.

Some of the men started shouting, "Here it is!"

The crowd parted and the judge walked through. I saw the gleaming metal of the gold cup in his hand. After a short speech, he handed it to me, saying, "Son, this makes me very proud. It's a great honor to present you with this championship cup."

The crowd exploded. The hunters' shouts were deafening.

I don't know from where the two silly old tears came. They just squeezed their way out. I felt them as they rolled down my cheeks. One dropped on the smooth surface of the cup and splattered. I wiped it away with my sleeve.

Turning to my dogs, I knelt down and showed the cup to them. Little Ann licked it. Old Dan sniffed one time, and then turned his head away.

The judge said, "Son, there's a place on the cup to engrave the names of your dogs. I can take it into Oklahoma City and have it done, or you can have it done yourself. The engraving charge has already been paid by the association."

Looking at the cup, it seemed that far down in the gleaming shadows I could see two wide blue eyes glued to a windowpane. I knew that my little sister was watching the road and waiting for our return. Looking back at the judge, I said, "If you don't mind, I'll take it with me. My grandfather can send it in for me."

Laughing, he said, "That's all right." Handing me a slip of paper, he said, "This is the address where you should send it."

Grandpa said, "Now that that's settled, I'm ready to go to town." Turning to Papa, he said, "You'll have to bring the buggy, and I wish you'd look after my stock. I know Grandma will want to go in with us and there'll be no one there to feed them. Tell Bill Lowery to come up and take care of the store. You'll find the keys in the usual place."

"We'll take care of everything," Papa said. "Don't worry about a thing. I don't intend to stop until we get back, because it looks like we're in for some more bad weather."

I went over and kissed Grandpa good-bye. He pinched my cheek, and whispered, "We'll teach these city slickers that they can't come up here and beat our dogs."

I smiled.

Grandpa was carried out and made comfortable in the back seat of Dr. Lathman's car. I stood and watched as it wheezed and bounced its way out of sight.

"While I'm harnessing the team," Papa said, "you take the tent down and pack our gear."

On the back seat of the buggy, I made a bed out of our bed-clothes. Down on the floor boards, I fixed a nice place for my dogs.

All through the night, the creaking wheels of our buggy moved on. Several times I woke up. My father had wrapped a tarp around himself. Reaching down, I could feel my dogs. They were warm and comfortable.

Early the next morning, we stopped for breakfast. While Papa tended to the team, I turned my dogs loose and let them stretch.

"We made good time last night," Papa said. "If everything goes right, we'll be home long before dark."

Reaching Grandpa's store in the middle of the afternoon, Papa said, "I'll put the team in the barn and feed the stock while you unload the buggy."

Coming back from the barn, he said, "In the morning, I'll go over and tell Bill Lowery to come up and open the store."

Looking around, he said, "It snowed more here than it did where we were hunting."

Feeling big and important, I said, "I don't like the looks of this weather. We'd better be scooting for home."

Papa laughed. "Sure you're not in a hurry to get home to show off the gold cup?" he asked.

A smile was my only answer.

Two hundred yards this side of our home, the road made a turn around a low foothill shutting our house off from view.

Papa said, "You're going to see a scramble as soon as we round that bend."

It was more of a stampede than a scramble. The little one came out first, and all but tore the screen door from its hinges. The older girls passed her just beyond the gate. In her hurry, she slipped and fell face down in the snow. She started crying.

The older girls ran up asking for the cup.

Holding it high over my head, I said, "Now wait a minute. I've got another one for you two." I held the small silver cup out to them.

While they were fighting over it, I ran to the little one. Picking her up, I brushed the snow from her long, braided hair and her tear-stained face. I told her there was no use to cry. I had brought the gold cup to her, and no one else was going to get it.

Reaching for the cup, she wrapped her small arms around it.

Squeezing it up tight, she ran for the house to show it to Mama.

Mama came out on the porch. She was just as excited as the girls were. She held out her arms. I ran to her. She hugged me and kissed me.

"It's good to have you home again," she said.

"Look what I have, Mama," the little one cried, "and it's all mine."

She held the golden cup out in her two small hands.

As Mama took the beautiful cup, she looked at me. She started to say something but was interrupted by the cries from the other girls.

"We have one, too, Mama," they cried, "and it's just as pretty as that one."

"It's not either," the little one piped in a defiant voice. "It's not even as big as mine."

"Two cups!" Mama exclaimed. "Did you win two?"

"Yes, Mama," I said. "Little Ann won that one all by herself."

The awed expression on my mother's face was wonderful to see. Holding a cup in each hand, she held them out in front of her.

"Two," she said. "A gold one and a silver one. Who would have thought anything so wonderful could have happened to us. I'm so proud; so very proud."

Handing the cups back to the girls, she walked over to Papa. After kissing him, she said, "I just can't believe everything that has happened. I'm so glad you went along. Did you enjoy yourself?"

With a smile on his face, Papa almost shouted, "Enjoy myself? Why, I never had such a time in my life."

His voice trailed off to a low calm, "That is, except for one thing. Grandpa had a bad accident."

"Yes, I know," Mama said. "One of Tom Logan's boys was at the store when they arrived. He came by and told us all about it. The doctor said it wasn't as bad as it looked, and he was pretty sure Grandpa would be home in a few days."

I was happy to hear this news, and could tell by the pleased look on my father's face, he was glad to hear it, too.

On entering the house, Papa said, "Oh, I almost forgot." He handed the box of money to Mama.

"What's this?" she asked.

"Oh, it's just a little gift from Old Dan and Little Ann," Papa said.

Mama opened the box. I saw the color drain from her face. Her hands started trembling. Turning her back to us, she walked over and set it on the mantel. A peaceful silence settled over the room. I could hear the clock ticking away. The fire in the fireplace crackled and popped.

Turning from the mantel, Mama looked straight at us. Her lips were tightly pressed together to keep them from quivering. Walking slowly to Papa, she buried her face in his chest. I heard her say, "Thank God, my prayers have been answered."

There was a celebration in our home that night. To me it was like a second Christmas.

Mama opened a jar of huckleberries and made a large cobbler. Papa went to the smokehouse and came back with a hickory-cured ham. We sat down to a feast of the ham, huge plates of fried potatoes, ham gravy, hot corn bread, fresh butter, and wild bee honey.

During the course of the meal, the entire story of the championship hunt was told, some by Papa but mostly by me.

Just when everything was so perfect and peaceful, an argument sprang up between the two oldest girls. It seemed that each wanted to claim the silver cup. Just when they were on the verge of sawing it in two, so each would have her allotted share, Papa settled the squabble by giving the oldest one a silver dollar. Once again peace and harmony was restored.

That night as I was preparing for bed, a light flashed by my window. Puzzled, I tiptoed over and peeked through the pane. It was Mama. Carrying my lantern and two large plates heaped high with food, she was heading for the doghouse. Setting the light down on the ground in front of it, she called to my dogs. While they were eating, Mama did something I couldn't understand. She knelt down on her knees in prayer.

After they had eaten their food, Mama started petting them. I could hear her voice but couldn't make out her words. Whatever she was saying must have pleased them. Little Ann wiggled and twisted. Even Old Dan wagged his long red tail, which was very unusual.

Papa came out. I saw him put his arm around Mama. Side by

side they stood for several minutes looking at my dogs. When they turned to enter the house, I saw Mama dab at her eyes with her apron.

Lying in bed, staring into the darkness, I tried hard to figure out the strange actions of my parents. Why had Mama knelt in prayer in front of my dogs? Why had she wept?

I was running all the why's around in my mind when I heard them talking.

"I know," Papa said, "but I think there's a way. I'm going to have a talk with Grandpa. I don't think that old foot of his is ever going to be the same again. He's going to need some help around the store."

I knew they were talking about me, but I couldn't understand what they meant. Then I thought, "Why, that's it. They want me to help Grandpa." That would be all right with me. I could still hunt every night.

Feeling smart for figuring out their conversation, I turned over and fell asleep.

XIX

ALTHOUGH THE WINNING of the cups and the money was a big event in my life, it didn't change my hunting any. I was out after the ringtails every night.

I had been hunting the river bottoms hard for about three weeks. On that night, I decided to go back to the Cyclone Timber country. I had barely reached the hunting ground when my dogs struck a trail. Old Dan opened up first.

They struck the trail on a ridge and then dropped down into a deep canyon, up the other side, and broke out into some flats. I could tell that the scent was hot from their steady bawling. Three times they treed the animal.

Every time I came close to the tree, the animal would jump, and the race would be on. After a while, I knew it wasn't a coon. I decided it was a bobcat.

I didn't like to have my dogs tree the big cats, for their fur wasn't any good, and all I could expect was two cut-up hounds.

They could kill the largest bobcat in the hills, and had on several occasions, but to me it was useless. The only good I could see in killing one was getting rid of a vicious predatory animal.

The fourth time they treed, they were on top of a mountain. After the long chase, I figured the animal was winded and would stay in the tree. In a trot I started to them.

As I neared the tree, Little Ann came to me, reared up, and whined. By her actions, I knew something was wrong. I stopped. In the moonlight, I could see Old Dan sitting on his haunches, staring up at the tree and bawling.

The tree had lots of dead leaves on it. I knew it was a large white oak because it is one of the last trees in the mountains to lose its leaves.

Old Dan kept bawling. Then he did something he had never done before. For seconds his deep voice was still, and silence settled over the mountains. My eyes wandered from the tree to him. His lips were curled back and he snarled as he stared into the dark foliage of the tree. His teeth gleamed white in the moonlight. The hair on his neck and along his back stood on end. A low, deep, rumbling growl rolled from his throat.

I was scared and I called to him. I wanted to get away from there. Again I called, but it was no use. He wouldn't leave the tree, for in his veins flowed the breeded blood of a hunting hound. In his fighting heart, there was no fear.

I set the lantern down and tightened my grip on the handle of the ax. Slowly I started walking toward him. I thought, "If I can get close enough to him, I can grab his collar." I kept my eyes on the tree as I edged forward. Little Ann stayed by my side. She, too, was watching the tree.

Then I saw them—two burning, yellow eyes—staring at me from the shadowy foliage of the tree. I stopped, petrified with fear.

The deep baying of Old Dan stopped and again the silence closed in.

I stared back at the unblinking eyes.

I could make out the bulk of a large animal, crouched on a huge branch, close to the trunk of the big tree. Then it moved. I heard the scratch of razor-sharp claws on the bark. It stood up and moved out of the shadows on to the limb. I saw it clearly as it passed between the moon and me. I knew what it was. It was the devil cat of the Ozarks, the mountain lion.

The silence was shattered by one long, loud bawl from Old Dan. I'd never heard my dog bawl like that. It was different. His voice rang out over the mountains, loud and clear. The vibration of the deep tones rolled in the silence of the frosty night, on and on, out over the flats, down in the canyons, and died away in the rimrocks, like the cry of a lost soul. Old Dan had voiced his challenge to the devil cat.

There was a low cough and a deep growl from the lion. I saw him crouch. I knew what was coming. My hands felt hot and sweaty on the smooth ash handle of the ax. With a bloodcurdling scream he sprang from the tree with claws outspread and long, yellow fangs bared.

Old Dan didn't wait. Rearing up on his hind legs, he met the lion in the air. The heavy weight bowled him over and over. He wound up in a fallen treetop.

The impact of the two bodies threw the lion off balance. Little Ann darted in. Her aim was true. I heard the snap of her steel-trap jaws as they closed on his throat.

With a squall of pain and rage, the big cat rolled over on his side, dragging Little Ann with him. His right paw reached out and curved over her shoulder. Sinews tightened and razor-sharp claws dug inward. With a cry of pain, she loosened her hold. I saw the blood squirting from the deep wound in her shoulder. She ignored it and bored back into the fight.

Old Dan, stunned for an instant from the impact of the lion's body, fought his way from the treetop. Bawling the cry of the damned, he charged back in.

I went berserk, and charged into the fight.

There in the flinty hills of the Ozarks, I fought for the lives of my dogs. I fought with the only weapon I had, the sharp cutting blade of a double-bitted ax.

Screaming like a madman, with tears running down my face, I hacked and chopped at the big snarling mountain cat.

Once, feeling the bite of the sharp blade, the devil cat turned on me. His yellow slitted eyes burned with hate. The long, lithe body dipped low to the ground. The shoulder muscles knotted and bulged. I tried to jump back but my foot slipped and I dropped to my knees. I knew I was trapped. With a terrifying scream he sprang.

I never saw my dogs when they got between the lion and me, but they were there. Side by side, they rose up from the ground as one. They sailed straight into those jaws of death, their small, red bodies taking the ripping, slashing claws meant for me.

I screamed and charged back into the fight, swinging my ax, but I was careful not to hit one of my dogs.

The battle raged on and on, down the side of the mountain, over huckleberry bushes, fallen logs, and rocks. It was a rolling, tumbling mass of fighting fury. I was in the middle of it all, falling, screaming, crying and hacking away at every opportunity.

I had cut the big cat several times. Blood showed red on the bit of the ax, but as yet I had not gotten in the fatal lick. I knew it had to be soon for my dogs were no match against the razor-sharp claws and the long, yellow fangs.

The screams of the big cat and the deep bellowing voices of my dogs echoed through the mountains as if the demons of hell had been turned loose. Down the side of the mountain, the terrible fight went on, down to the very bottom of the canyon.

The big cat had Old Dan by the throat. I knew he was seeking to cut the all-important vein, the jugular. At the pitiful bawl of Old Dan, Little Ann, throwing caution to the wind, ran in and sank her teeth in the lion's tough neck.

With her claws digging into the mountain soil, she braced herself, and started pulling. The muscles in her small legs knotted and quivered. She was trying hard to pull the devil cat's fangs from the throat of Old Dan.

In the rays of a bright Ozark moon, I could see clearly. For an instant I saw the broad back of the big cat. I saw the knotty bulge of steel-bound muscle, the piston-like jerk of the deadly hind claws, trying for the downward stroke that could disembowel a dog.

Raising the ax high over my head, I brought it down with all the strength in my body. My aim was true. Behind the shoulders, in the broad muscular back, the heavy blade sank with a sickening sound. The keen edge cleaved through the tough skin. It seemed to hiss as it sliced its way through bone and gristle.

I left the ax where it was, sunk to the eye in the back of the devil cat.

He loosened his hold on the throat of Old Dan. With a scream of pain, he reared up on his hind legs and started pawing the air. Little Ann dangled from his neck, still holding on. Her eyes were shut tight and her small feet were digging and clawing at the body.

Old Dan, spewing blood from a dozen wounds, leaped high in the air. His long, red body sailed in between the outspread paws of the lion. I heard the snap of his powerful jaws as they closed on the throat.

The big cat screamed again. Blood gurgled and sprayed. In a bright red mist, it rained out over the underbrush and rattled like sleet on the white oak leaves. In a boxer's stance, he stood and clawed the air. His slitted eyes turned green with hate. He seemed to be unaware of the two hounds hanging from his body, and kept staring at me. I stood in a trance and stared back at the ghastly scene.

The breath of life was slowly leaving him. He was dying on his feet but refusing to go down. My ax handle stuck straight out from his back. Blood, gushing from the mortal wound, glistened in the moonlight. A shudder ran through his body. He tried once again to scream. Blood gurgled in his throat.

It was the end of the trail for the scourge of the mountains. No more would he scream his challenge from the rimrocks to the valley below. The small, harmless calves and the young colts would be safe from his silent stalk.

He fell toward me. It seemed that with his last effort he was still trying to get at me.

As his heavy body struck the ground, something exploded in my head. I knew no more.

When I came to, I was sitting down. It was silent and still. A bird, disturbed by the fight, started chirping far up on the side of the mountain. A small winter breeze rustled some dead leaves in the deep canyon. A cold, crawling chill crept over my body.

I looked over at the lion. My dogs were still glued to his lifeless body. In his dying convulsions the ax had become dislodged from the wound. It lay there in the moonlight, covered with blood.

My numb brain started working. I thought of another time the ax had been covered with blood. I don't know why I thought of Rubin Pritchard at that time, or why I thought of these words I had often heard: "There is a little good in all evil."

I got to my feet and went over to my dogs. I knew I had to inspect them to see how badly they were hurt. It wasn't too hard to get Little Ann to loosen her hold. I examined her body. She was cut in several places, but nothing fatal. The only bad wound she had was in her shoulder. It was nine inches long and down to the clean, white bone. She started licking it immediately.

It was different with Old Dan. Try as I might, he wouldn't turn loose. Maybe he could remember the night in the cave when he was a pup. How the big cat had screamed and how he had bawled back at him.

I took hold of his hind legs and tried to pull him loose. It was no use. He knew that the hold he had was a deadly one and he wasn't going to let go. I tried to tell him it was all over, that the lion was dead, to turn loose as I wanted to see how badly he was hurt. He couldn't understand and wouldn't even open his eyes. He was determined to hold on until the body turned cold and stiff.

With my ax handle, I pried apart his locked jaws. Holding on to his collar, I led him off to one side. I couldn't turn him loose as I knew if I did, he would go back to the lion.

With one hand I started examining him. I ran my fingers through the short, red hair. I could feel the quivering muscles and the hot, sweaty skin. He was a bloody mess. His long, velvety ears were shredded. His entire body was a mass of deep, raw, red wounds. On both sides of his rib carriage, the sharp claws had laid the flesh open to the bone.

His friendly old face was pitiful to see. A razor-sharp claw had ripped down on an angle across his right eye. It was swollen shut. I wondered if he would ever see from that eye again.

Blood dripped from his wounds and fell on the white oak leaves. I saw he was bleeding to death. With tears running down my cheeks, I did the only thing a hunter could do. I raked the leaves away and let his blood drip on the black mountain soil. Mixing it into a mud, I worked it into his wounds to stop the flow of blood.

With my ax in one hand and holding onto his collar with the other, we climbed out of the canyon. I knew if I could get him far enough away from the lion he wouldn't go back.

On reaching the top, I saw the yellow glow of my lantern. I turned Old Dan loose and walked over and picked it up.

Not knowing exactly where I was, I looked down out of the mountains to get my bearings. Beyond the foothills and fields I could see the long, white, crooked line of steam, marking the river's course. Following the snakelike pattern with my eyes, in no time I knew exactly where I was, for I knew every bend in the river.

Anxious to get home so I could take care of my dogs, I turned to call to them. Little Ann was close by. She was sitting down, licking at the wound in her shoulder. I saw the shadowy form of Old Dan sniffing around the tree where the lion had been treed.

As I stood and watched him in the moonlight, my heart swelled with pride. Wounded though he was, he wanted to make sure there were no more lions around.

I called to him. In a stiff-legged trot he came to me. I caught hold of his collar and gave him another inspection. In the lantern light I could see the mud-caked wounds clearly. The bleeding had almost stopped. I felt much better.

Little Ann came over. I knelt down and put my arms around them. I knew that if it hadn't been for their loyalty and unselfish courage I would have probably been killed by the slashing claws of the devil cat.

"I don't know how I'll ever pay you back for what you've done," I said, "but I'll never forget it."

Getting up, I said, "Come on, let's go home so I can take care of those wounds."

I hadn't gone far when I heard a cry. At first I thought it was a bird, or a night hawk. I stood still and listened. I glanced at Little Ann. She was looking behind me. I turned around and looked for Old Dan. He was nowhere in sight.

The cry came again, low and pitiful. Instantly Little Ann started back the way we had come. I followed as fast as I could run.

I found Old Dan lying on his side, pleading for help. What I saw was almost more than I could stand. There, tangled in the low branches of a huckleberry bush, were the entrails of my dog. With a gasping cry I knelt down by his side.

I knew what had happened. Far back in the soft belly, the slashing, razor-sharp claws of the lion had cut into the hollow. In my inspections I had overlooked the wound. His entrails had worked out and had become entangled in the bush. The forward motion of his body had done the rest.

He whimpered as I laid my hand on his head. A warm, red tongue flicked out at it. With tears in my eyes, I started talking to him. "Hang on, boy," I said. "Everything will be all right. I'll take care of you."

With trembling hands, I unwound the entrails from the bush. With my handkerchief I wiped away the gravel, leaves, and pine needles. With fingers that shook, I worked the entrails back into the wound.

Knowing that I couldn't carry him and the ax and lantern, I stuck the ax deep in the side of a white oak tree. I blew out the lantern and hung the handle over the other blade. I wrapped my dog in my old sheepskin coat and hurried for home.

Arriving home, I awakened my mother and father. Together

we doctored my dogs. Old Dan was taken care of first. Very gently Mama worked the entrails out and in a pan of warm soapy water, washed them clean of the pine needles, leaves, and grit.

"If I only knew what I was doing," Mama said, as she worked, "I'd feel better."

With gentle hands, she worked the entrails back through the opening. The wound was sewn up and bandaged with a clean white cloth.

Little Ann wasn't hard to doctor. I held her head while Mama cleaned her wounds with peroxide. Feeling the bite of the strong liquid, she whined and licked at my hands.

"It's all right, little girl," I said. "You'll be well in no time."

I opened the door and watched her as she limped off to the doghouse.

Hearing a whimper, I turned around. There in the doorway to the room stood my sisters. I could tell by the looks on their faces that they had been watching for some time. They looked pitiful standing there in their long white gowns. I felt sorry for them.

"Will Little Ann be all right?" my oldest sister asked.

"Yes," I said, "she'll be all right. She only had one bad wound and we've taken care of that."

"Old Dan's hurt bad, isn't he?" she said.

I nodded my head.

"How bad is it?" she asked.

"It's bad," I said. "He was cut wide open."

They all started crying.

"Now here," Mama said, going over, "you girls get back in bed. You'll take a death of cold being up like this in your bare feet."

"Mommie," the little one said. "God won't let Old Dan die, will He?"

"I don't think so, honey," Mama said. "Now off to bed."

They turned and walked slowly back to their room.

"The way your dogs are cut up," Papa said, "it must have been a terrible fight."

"It was, Papa," I said. "I never saw anything like it. Little Ann wouldn't have fought the lion if it hadn't been for Old Dan. All she was doing was helping him. He wouldn't quit. He just stayed right in there till the end. I even had to pry his jaws loose from the lion's throat after the lion was dead."

Glancing at Old Dan, Papa said, "It's in his blood, Billy. He's a hunting hound, and the best one I ever saw. He only has two loves—you and hunting. That's all he knows."

"If it hadn't been for them, Papa," I said, "I probably wouldn't be here now."

"What do you mean," Mama said, "you wouldn't be here now?"

I told them how the lion had leaped at me and how my dogs had gotten between him and me.

"They were so close together," I said, "when they came up off the ground they looked just like one."

There was a moaning sigh from Mama. She covered her face with her hands and started crying.

"I don't know," she sobbed, "I just don't know. To think how close you came to being killed. I don't think I can stand any more."

"Now, now," Papa said, as he walked over and put his arms around her. "Don't go all to pieces. It's all over. Let's be thankful and do our best for Old Dan."

"Do you think he'll die, Papa?" I asked.

"I don't know, Billy," Papa said, shaking his head. "He's lost an awful lot of blood and he's a mighty sick dog. All we can do now is wait and see."

Our wait wasn't long. My dog's breathing grew faster and faster, and there was a terrible rattling in his throat. I knelt down and laid his head in my lap.

Old Dan must have known he was dying. Just before he drew his last breath, he opened his eyes and looked at me. Then with one last sigh, and a feeble thump of his tail, his friendly gray eyes closed forever.

At first I couldn't believe my dog was dead. I started talking to him. "Please don't die, Dan," I said. "Don't leave me now."

I looked to Mama for help. Her face was as white as the bark on a sycamore tree and the hurt in her eyes tore at my heart. She opened her mouth to say something but words wouldn't come out.

Feeling as cold as an arctic wind, I got up and stumbled to a chair. Mama came over and said something. Her words were only a murmur in my ears.

Very gently Papa picked Old Dan up in his arms and carried him out on the porch. When he came back in the house, he said, "Well, we did all we could do, but I guess it wasn't enough."

I had never seen my father and mother look so tired and weary as they did on that night. I knew they wanted to comfort me, but didn't know what to say.

Papa tried. "Billy," he said, "I wouldn't think too much about this if I were you. It's not good to hurt like that. I believe I'd just try to forget it. Besides, you still have Little Ann."

I wasn't even thinking about Little Ann at that moment. I knew she was all right.

"I'm thankful that I still have her," I said, "but how can I forget Old Dan? He gave his life for me, that's what he did—just laid down his life for me. How can I ever forget something like that?"

Mama said, "It's been a terrible night for all of us. Let's go to bed and try to get some rest. Maybe we'll all feel better tomorrow."

"No, Mama," I said. "You and Papa go on to bed. I think I'll stay up for a while. I couldn't sleep anyway."

Mama started to protest, but Papa shook his head. Arm in arm they walked from the room.

Long after my mother and father had retired, I sat by the fire trying to think and couldn't. I felt numb all over. I knew my dog was dead, but I couldn't believe it. I didn't want to. One day they were both alive and happy. Then that night, just like that, one of them was dead.

I didn't know how long I had been sitting there when I heard a noise out on the porch. I got up, walked over to the door, and listened. It came again, a low whimper and a scratchy sound.

I could think of only one thing that could have made the noise. It had to be my dog. He wasn't dead. He had come back to life. With a pounding heart, I opened the door and stepped out on the porch.

What I saw was more than I could stand. The noise I had heard had been made by Little Ann. All her life she had slept by Old Dan's side. And although he was dead, she had left the doghouse, had come back to the porch, and snuggled up close to his side.

She looked up at me and whimpered. I couldn't stand it. I didn't know I was running until I tripped and fell. I got to my feet and ran on and on, down through our fields of shocked corn, until I fell face down on the river's bank. There in the gray shadows of a breaking dawn, I cried until I could cry no more.

The churring of gray squirrels in the bright morning sun told me it was daylight. I got to my feet and walked back to the house.

Coming up through our barn lot, I saw my father feeding our stock. He came over and said, "Breakfast is about ready."

"I don't want any breakfast, Papa," I said. "I'm not hungry and I have a job to do. I'll have to bury my dog."

"I tell you what," he said, "I'm not going to be very busy today, so let's have a good breakfast and then I'll help you."

"No, Papa," I said. "I'll take care of it. You go and eat breakfast. Tell Mama I'm not hungry."

I saw a hurt look in my father's eyes. Shaking his head, he turned and walked away.

From rough pine slabs, I made a box for my dog. It was a crude box but it was the best I could do. With strips of burlap and corn shucks, I padded the inside.

Up on the hillside, at the foot of a beautiful red oak tree, I dug his grave. There where the wild mountain flowers would grow in the spring, I laid him away.

I had a purpose in burying my dog up there on the hillside. It was a beautiful spot. From there one could see the country for miles, the long white crooked line of the river, the tall thick timber of the bottoms, the sycamore, birch, and box elder. I thought perhaps that on moonlight nights Old Dan would be able to hear the deep voices of the hounds as they rolled out of the river bottoms on the frosty air.

After the last shovel of dirt was patted in place, I sat down and let my mind drift back through the years. I thought of the old K. C. Baking Powder can, and the first time I saw my pups in the box at the depot. I thought of the fifty dollars, the nickels and dimes, and the fishermen and blackberry patches.

I looked at his grave and, with tears in my eyes, I voiced these words: "You were worth it, old friend, and a thousand times over."

In my heart I knew that there in the grave lay a man's best friend.

Two days later, when I came in from the bottoms where my father and I were clearing land, my mother said, "Billy, you had better look after your dog. She won't eat."

I started looking for her. I went to the barn, the corncrib, and looked under the porch. I called her name. It was no use.

I rounded up my sisters and asked if they had seen Little Ann. The youngest one said she had seen her go down into the garden. I went there, calling her name. She wouldn't answer my call.

I was about to give up, and then I saw her. She had wiggled her way far back under the thorny limbs of a blackberry bush in the corner of the garden. I talked to her and tried to coax her out. She wouldn't budge. I got down on my knees and crawled back to her. As I did, she raised her head and looked at me.

Her eyes told the story. They weren't the soft gray eyes I had looked into so many times. They were dull and cloudy. There was no fire, no life. I couldn't understand.

I carried her back to the house. I offered her food and water. She wouldn't touch it. I noticed how lifeless she was. I thought perhaps she had a wound I had overlooked. I felt and probed with my fingers. I could find nothing.

My father came and looked at her. He shook his head and said, "Billy, it's no use. The life has gone out of her. She has no will to live."

He turned and walked away.

I couldn't believe it. I couldn't.

With eggs and rich cream, I made a liquid. I pried her mouth open and poured it down. She responded to nothing I did. I carried her to the porch, and laid her in the same place I had laid the body of Old Dan. I covered her with gunny sacks.

All through the night I would get up and check on her. Next morning I took warm fresh milk and again I opened her mouth and fed her. It was a miserable day for me. At noon it was the same. My dog had just given up. There was no will to live.

That evening when I came in from the fields, she was gone. I hurried to my mother. Mama told me she had seen her go up the hollow from the house, so weak she could hardly stand. Mama had watched her until she had disappeared in the timber.

I hurried up the hollow, calling her name. I called and called. I went up to the head of it, still calling her name and praying she would come to me. I climbed out onto the flats; looking, searching, and calling. It was no use. My dog was gone.

I had a thought, a ray of hope. I just knew I'd find her at the grave of Old Dan. I hurried there.

I found her lying on her stomach, her hind legs stretched out straight, and her front feet folded back under her chest. She had laid her head on his grave. I saw the trail where she had dragged herself through the leaves. The way she lay there, I thought she was alive. I called her name. She made no movement. With the last ounce of strength in her body, she had dragged herself to the grave of Old Dan.

Kneeling down by her side, I reached out and touched her. There was no response, no whimpering cry or friendly wag of her tail. My little dog was dead.

I laid her head in my lap and with tear-filled eyes gazed up into the heavens. In a choking voice, I asked, "Why did they have to die? Why must I hurt so? What have I done wrong?"

I heard a noise behind me. It was my mother. She sat down and put her arm around me.

"You've done no wrong, Billy," she said. "I know this seems terrible and I know how it hurts, but at one time or another, everyone suffers. Even the Good Lord suffered while He was here on earth."

"I know, Mama," I said, "but I can't understand. It was bad enough when Old Dan died. Now Little Ann is gone. Both of them gone, just like that."

"Billy, you haven't lost your dogs altogether," Mama said. "You'll always have their memory. Besides, you can have some more dogs."

I rebelled at this. "I don't want any more dogs," I said. "I won't ever want another dog. They wouldn't be like Old Dan and Little Ann."

"We all feel that way, Billy," she said. "I do especially. They've fulfilled a prayer that I thought would never be answered."

"I don't believe in prayers any more," I said. "I prayed for my dogs, and now look, both of them are dead."

Mama was silent for a moment; then, in a gentle voice, she said, "Billy, sometimes it's hard to believe that things like this can happen, but there's always an answer. When you're older, you'll understand better."

"No, I won't," I said. "I don't care if I'm a hundred years old, I'll never understand why my dogs had to die."

As if she were talking to someone far away, I heard her say in a low voice, "I don't know what to say. I can't seem to find the right words."

Looking up to her face, I saw that her eyes were flooded with tears.

"Mama, please don't cry," I said. "I didn't mean what I said."

"I know you didn't," she said, as she squeezed me up tight. "It's just your way of fighting back."

I heard the voice of my father calling to us from the house.

"Come now," Mama said. "I have supper ready and your father wants to talk to you. I think when you've heard what he has to say, you'll feel better."

"I can't leave Little Ann like this, Mama," I said. "It'll be cold tonight. I think I'll carry her back to the house."

"No, I don't think you should do that," Mama said. "Your sisters would go all to pieces. Let's make her comfortable here."

Raking some dead leaves into a pile, she picked Little Ann up and laid her in them. Taking off my coat, I spread it over her body. I dreaded to think of what I had to do on the morrow.

My father and sisters were waiting for us on the porch. Mama told them the sad story. My sisters broke down and started crying. They ran to Mama and buried their faces in her long cotton dress.

Papa came over and laid his hand on my shoulder. "Billy," he said, "there are times in a boy's life when he has to stand up like a man. This is one of those times. I know what you're going through and how it hurts, but there's always an answer. The Good Lord has a reason for everything He does."

"There couldn't be any reason for my dogs to die, Papa," I said. "There just couldn't. They hadn't done anything wrong."

Papa glanced at Mama. Getting no help from her, he said, "It's getting cold out here. Let's go in the house. I have something to show you."

"Guess what we're having for supper," Mama said, as we turned to enter the house. "Your favorite, Billy, sweet potato pie. You'll like that, won't you?"

I nodded my head, but my heart wasn't in it.

Papa didn't follow us into the kitchen. He turned and entered his bedroom.

When he came into the room, he had a small shoe box in his hand. I recognized the box by the bright blue ribbon tied around it. Mama kept her valuables in it.

A silence settled over the room. Walking to the head of the table, Papa set the box down and started untying the ribbon. His hands were trembling as he fumbled with the knot. With the lid off, he reached in and started lifting out bundles of money.

After stacking them in a neat pile, he raised his head and looked straight at me. "Billy," he said, "you know how your mother has prayed that some day we'd have enough money to move out of these hills and into town so that you children could get an education."

I nodded my head.

"Well," he said, in a low voice, "because of your dogs, her prayers have been answered. This is the money earned by Old Dan and Little Ann. I've managed to make the farm feed us and clothe us and I've saved every cent your furs brought in. We now have enough."

"Isn't it wonderful," Mama said. "It's just like a miracle."

"I think it is a miracle," Papa said. "Remember, Billy said a prayer when he asked for his pups and then there were your prayers. Billy got his pups. Through those dogs your prayers were answered. Yes, I'm sure it is a miracle."

"If he gave them to me, then why did he take them away?" I asked.

"I think there's an answer for that, too," Papa said. "You see, Billy, your mother and I had decided not to separate you from your dogs. We knew how much you loved them. We decided that when we moved to town we'd leave you here with your grandpa for a while. He needs help anyway. But I guess the Good Lord didn't want that to happen. He doesn't like to see families split up. That's why they were taken away."

I knew my father was a firm believer in fate. To him everything that happened was the will of God, and in his Bible he could always find the answers.

Papa could see that his talk had had very little effect on me. With a sorrowful look on his face, he sat down and said, "Now let us give thanks for our food and for all the wonderful things God has done for us. I'll say a special prayer and ask Him to help Billy."

I barely heard what Papa had to say.

During the meal, I could tell that no one was enjoying the food. As soon as it was over, I went to my room and lay down on the bed.

Mama came in. "Why don't you go to bed," she said, "and get a good night's sleep. You'll feel better tomorrow."

"No, I won't, Mama," I said. "I'll have to bury Little Ann tomorrow."

"I know," she said, as she turned my covers down. "I'll help if you want me to."

"No, Mama," I said, "I don't want anyone to help. I'd rather do it all by myself."

"Billy, you're always doing things by yourself," Mama said. "That's not right. Everyone needs help some time in his life."

"I know, Mama," I said, "but, please, not this time. Ever since my dogs were puppies, we've always been together—just us three. We hunted together and played together. We even went swimming together.

"Did you know, Mama, that Little Ann used to come every night and peek in my window just to see if I was all right? I guess that's why I want to be by myself when I bury her."

"Now say your prayers and go to sleep. I'm sure you'll feel better in the morning."

I didn't feel like saying any prayers that night. I was hurting too much. Long after the rest of the family had gone to bed, I lay staring into the darkness, trying to think and not able to.

Some time in the night I got up, tiptoed to my window, and looked out at my doghouse. It looked so lonely and empty sitting there in the moonlight. I could see that the door was slightly ajar. I thought of the many times I had lain in my bed and listened to the squeaking of the door as my dogs went in and out. I didn't know I was crying until I felt the tears roll down my cheeks.

Mama must have heard me get up. She came in and put her arms around me. "Billy," she said, in a quavering voice, "you'll just have to stop this. You're going to make yourself sick and I don't think I can stand any more of it."

"I can't, Mama," I said. "It hurts so much, I just can't. I don't want you to feel bad just because I do."

"I can't help it, Billy," she said. "Come now and get back in bed. I'm afraid you'll catch cold."

After she had tucked me in, she sat on the bed for a while. As if she were talking to the darkness, I heard her say, "If only there were some way I could help—something I could do."

"No one can help, Mama," I said. "No one can bring my dogs back."

"I know," she said, as she got up to leave the room, "but there must be something—there just has to be."

After Mama had left the room, I buried my face in my pillow and cried myself to sleep.

The next morning I made another box. It was smaller than the first one. Each nail I drove in the rough pine boards caused the knot in my throat to get bigger and bigger.

My sisters came to help. They stood it for a while, then with tears streaming, they ran for the house.

I buried Little Ann by the side of Old Dan. I knew that was where she wanted to be. I also buried a part of my life along with my dog.

Remembering a sandstone ledge I had seen while prowling the woods, I went there. I picked out a nice stone and carried it back to the graves. Then, with painstaking care, I carved their names deep in its red surface.

As I stood looking at the two graves, I tried hard to understand some of the things my father had told me, but I couldn't—I was still hurting and still had that empty feeling.

I went to Mama and had a talk with her.

"Mama," I asked, "do you think God made a heaven for all good dogs?"

"Yes," she said, "I'm sure He did."

"Do you think He made a place for dogs to hunt? You know— just like we have here on our place—with mountains and sycamore trees, rivers and cornfields, and old rail fences? Do you think He did?"

"From what I've read in the Good Book, Billy," she said, "He put far more things up there than we have here. Yes, I'm sure He did."

I was thinking this over when Mama came up to me and started tucking my shirt in. "Do you feel better now?" she asked.

"It still hurts, Mama," I said, as I buried my face in her dress, "but I do feel a little better."

"I'm glad," she said, as she patted my head. "I don't like to see my little boy hurt like this."

XX

THE FOLLOWING SPRING we left the Ozarks. The day we moved I
thought everyone would be sad, but it was just the opposite. Mama
seemed to be the happiest one of all. I could hear her laughing
and joking with my sisters as they packed things. She had a glow in
her eyes I had never seen before and it made me feel good.

I even noticed a change in Papa. He didn't have that whipped
look on his face any more. He was in high spirits as we carried the
furniture out to our wagon.

After the last item was stored in the wagon, Papa helped Mama
to the spring seat and we were ready to go.

"Papa, would you mind waiting a few minutes?" I asked. "I'd
like to say good-bye to my dogs."

"Sure," he said, smiling. "We have plenty of time. Go right
ahead."

Nearing the graves, I saw something was different. It looked like
a wild bush had grown up and practically covered the two little
mounds. It made me angry to think that an old bush would dare
grow so close to the graves. I took out my knife, intending to cut it
down.

When I walked up close enough to see what it was, I sucked in a
mouthful of air and stopped. I couldn't believe what I was seeing.
There between the graves, a beautiful red fern had sprung up from
the rich mountain soil. It was fully two feet tall and its long red
leaves had reached out and in rainbow arches curved over the
graves of my dogs.

I had heard the old Indian legend about the red fern. How a
little Indian boy and girl were lost in a blizzard and had frozen to

death. In the spring, when they were found, a beautiful red fern had grown up between their two bodies. The story went on to say that only an angel could plant the seeds of a red fern, and that they never died; where one grew, that spot was sacred.

Remembering the meaning of the legend, I turned and started hollering for Mama.

"Mama! Mama!" I shouted. "Come here! And hurry! You won't believe it."

In a frightened voice, she shouted back, "What is it, Billy? Are you all right?"

"I'm all right, Mama," I shouted, "but hurry. You just won't believe it."

Holding her long skirt in her hand and with a frightened look on her face, Mama came puffing up the hillside. Close behind her came Papa and my sisters.

"What is it, Billy?" Mama asked, in a scared voice. "Are you all right?"

"Look!" I said, pointing at the red fern.

Staring wide-eyed, Mama gasped and covered her mouth with her hand. I heard her say, almost in a whisper, "Oh-h-h-h, it's a red fern—a sacred red fern."

She walked over and very tenderly started fingering the long red leaves. In an awed voice, she said, "All my life I've wanted to see one. Now I have. It's almost unbelievable."

"Don't touch it, Mama," my oldest sister whispered. "It was planted by an angel."

Mama smiled and asked, "Have you heard the legend?"

"Yes, Mama," my sister said. "Grandma told me the story, and I believe it, too."

With a serious look on his face, Papa said, "These hills are full of legends. Up until now I've never paid much attention to them, but now I don't know. Perhaps there is something to the legend of the red fern. Maybe this is God's way of helping Billy understand why his dogs died."

"I'm sure it is, Papa," I said, "and I do understand. I feel different now, and I don't hurt any more."

"Come," Mama said, "let's go back to the wagon. Billy wants to be alone with his dogs for a while."

Just as they turned to leave, I heard Papa murmur in a low voice, "Wonderful indeed is the work of our Lord."

As I stood looking at the two graves, I noticed things I hadn't seen before. Wild violets, rooster heads, and mountain daisies had completely covered the two little mounds. A summer breeze gushed down from the rugged hills. I felt its warm caress as it fanned my face. It hummed a tune in the underbrush and rustled the leaves on the huge red oak. The red fern wavered and danced to the music of the hills.

Taking off my cap, I bowed my head. In a choking voice, I said, "Good-bye, Old Dan and Little Ann. I'll never forget you; and this I know—if God made room in heaven for all good dogs, I know he made a special place for you."

With a heavy heart, I turned and walked away. I knew that as long as I lived I'd never forget the two little graves and the sacred red fern.

Not far from our home, the road wound its way up and over a hill. At the top Papa stopped the team. We all stood up and looked back. It was a beautiful sight, one I'll never forget.

As I stood and looked at the home of my birth, it looked sad and lonely. There was no spiral of lazy blue smoke twisting from the rock chimney, no white leghorn hen chasing a June bug, no horse or cow standing with head down and tail switching.

I saw I had left the door to the barn loft open. A tuft of hay hung out. It wavered gently in the warm summer breeze.

Something scurried across the vacant yard and disappeared under the barn. It was Samie, our house cat. I heard my little sister say in a choking voice, "Mommie, we forgot Samie."

There was no answer.

To the left, I could see our fields and the zigzag lines of rail fences. Farther down, I could see the shimmering whiteness of the tall sycamores. My vision blurred as tears came to my eyes.

The sorrowful silence was broken by my mother's voice. She asked, "Billy, can you see it?"

"See what, Mama?" I asked.

"The red fern," she said.

My oldest sister spoke up. "I can see it," she said.

Rubbing my eyes, I looked to the hillside above our home. There it stood in all its wild beauty, a waving red banner in a carpet of green. It seemed to be saying, "Good-bye, and don't worry, for I'll be here always."

Hearing a sniffling, I turned around. My three little sisters had started crying. Mama said something to Papa. I heard the jingle of the trace chains as they tightened in the singletrees.

Our wagon moved on.

I have never been back to the Ozarks. All I have left are my dreams and memories, but if God is willing, some day I'd like to go back—back to those beautiful hills. I'd like to walk again on trails I walked in my boyhood days.

Once again I'd like to face a mountain breeze and smell the wonderful scent of the redbuds, the papaws, and the dogwoods. With my hands I'd like to caress the cool white bark of a sycamore.

I'd like to take a walk far back in the flinty hills and search for a souvenir, an old double-bitted ax stuck deep in the side of a white oak tree. I know the handle has long since rotted away with time. Perhaps the rusty frame of a coal-oil lantern still hangs there on the blade.

I'd like to see the old home place, the barn and the rail fences. I'd like to pause under the beautiful red oaks where my sisters and I played in our childhood. I'd like to walk up the hillside to the graves of my dogs.

I'm sure the red fern has grown and has completely covered the two little mounds. I know it is still there, hiding its secret beneath those long, red leaves, but it wouldn't be hidden from me for part of my life is buried there, too.

Yes, I know it is still there, for in my heart I believe the legend of the sacred red fern.

CONNECTIONS

Do you remember reading the American Indian legend about the red fern in Where the Red Fern Grows? *Here's a story from Japan that may remind you of that legend. If you're ready for a story about the power of love and the power of music, read on.*

The Pine of Akoya
a Japanese folk tale
retold by Rafe Martin

More than a thousand years ago, there lived a governor named Fujiwara Toyomitsu with his daughter, Akoya. Not only was she beautiful, but she was a talented and accomplished musician.

Each night, but especially when the moon was bright, Akoya loved to sit near the polished wooden deck, just inside the opened sliding *shoji* screens. Facing into the garden, she would play the stringed *koto*. The music floated up, each note resonant and still. It seemed to her, as she played, that the bushes and trees swayed, their leaves rustled and whispered in time to her music.

One night when her father was away and Akoya played her *koto* in the moonlight, someone began playing a flute nearby. The harmonies the flute made with the *koto* were exquisite. Akoya's heart beat with excitement and wonder. The music ended. All she heard was the wind moving through the trees. She hoped the flute player would appear. But no one did.

The next night Akoya played again. The night was calm and still, the moon's light still bright. She began to play and, as she played, her music seemed to clearly express her truest feelings—her love for the garden, her yearnings for true friend-ship, the sadness she still felt over her mother's death two years before. The clouds, the moon, the flowers, and trees all seemed to listen. Then from the velvety darkness arose once more the notes of the mysterious flute. Its eerie, tender notes matched her music perfectly. Flute and *koto* soared and harmonized. Akoya's loneliness left her completely.

When the music ended she waited expectantly. "Please," she said, "won't you step from the shadows? Let us meet."

A young man wearing a green robe stepped from beneath the trees. In his hand was a silver flute. "My name is Natori Taro. I live alone at the foot of Chitose Mountain. I was traveling through these parts when I heard of you and your music. Several nights ago I came to listen and was entranced. Never had I heard such beautiful music! I longed to play along with you. Last night I had the courage to do so."

"You are too kind," murmured Akoya.

Natori came closer. He lifted his flute and began to play. Akoya plucked the strings of the *koto*. Music of such haunting beauty filled the garden that the trees and bushes seemed to sway to it. The twinkling stars and wandering clouds seemed to move in rhythm to it. The night flew by and then, just before the dawn, Natori ceased. "Dear Akoya, now I must leave."

Akoya paled. "But you will return?" she asked, her heart skipping, losing its rhythm.

"If you wish it," Natori answered quietly.

And Akoya said, "Yes."

And so he returned the next night. Once more their music filled the garden. And their love grew. It grew and grew. And Akoya was happy.

One night, as the moon's light was fading, Natori, seated beside Akoya, spoke. And his voice this night was filled with sorrow. "Dear Akoya, I cannot stay with you. It is not because I wish to leave, and there is no other who has a place in my heart. I must return home because I have agreed to help my people. And when I return, I shall die."

Akoya gasped, but Natori went on, "My days here with you have been the happiest of my life. Our music will not end. Do not doubt me. Come to the foot of Chitose Mountain and you will know the truth of my words."

Then Natori rose and quickly stepped through the open *shoji*. As he passed along the paper wall, he cast a shadow in the torchlight. Akoya gasped. The shadow was not that of a man but of a pine tree.

Akoya ran out. The torches smoked and flared but there was no sign of Natori. From off in the distance came the sound of his silver flute, so beautiful and haunting. The notes trailed off and were gone.

Several days later Akoya's father returned. "Daughter, a strange thing has happened at Chitose Mountain."

When Akoya heard that name her heart began to beat very fast. "What is it?" she managed to ask.

"As you know the famous wooden bridge over the Natori River was damaged this spring in the floods. It must be repaired soon or it may collapse. A great pine tree was found growing at the foot of Chitose Mountain, not far from the river. Huge, straight, and solid, it will provide the perfect log to repair the bridge. So I gave the order for it to be cut."

"Yes, Father," Akoya stammered, "go on."

"The tree was felled and the branches cut away. But it is so huge and heavy that a hundred men have been tugging at the log and it will not budge. I am sending more men and will go back myself in another day to oversee the work. Imagine! One hundred men and still the log cannot be moved! Not even an inch. No one has ever seen such a thing."

"Take me with you, Father," Akoya said.

They left the next day, and after several days traveling, arrived at the foot of Chitose Mountain. The great pine lay where it had fallen. Many hundreds of people—in addition to the hundreds of workmen sent by Akoya's father—had gathered there. Men, women, and children; lords and noblewomen, samurai, peasants, and working people—all had come to see the great log that could not be moved. It was like a holiday.

Akoya approached and ran her hands along the log. It seemed to shiver.

"Do you see! Do you see that!" cried the people. "The log moved!"

Akoya seemed to hear the music of a silver flute. "I am here, Natori," she said quietly, "and I do not doubt you."

She bent down, reached her arms around the log, and lifted it up. The crowd surged around her, and hundreds of hands took hold. They carried the log to the river and set it in the water. The great log floated easily. "We can float it to the bridge now," the workmen said. "The bridge will be repaired. It is a miracle."

Akoya sat where the log had lain. Its shape showed as a great hollow pressed into the earth and bent grasses. There, in the hollow, lay Natori's silver flute. Cut into its surface, the way the names of lovers are cut into the bark of a tree, were the names *Akoya* and *Natori*.

Akoya kept the flute beside her always. Generations passed. In time another great pine grew at the foot of Chitose Mountain. It is known, even today, as the Pine of Akoya.

■ ■ ■

Both Billy in Where the Red Fern Grows *and Tom in this
story want to become grown-up hunters. What else makes them
alike—and how are they different? See what clues you can
hunt down as you read.*

The Christmas Hunt
Borden Deal

It should have been the best Christmas of them all, that year at
Dog Run. It started out to be, anyway. I was so excited,
watching my father talking on the telephone, that I couldn't
stand still. For I was ten years old, and I had never been on a
quail shoot in my whole life. I wanted to go on the big
Christmas Day hunt even more than I wanted that bicycle I
was supposed to get. And I really needed the bicycle to cover
with speed and ease the two miles I had to walk to school.

The Christmas Day hunt was always the biggest and best
of the season. It was almost like a field trial; only the best
hunters and the finest dogs were invited by my father. All my
life I had been hearing great tales of past Christmas Day hunts.
And now I knew with a great ten-year-old certainty that I was
old enough to go.

My father hung up the phone and turned around, grinning.
"That was Walter," he said. "There'll be ten of them this year.
And Walter is bringing his new dog. If all he claims for that
dog is true—"

"Papa," I said.

"Lord," my mother said. "That'll be a houseful to feed."

My father put his arm around her shoulders, hugging her.
"Oh, you know you like it," he said. "They come as much for
your cooking as they do for the hunting, I think."

My mother pursed her lips in the way she had and then smiled. "Wild turkey," she said. "You think you could shoot me four or five nice fat wild turkeys?"

I wanted to jump up and down to attract attention. But that was kid stuff, a tactic for the five-year-olds, though I had to admit it was effective. But I was ten. So I said, "Papa."

My father laughed. "I think I can," he said. "I'll put in a couple of mornings trying."

"Papa," I said desperately.

"Wild turkey stuffed with wild rice," my mother said quickly, thoughtfully, in her planning voice. "Giblet gravy, mashed potatoes, maybe a nice potato salad—"

"If I don't fail on the turkeys," my father said.

"Papa!" I said.

My father turned to me. "Come on, Tom," he said. "We've got to feed those dogs."

That's the way parents are, even when you're ten years old. They can talk right on and never hear a word you say. I ran after my father as he left the kitchen, hoping for a chance to get my words in edgewise. But my father was walking fast, and already the clamor of the bird dogs was rising up to cover any speech I might want to make.

The dogs were standing on the wire fence in long, dappled rows, their voices lifted in greeting. Even in my urgent need I had to stop and admire them. There's nothing prettier in the whole world than a good bird dog. There's a nobleness to its head, an intelligence in its eyes, that no other animal has. Just looking at them sent a shiver down my backbone, and the thought of shooting birds over them—well, the shiver just wasn't in my backbone now; I was shaking all over.

All of the dogs except one were in the same big run. But my father kept Calypso Baby in her own regal pen. I went to her and looked into her soft brown eyes. She stood up tall on the fence, her strong, lithe body stretched to its full height, as tall as I was.

"Hello, Baby," I whispered, and she wagged her tail. "You gonna find me some birds this Christmas, Baby? You gonna hunt for me like you do for Papa?"

She lolled her tongue, laughing at me. We were old friends. Calypso Baby was the finest bird dog in that part of the country. My father owned a number of dogs and kept and trained others for his town friends. But Calypso Baby was his personal dog, the one that he took to the field trials, the one he shot over in the big Christmas Day hunt held at Dog Run.

My father was bringing the sack of feed from the shed. I put out my hand, holding it against the wire so Calypso Baby could lick my fingers.

"This year," I whispered to her. "This year I'm going." I left Calypso Baby, went with determination toward my father. "Papa," I said, in a voice not to be denied this time.

My father was busy opening the sack of dog food.

"Papa," I said firmly. "I want to talk to you." It was the tone and the words my father used often toward me, so much of mimicry that my father looked down at me in surprise, at last giving me his attention.

"What is it?" he said. "What do you want?"

"Papa, I'm ten years old," I said.

My father laughed. "Well, what of it?" he said. "Next year you'll be eleven. And the next year twelve."

"I'm old enough to go on the Christmas hunt," I said.

Incredibly, my father laughed. "At ten?" he said. "I'm afraid not."

I stood, stricken. "But—" I said.

"No," my father said, in the voice that meant No, and no more talking about it. He hoisted the sack of feed and took it into the wire dog pen, the bird dogs crowding around him, rearing up on him in their eagerness.

"Well, come on and help me," my father said impatiently. "I've got a lot of things to do."

Usually I enjoyed the daily feeding of the dogs. But not today; I went through the motions dumbly, silently, not paying any attention to the fine bird dogs crowding around me. I cleaned the watering troughs with my usual care, but my heart was not in it.

After the feeding was over, I scuffed stubbornly about my other tasks and then went up to my room, not even coming down when my father came home at dusk excited with the two wild turkeys he had shot. I could hear him talking to my mother in the kitchen, and the ring of their voices had already the feel of Christmas, a hunting cheer that made them brighter, livelier, than usual. But none of the cheer and the pleasure came into me, even though Christmas was almost upon us and yesterday had been the last day of school.

That night I hunted. In my dreams I was out ahead of all the other men and dogs, Calypso Baby quartering the field in her busy way, doing it so beautifully I ached inside to watch her. All the men and dogs stopped their own hunting to watch us, as though it were a field trial. When Calypso Baby pointed, I raised the twelve-gauge shotgun, moved in on her on the ready, and Calypso Baby flushed the birds in her fine, steady way. They came up in an explosive whir, and I had the gun to my shoulder, squeezing off the shot just the way I'd been told to do. Three quail dropped like stones out of the covey, and I swung the gun, following a single. I brought down the single with the second barrel, and Calypso Baby was already bringing the first bird to me in her soft, unbruising mouth. I knelt to pat her for a moment, and Baby whipped her tail to tell me how fine a shot I was, how much she liked for me to be the one shooting over her today.

Soon there was another covey, and I did even better on this one, and then another and another; and nobody was hunting at all, not even my father, who was laughing and grinning at the other men, knowing this was his boy, Tom, and his dog, Calypso Baby, and just full of pride with it all. When it was over, the men crowded around and patted me on the shoulder, hefting the full game bag in admiration; and then there was my father's face close before me, saying, "I was wrong, son, when I said a ten-year-old boy isn't old enough to go bird hunting with the best of us."

Then I was awake, and my father, dressed in his hunting clothes, was shaking me, and it was morning. I looked up dazedly into his face, unable to shake off the dream, and I knew what it was I had to do. I had to show my father. Only then would he believe.

"Are you awake?" my father said. "You'll have to change the water for the dogs. I'm going to see if I can get some more turkeys this morning."

"All right," I said. "I'm awake now."

My father left. I got up and ate breakfast in the kitchen, close to the warm stove. I didn't say anything to my mother about my plans. I went out and watered the dogs as soon as the sun was up, but I didn't take the time, as I usually did, to play with them.

"Me and you are going hunting," I told Calypso Baby as I changed her water. She jumped and quivered all over, knowing the word as well as I did.

I went back into the house, listening for my mother. She was upstairs, making the beds. I went into the spare room where my father kept all the hunting gear. I was trembling, remembering the dream, as I went to the gun rack and touched the cold steel of the double-barreled twelve-gauge. But I knew it would be very heavy for me. I took the single-barrel instead, though I knew that pretty near ruined my chances for a second shot unless I could reload very quickly.

I picked up a full shell bag and hung it under my left arm. I found a game bag and hung it under my right arm. The strap was too long, and the bag dangled emptily to my knees, banging against me as I walked. I tied a knot in the strap so the bag would rest comfortably on my right hip. The gun was heavy in my hands as I walked into the hallway, listening for my mother. She was still upstairs.

"Mamma, I'm gone," I shouted up to her. "I'll be back in a little while." That was so she wouldn't be looking for me.

"All right," she called. "Don't wander far off. Your father will be back in an hour or two and might have something for you to do."

I hurried out of the house, straight to Calypso Baby's pen. I did not look up, afraid that my mother might be watching out of the window.

That was a danger I could do nothing about, so I just ignored it. I opened the gate to Baby's pen, and she came out, circling and cavorting.

"Come on, Baby," I whispered. "Find me some birds now. Find me a whole lot of birds."

We started off, circling the barn so we would not be seen from the house and going straight away in its shadow as far as we could. Beyond the pasture we crossed a cornfield, Calypso Baby arrowing straight for the patch of sedge grass beyond. Her tail was whiplike in its thrash, her head high as she plunged toward her work, and I had to hurry to keep up. The gun was clumsy in my hands, and the two bags banged against my hips. But I remembered not to run with the gun, remembered to keep the breech open until I was ready to shoot. I knew all about hunting; I just hadn't had a chance to practice what I knew. When I came home with a bag full of fine birds, my father would have to admit that I knew how to hunt, that I was old enough for the big Christmas Day hunt when all the great hunters came out from town for the biggest day of the season.

When I ducked through the barbed-wire fence, Calypso Baby was waiting for me, standing a few steps into the sedge grass, her head up watching me alertly. Her whole body quivered with her eagerness to be off. I swept my arm in the gesture I had seen my father use so many times, and Calypso Baby plunged instantly into the grass. She was a fast worker, quartering back and forth with an economical use of her energy. She could cover a field in half the time it took any other dog. The first field was empty, and we passed on to the second one. Somehow Calypso Baby knew that birds were here. She steadied down, hunting slowly, more thoroughly.

Then, startling me though I had been expecting it, she froze into a point, one foot up, her tail straight back, her head flat with the line of her backbone. I froze too. I couldn't move; I couldn't even remember to breech the gun and raise it to my shoulder. I stood as still as the dog, all of my knowledge flown out of my head; and yet far back under the panic, I knew that the birds weren't going to hold, they were going to rise in just a moment. Calypso Baby, surprised at my inaction, broke her point to look at me in inquiry. Her head turned toward me, and she asked the question as plain as my father's voice: *Well, what are you going to do about these fine birds I found for you?*

I could move then. I took a step or two, fumblingly breeched the gun, raised it to my shoulder. The birds rose of their own accord in a sudden wild drum of sound. I yanked at the trigger, unconsciously bracing myself against the blast and the recoil. Nothing happened. Nothing at all happened. I tugged at the trigger wildly, furiously, but it was too late, and the birds were gone.

I lowered the gun, looking down at it in bewilderment. I had forgotten to release the safety. I wanted to cry at my own stupidity; I could feel the tears standing in my eyes. This was not at all like my dream of last night, when I and the dog and the birds had all been so perfect.

Calypso Baby walked back to me and looked up into my face. I could read the puzzled contempt in her eyes. She lay down at my feet, putting her muzzle on her paws. I looked down at her, ashamed of myself and knowing that she was ashamed. She demanded perfection, just as my father did.

"It was my fault, Baby," I told her. I leaned over and patted her on the head. "You didn't do anything wrong. It was me."

I started off then, looking back at the bird dog. She did not follow me. "Come on," I told her. "Hunt."

She got up slowly and went out ahead of me again. But she worked in a puzzled manner, checking back to me frequently. She no longer had the joy, the confidence, with which she had started out.

"Come on, Baby," I coaxed her. "Hunt, Baby. Hunt."

We crossed into another field, low grass this time, and when we found the covey, there was very little time for setting myself. Calypso Baby pointed suddenly; I jerked the gun to my shoulder, remembering the safety this time, and then Calypso Baby flushed the birds. They rose up before me, and I pulled the trigger, hearing the blast of the gun, feeling the shock of it into my shoulder knocking me back a step.

But not even one bird dropped like a fateful stone out of the covey. The covey had gone off low and hard on an angle to the left, and I had completely missed the shot, aiming straight ahead instead of swinging with the birds. Calypso Baby did not even attempt to point singles. She dropped her head and her tail and started away from me, going back toward the house.

I ran after her, calling her, crying now but with anger rather than hurt. Baby would never like me again; she would hold me in the indifference she felt toward any person who was not a bird hunter. She would tolerate me as she tolerated my mother and the men who came out with shiny new hunting clothes and walked all over the land talking about how the dogs didn't hold the birds properly so you could get a decent shot.

I couldn't be one of those. I ran after the dog, calling her, until at last she suffered me to come near. I knelt, fondling her head, talking to her, begging her for another chance.

"I'll get some birds next time," I told her. "You just watch. You hear?"

At last, reluctantly, she consented to hunt again. I followed her, my hands gripping the heavy gun, determined this time. I knew it was my last chance; she would not give me another. I could not miss this time.

We hunted for an hour before we found another covey of birds. I was tired, the gun and the frustration heavier with every step. But, holding only last night's dream in my mind, I refused to quit. At last Calypso Baby froze into a beautiful point. I could feel myself sweating, my teeth gritted hard. I had to bring down a bird this time.

It seemed to be perfect. I had plenty of time, but I hurried anyway, just to be sure. Then the birds were rising in a tight cluster, and I was pulling the trigger before I had the heavy gun lined up—and in the midst of the thundering blast I heard Calypso Baby yell with pain as the random shot tore into her hip.

I threw down the gun and ran toward her, seeing the blood streaking down her leg as she staggered away from me, whimpering. I knelt, trying to coax her to me, but she was afraid. I was crying, feeling the full weight of the disaster. I had committed the worst crime of any bird hunter; I had shot my own dog.

Calypso Baby was trying to hide in a clump of bushes. She snapped at me in her fear when I reached in after her, but I did not feel the pain in my hand. I knelt over her, looking at the shredded hip. It was a terrible wound; I could see only blood and raw flesh. I snatched off the empty hunting bag I had donned so optimistically, the shell bag, and took off my coat. I wrapped her in the coat and picked her up in my arms. She was very heavy, hurting, whining with each jolting step as I ran toward the house.

I came into the yard doubled over with the catch in my side from the running, and my legs were trembling. My father was sitting on the back porch with three wild turkeys beside him, cleaning his gun. He jumped to his feet when he saw the wounded dog.

"What happened?" he said. "Did some fool hunter shoot her?"

I stopped, standing before my father and holding the wounded dog; I looked into his angry face. They were the most terrible words I had ever had to say. "I shot her, Papa," I said.

My father stood very still. I did not know what would happen. I had never done anything so bad in my whole life, and I could not even guess how my father would react. The only thing justified would be to wipe me off the face of the earth with one irate gesture of his hand.

I gulped, trying to move the pain in my throat out of the way of the words. "I took her out bird hunting," I said. "I

wanted to show you—if I got a full bag of birds, I thought
you'd let me go on the Christmas Day hunt—"

"I'll talk to you later," my father said grimly, taking the dog
from me and starting into the kitchen. "I've got to try to save
this dog's life now."

I started into the kitchen behind my father. He turned.
"Where's the gun you shot her with?" he said.

"I—left it."

"Don't leave it lying out there in the field," my father said
in a stern voice.

I wanted very badly to go into the kitchen, find out that
the dog would live. But I turned instead, and went back
the way I had come, walking with my head down, feeling
shrunken inside myself. I had overreached; I had risen up
today full of pride beyond my ability, and in the stubbornness
of the pride I had been blind until the terrible accident had
opened my eyes so that I could see myself clearly—too
clearly. I found the gun, the two bags, where I had dropped
them. I picked them up without looking at the smear of blood
where Calypso had lain. I went back to the house slowly, not
wanting to face it, reluctant to see the damage I had wrought.

When I came into the kitchen, my father had the dog
stretched out on the kitchen table. My mother stood by his
side with bandages and ointment in her hands. The wound
was cleaned of the birdshot and dirt and blood. Calypso Baby
whined when she saw me, and I felt my heart cringe with
the rejection.

My father looked at me across the dog. The anger was
gone out of him; his voice was slow and searching and not to
be denied. "Now I want to know why you took my gun and
my dog without permission," he said.

"David," my mother said to him.

My father ignored her, kept his eyes hard on my face.
I knew it wouldn't do any good to look toward my mother.
This was between me and my father, and there was no refuge
for me anywhere in the world. I didn't want a refuge; I knew
I had to face not only my father but myself.

"I—I wanted to go on the Christmas Day hunt," I said
again. "I thought if I—" I stopped. It was all that I had to say;
it seemed pretty flimsy to me now.

My father looked down at the dog. I was surprised at the
lack of anger in him. I could read only sadness in his voice.
"She may be ruined for hunting," he said. "Even if the wound
heals good, if she doesn't lose the use of her leg, she may be
gun-shy for the rest of her life. At best, I'll never be able to
show her in field trials again. You understand what you've
done?"

"Yes, sir," I said. I wanted to cry. But that would not help,
any more than anger from my father would help.

"You see now why I said you weren't old enough?" my
father said. "You've got to be trained for hunting, just like
a dog is trained. Suppose other men had been out there;
suppose you had shot a human being?"

"David!" my mother said.

My father turned angrily toward her. "He's got to learn!" he
said. "There's too many people in this world trying to do
things without learning how to do them first. I don't want my
boy to be one of them."

"Papa," I said. "I'm—I'm sorry. I wouldn't have hurt
Calypso Baby for anything in the world."

"I'm not going to punish you," my father said. He looked
down at the dog. "This is too bad for a whipping to settle. But
I want you to think about today. I don't want you to put it out
of your mind. You knew that when the time came ripe for it,
I intended to teach you, take you out like I'd take a puppy,

and hunt with you. After a while, you could hunt by yourself. Then if you were good enough—and only if you were good enough—you could go on the Christmas Day hunt. The Christmas Day hunt is the place you come to, not the place you start out from. Do you understand?"

"Yes, sir," I said. I would have been glad to settle for a whipping. But I knew that a mere dusting of the breeches would be inadequate for my brashness, my overconfidence, for the hurt I had given not only to the fine bird dog but also to my father—and to myself.

"You've got to take special care of Calypso Baby," my father said. "Maybe if you take care of her yourself while she's hurt, she'll decide to be your friend again."

I looked at the dog, and I could feel the need of her confidence and trust. "Yes, sir," I said. Then I said humbly, "I hope she will be friends with me again."

I went toward the hall, needing to be alone in my room. I stopped at the kitchen doorway, looking back at my father and mother watching me. I had to say it in a hurry if I was going to say it at all.

"Papa," I said, the words rushing softly in my throat, threatening to gag there before I could get them out. "I— I don't think I deserve that bicycle this Christmas. I don't deserve it at all."

My father nodded his head. "All right, son," he said gravely. "This is your own punishment for yourself."

"Yes," I said, forcing the word, the loss empty inside me, and yet feeling better too. I turned and ran out of the room and up the stairs.

Christmas came, but without any help from me at all. I went to bed on Christmas Eve heavy with the knowledge that tomorrow morning there would be no shiny new bicycle

under the tree; there would be no Christmas Day hunt for me.
I couldn't prevent myself from waking up at the usual excited
time, but I made myself turn over and go back to sleep. When
I did, reluctantly, go downstairs, the Christmas tree did not
excite me, nor the usual gifts I received every year, the heavy
sweater, the gloves, the scarf, the two new pairs of blue jeans.
I just wouldn't let myself think about the bicycle.

After my father had gone outside, my mother hugged me
to her in a sudden rush of affection. "He would have given
you the bicycle anyway," she said, "if you hadn't told him you
didn't want it."

I looked up at her. "I didn't deserve it," I said. "Maybe
next year I will."

She surprised me then by holding me and crying. I heard
the first car arrive outside, the voices of the men excited with
the promise of hunting. My mother stood up and said briskly,
"Well, this is not getting that big dinner cooked," and went
into the kitchen without looking back.

I went out on the front porch. It was perfect quail-hunting
weather, cold but not too cold, with a smoky haze lying over
the earth. The dogs knew that today was for hunting; I could
hear them from around behind the house, standing on the
wire fence in broad-shouldered rows, their voices yelping and
calling. All except Calypso Baby. All except me.

I stood aside, watching the men arrive in their cars, my
father greeting them. Their breaths hung cloudy in the air, and
they moved with a sharp movement to their bodies. These
were the best hunters in the whole countryside, and today
would be a great comradeship and competition. Any man
invited on this hunt could be proud of the invitation alone.

I felt almost remote as I watched, as I went with them
around the side of the house to the dogs. They all went to

examine Calypso Baby, and I felt a freezing inside; but my
father only said, "She got shot by accident," and did not tell
the whole terrible story.

Then my father looked at his watch and said, "Let's wait
for a few more minutes. Walter ought to be here soon. Hate to
start without him."

One of the men called, "Here he comes now," and Walter
drove up in his battered car.

"Come here, son," my father said, speaking to me for the
first time this morning, and I went reluctantly to his side. I was
afraid it was coming now, the whole story, and all the men
would look at me in the same way that Calypso Baby had
after I had shot her.

My father drew me to the side of Walter's car, reached in,
and brought out a basket. "You wanted a bicycle," he said.
"Then you decided yourself you should wait. Because you
made the decision yourself, I decided you were old enough
for this."

I looked at the bird-dog puppy in the basket. All of a sudden Christmas burst inside me like a skyrocket, out of the
place where I had kept it suppressed all this time.

"Papa," I said. "Papa—"

"Take him," my father said.

I reached into the basket and took out the puppy. The
puppy licked my chin with his harsh, warm tongue. He was
long, gangly, his feet and head too big for his body—but
absolutely beautiful.

My father knelt beside me, one hand on the puppy. "I told
Walter to bring me the finest bird-dog puppy he could find,"
he said. "He's kin to Calypso Baby; he's got good blood."

"Thank you, Papa," I said in a choking voice. "I—I'd rather
have him than the bicycle. I'll name him Calypso Boy, I'll—"

"When this puppy is ready for birds, we'll train him," my

father said. "While we train the puppy, we'll train you too. When the time comes, you can both go on the Christmas Day hunt—if you're good enough."

"We'll be good enough," I said. "Both of us will be good enough."

"I hope so," my father said. He stood up and looked at the men standing around us, all of them smiling down at me and Calypso Boy. "Let's go," he said. "Those birds are going to get tired of waiting on us."

They laughed and hollered, and the dogs moiled and sounded in the excitement as they were let out of the pen. They fanned out across the pasture, each man or two men taking a dog. I stood watching, holding the puppy warm in my arms. I looked at Calypso Baby, standing crippled in her pen looking longingly after the hunters. I went over and spoke to her. She whined; then for the first time since the accident, she wagged her tail at me.

I looked down at the puppy in my arms. "We'll be going," I told him, as he licked at my chin. "One of these days, when you're a dog and I'm a man, we'll be right out there with the best of them."

It was three years more before I got to go on my first Christmas Hunt. Papa had been right, of course. In the time between I had learned a great deal myself while training Calypso Boy to hunt. With the good blood in him he turned out to be a great bird dog—second only, I guess, to Calypso Baby, who recovered well from her wound and was Papa's dog the day Calypso Boy and I made our first Christmas hunt.

But of all the Christmases, before and since, I guess I remember best the one when Calypso Baby was hurt—and Calypso Boy first came to me.

■ ■ ■

The animals' point of view is not presented in Where the Red
Fern Grows. *In* Bambi: A Life in the Woods, *the animals think of
human hunters as "Him," a mysterious but deadly power. Read on
to find out what happens when "He" visits the woods one day.*

Him

from Bambi: A Life in the Woods

Felix Salten

Ronno, who had settled himself a little to one side in the snow,
suddenly sprang up. "I don't know what it is," he mumbled and
gazed around.

Everyone grew watchful. "What is it?" they asked.

"I don't know," Ronno repeated. "But I'm restless. I suddenly
felt restless as if something were wrong."

Karus was snuffing the air. "I don't smell anything strange,"
he declared.

They all stood still, listening and snuffing the air. "It's nothing, there's absolutely nothing to smell," they agreed one after
another.

"Nevertheless," Ronno insisted, "You can say what you like,
something is wrong."

Marena said, "The crows are calling."

"There they go calling again," Faline added quickly, but the
others had already heard them.

"They are flying," said Karus and the others.

Everybody looked up. High above the treetops a flock of
crows flapped by. They came from the farthest edge of the
forest, the direction from which danger always came, and they
were complaining to one another. Apparently something unusual
had happened.

"Wasn't I right?" asked Ronno. "You can see that something is happening."

"What shall we do?" Bambi's mother whispered anxiously.

"Let's get away," Aunt Ena urged in alarm.

"Wait," Ronno commanded.

"But the children," Aunt Ena replied, "the children. Gobo can't run."

"Go ahead," Ronno agreed, "go off with your children. I don't think there's any need for it, but I don't blame you for going." He was alert and serious.

"Come, Gobo. Come, Faline. Softly now, go slowly. And keep behind me," Aunt Ena warned them. She slipped away with the children.

Time passed. They stood still, listening and trembling.

"As if we hadn't suffered enough already," old Nettla began. "We still have this to go through. . . ." She was very angry. Bambi looked at her, and he felt that she was thinking of something horrible.

Three or four magpies had already begun to chatter on the side of the thicket from which the crows had come. "Look out! Look out, out, out!" they cried. The deer could not see them, but could hear them calling and warning each other. Sometimes one of them, and sometimes all of them together, would cry, "Look out, out, out!" Then they came nearer. They fluttered in terror from tree to tree, peered back and fluttered away again in fear and alarm.

"Akh!" cried the jays. They screamed their warning loudly.

Suddenly all the deer shrank together at once as though a blow had struck them. Then they stood still snuffing the air.

It was He.

A heavy wave of scent blew past. There was nothing they could do. The scent filled their nostrils, it numbed their senses and made their hearts stop beating.

The magpies were still chattering. The jays were still screaming overhead. In the woods around them everything had
sprung to life. The titmice flitted through the branches, like tiny
feathered balls, chirping, "Run! Run!"

The blackbirds fled swiftly and darkly above them with long-
drawn twittering cries. Through the dark tangle of bare bushes,
they saw on the white snow a wild aimless scurrying of smaller,
shadowy creatures. These were the pheasants. Then a flash of red
streaked by. That was the fox. But no one was afraid of him now.
For that fearful scent kept streaming on in a wider wave, sending
terror into their hearts and uniting them all in one mad fear, in a
single feverish impulse to flee, to save themselves.

That mysterious overpowering scent filled the woods with
such strength that they knew that this time He was not alone,
but had come with many others, and there would be no end to
the killing.

They did not move. They looked at the titmice, whisking
away in a sudden flutter, at the blackbirds and the squirrels who
dashed from treetop to treetop in mad bounds. They knew that
all the little creatures on the ground had nothing to fear. But
they understood their flight when they smelled Him, for no forest
creature could bear His presence.

Presently Friend Hare hopped up. He hesitated, sat still and
then hopped on again.

"What is it?" Karus called after him impatiently.

But Friend Hare only looked around with bewildered eyes
and could not even speak. He was completely terrified.

"What's the use of asking?" said Ronno gloomily.

Friend Hare gasped for breath. "We are surrounded," he
said in a lifeless voice. "We can't escape on any side. He is
everywhere."

At the same instant they heard His voice. Twenty or thirty
strong, He cried, "Ho! ho! Ha! ha!" It roared like the sound of

winds and storms. He beat on the tree trunks as though they were drums. It was wracking and terrifying. A distant twisting and rending of parted bushes rang out. There was a snapping and cracking of broken boughs.

He was coming.

He was coming into the heart of the thicket.

Then short whistling flutelike trills sounded together with the loud flap of soaring wings. A pheasant rose from under His very feet. The deer heard the wing beats of the pheasant grow fainter as he mounted into the air. There was a loud crash like thunder. Then silence. Then a dull thud on the ground.

"He is dead," said Bambi's mother, trembling.

"The first," Ronno added.

The young doe, Marena, said, "In this very hour many of us are going to die. Perhaps I shall be one of them." No one listened to her, for a mad terror had seized them all.

Bambi tried to think. But His savage noises grew louder and louder and paralyzed Bambi's senses. He heard nothing but those noises. They numbed him while amidst the howling, shouting and crashing he could hear his own heart pounding. He felt nothing but curiosity and did not even realize that he was trembling in every limb. From time to time his mother whispered in his ear, "Stay close to me." She was shouting, but in the uproar it sounded to Bambi as if she were whispering. Her "Stay close to me" encouraged him. It was like a chain holding him. Without it he would have rushed off senselessly, and he heard it at the very moment when his wits were wandering and he wanted to dash away.

He looked around. All sorts of creatures were swarming past, scampering blindly over one another. A pair of weasels ran by like thin snakelike streaks. The eye could scarcely follow them. A ferret listened as though bewitched to every shriek that desperate Friend Hare let out.

A fox was standing in a whole flurry of fluttering pheasants. They paid no attention to him. They ran right under his nose and he paid no attention to them. Motionless, with his head thrust forward, he listened to the onrushing tumult, lifting his pointed ears, and snuffed the air with his nose. Only his tail moved, slowly wagging with his intense concentration.

A pheasant dashed up. He had come from where the danger was worst and was beside himself with fear.

"Don't try to fly," he shouted to the others. "Don't fly, just run! Don't lose your head! Don't try to fly! Just run, run, run!"

He kept repeating the same thing over and over again as though to encourage himself. But he no longer knew what he was saying.

"Ho! ho! Ha! ha!" came the death cry, from quite near apparently.

"Don't lose your head," screamed the pheasant. And at the same time his voice broke in a whistling gasp and, spreading his wings, he flew up with a loud whir. Bambi watched how he flew straight up, directly between the trees, beating his wings. The dark metallic blue and greenish-brown markings on his body gleamed like gold. His long tail feathers swept proudly behind him. A short crash like thunder sounded sharply. The pheasant suddenly crumpled up in mid-flight. He turned head over tail as though he wanted to catch his claws with his beak, and then dropped violently to earth. He fell among the others and did not move again.

Then everyone lost his senses. They all rushed toward one another. Five or six pheasants rose at one time with a loud whir. "Don't fly," cried the rest and ran. The thunder cracked five or six times and more of the flying birds dropped lifeless to the ground.

"Come," said Bambi's mother. Bambi looked around. Ronno and Karus had already fled. Old Nettla was disappearing. Only

Marena was still beside them. Bambi went with his mother, Marena following them timidly. All around them was a roaring and shouting, and the thunder was crashing. Bambi's mother was calm. She trembled quietly, but she kept her wits together.

"Bambi, my child," she said, "keep behind me all the time. We'll have to get out of here and across the open place. But now we'll go slowly."

The din was maddening. The thunder crashed ten, twelve times as He hurled it from His hands.

"Watch out," said Bambi's mother. "Don't run. But when we have to cross the open place, run as fast as you can. And don't forget, Bambi, my child, don't pay any attention to me when we get out there. Even if I fall, don't pay any attention to me, just keep on running. Do you understand, Bambi?"

His mother walked carefully step by step amidst the uproar. The pheasants were running up and down, burying themselves in the snow. Suddenly they would spring out and begin to run again. The whole Hare family was hopping to and fro, squatting down and then hopping again. No one said a word. They were all spent with terror and numbed by the din and thunderclaps.

It grew lighter in front of Bambi and his mother. The clearing showed through the bushes. Behind them the terrifying drumming on the tree trunks came crashing nearer and nearer. The breaking branches snapped. There was a roaring of "Ha, ha! Ho, ho!"

Then Friend Hare and two of his cousins rushed past them across the clearing. Bing! Ping! Bang! roared the thunder. Bambi saw how one hare struck an elder in the middle of his flight and lay with his white belly turned upward. He quivered a little and then was still. Bambi stood petrified. But from behind him came the cry, "Here they are! Run! Run!"

There was a loud clapping of wings suddenly opened. There were gasps, sobs, showers of feathers, flutterings. The pheasants took wing and the whole flock rose almost at one instant. The air was throbbing with repeated thunderclaps and the dull thuds of the fallen and the high, piercing shrieks of those who had escaped.

Bambi heard steps and looked behind him. He was there. He came bursting through the bushes on all sides. He sprang up everywhere, struck about Him, beat the bushes, drummed on the tree trunks and shouted with a fiendish voice.

"Now," said Bambi's mother. "Get away from here. And don't stay too close to me." She was off with a bound that barely skimmed the snow. Bambi rushed out after her. The thunder crashed around them on all sides. It seemed as if the earth would split in half. Bambi saw nothing. He kept running. A growing desire to get away from the tumult and out of reach of that scent which seemed to strangle him, the growing impulse to flee, the longing to save himself were loosed in him at last. He ran. It seemed to him as if he saw his mother hit but he did not know if it was really she or not. He felt a film come over his eyes from fear of the thunder crashing behind him. It had gripped him completely at last. He could think of nothing or see nothing around him. He kept running.

The open space was crossed. Another thicket took him in. The hue and cry still rang behind him. The sharp reports still thundered. And in the branches above him there was a light pattering like the first fall of hail. Then it grew quieter. Bambi kept running.

A dying pheasant, with its neck twisted, lay on the snow, beating feebly with its wings. When he heard Bambi coming he ceased his convulsive movements and whispered: "It's all over with me." Bambi paid no attention to him and ran on.

A tangle of bushes he blundered into forced him to slacken his pace and look for a path. He pawed the ground impatiently with his hoofs. "This way!" called someone with a gasping voice.

Bambi obeyed involuntarily and found an opening at once. Someone moved feebly in front of him. It was Friend Hare's wife who had called.

"Can you help me a little?" she said. Bambi looked at her and shuddered. Her hind leg dangled lifelessly in the snow, dyeing it red and melting it with warm, oozing blood. "Can you help me a little?" she repeated. She spoke as if she were well and whole, almost as if she were happy. "I don't know what can have happened to me," she went on. "There's really no sense to it, but I just can't seem to walk . . ."

In the middle of her words she rolled over on her side and died. Bambi was seized with horror again and ran.

"Bambi!"

He stopped with a jolt. A deer was calling him. Again he heard the cry. "Is that you, Bambi?"

Bambi saw Gobo floundering helplessly in the snow. All his strength was gone; he could no longer stand on his feet. He lay there half buried and lifted his head feebly. Bambi went up to him excitedly.

"Where's your mother, Gobo?" he asked, gasping for breath. "Where's Faline?" Bambi spoke quickly and impatiently. Terror still gripped his heart.

"Mother and Faline had to go on," Gobo answered resignedly. He spoke softly, but as seriously and as well as a grown deer. "They had to leave me here. I fell down. You must go on, too, Bambi."

"Get up," cried Bambi. "Get up, Gobo! You've rested long enough. There's not a minute to lose now. Get up and come with me!"

"No, leave me," Gobo answered quietly. "I can't stand up. It's impossible. I'd like to, but I'm too weak."

"What will happen to you?" Bambi persisted.

"I don't know. Probably I'll die," said Gobo simply.

The uproar began again and re-echoed. New crashes of thunder followed. Bambi shrank together. Suddenly a branch snapped. Young Karus pounded swiftly through the snow, galloping ahead of the din.

"Run," he called when he saw Bambi. "Don't stand there if you can run!" He was gone in a flash and his headlong flight carried Bambi along with it. Bambi was hardly aware that he had begun to run again, and only after an interval did he say, "Goodbye, Gobo." But he was already too far away. Gobo could no longer hear him.

He ran till nightfall through the woods that was filled with shouting and thunder. As darkness closed in, it grew quiet. Soon a light wind carried away the horrible scent that spread everywhere. But the excitement remained.

The first friend whom Bambi saw again was Ronno. He was limping more than ever.

"Over in the oak grove the fox has a burning fever from his wound," Ronno said. "I just passed him. He's suffering terribly. He keeps biting the snow and the ground."

"Have you seen my mother?" asked Bambi.

"No," answered Ronno evasively, and walked quickly away.

Later during the night Bambi met old Nettla with Faline. All three were delighted to meet.

"Have you seen my mother?" asked Bambi.

"No," Faline answered. "I don't even know where my own mother is."

"Well," said old Nettla cheerfully. "Here's a nice mess. I was so glad that I didn't have to bother with children any more and now I have to look after two at once. I'm heartily grateful."

Bambi and Faline laughed.

They talked about Gobo. Bambi told how he had found him, and they grew so sad they began to cry. But old Nettla would not have them crying. "Before everything else you have got to get something to eat. I never heard of such a thing. You haven't had a bite to eat this livelong day!"

She led them to places where there were still a few leaves that had not completely withered. Old Nettla was wonderfully gentle. She ate nothing herself, but made Bambi and Faline eat heartily. She pawed away the snow from the grassy spots and ordered them to eat with, "The grass is good here." Or else she would say, "No, wait. We'll find something better farther on." But between whiles she would grumble. "It's perfectly ridiculous the trouble children give you."

Suddenly they saw Aunt Ena coming and rushed toward her. "Aunt Ena," cried Bambi. He had seen her first. Faline was beside herself with joy and bounded around her. "Mother," she cried. But Ena was weeping and nearly dead from exhaustion.

"Gobo is gone," she cried. "I've looked for him. I went to the little place where he lay when he broke down in the snow . . . there was nothing there . . . he is gone . . . my poor little Gobo . . ."

Old Nettla grumbled. "If you had looked for his tracks it would have been more sensible than crying," she said.

"There weren't any tracks," said Aunt Ena. "But . . . His . . . tracks were there. He found Gobo."

She was silent. Then Bambi asked despondently, "Aunt Ena, have you seen my mother?"

"No," answered Aunt Ena gently.

Bambi never saw his mother again.

■ ■ ■

These two stories are the kind of yarns that might have been spun at Billy's grandfather's general store.

Hunting Yarns

Mart Moody's Bird Dog
retold by Robert Bethke

Mart Moody from Tupper Lake used to tell this tale. "I went out one day and here was a big flock of ducks out on Tupper Lake. And I had this good dog. And I shot. And I sent the dog out there. She was heavy with pups, and I didn't know whether I should send her out there. It was a cold day in the fall. Well, she took right off and away she went. And it got dark and she never showed up. And I got to worrying about her. I worried about that dog. She was a good dog, a real good retriever. She'd get anything I'd shot at. So the next morning I woke up and I thought I'd go see if I could find her. And I got down by the shore of the lake and I looked out. And I see something coming. And this dog, she come into shore. She had three ducks in her mouth. And behind her she had seven pups. And each one of the pups had a duck in his mouth.

Davy Crockett Meets His Match

Well, Billy told me of a time when Davy Crockett was walkin' home in the late afternoon, right afore sunset. He hadn'a done much in the way of shootin', and knowin' Crockett's temper like folks around here did, Billy said he was mighty put out. "If you wanta make a hunter madder'n a bridled bull, jist keep him from bringin' meat home after a full day of walkin'," they say.

245

Billy told how Davy was passin' under a mighty tall tree near the Great Gap when he looked up and spied a fat furry coon starin' down at him. He was just about to raise his gun when he saw the coon lift his paw and say, "Excuse me, is your name Davy Crockett?"

"It is," Crockett said as he lowered his gun Old Betsy.

Well, Billy says that coon put on the saddest face you ever saw and he said to Davy, "Then, you needn't take any more trouble. I'm comin' down."

The coon climbed on down that tree just as slow and mournful as could be. He just plain considered himself shot. Davy got to thinkin' that such a courteous coon deserved better than bein' skinned, so when the coon waddled up to him he bent down and patted the little feller on the head.

"You're a right thoughtful feller," Crockett said. "I won't hurt you none."

The coon didn't seem surprised at all; instead he just started backin' himself off into the woods saying, "That's mighty kind, Mr. Crockett."

"Hey, now," said Davy, "what's yer hurry?"

"Well, Mr. Crockett, it's not that I doubt you. No, sir. It's just that you might change your mind."

And with that, the coon was gone. Billy said that Davy *did* change his mind, but by the time he did, that smart coon was long gone. Even Davy laughed. It was the first, and last, coon who ever out-talked Davy Crockett.

Hunters aren't the only ones who love to tell stories. One of the best-liked kind of story is the tall tale—full of exaggeration and humor. This tale features a character you may know.

Paul Bunyan's Cornstalk
retold by Harold Courlander

Paul Bunyan was the fellow who invented the ax with two edges so a man could stand between two trees and chop them both down at the same time. As it turned out, Paul was the only man who could do that trick, but the other lumberjacks used the double-bitted ax anyway, because they didn't have to sharpen the blades so often. Paul Bunyan also had other tricks. Most lumberjacks used to cut off the tops of the pines before they felled them. But when Paul was in a hurry, he'd wait till a tree started falling; then he'd get set with his ax and lop off the top of the tree as it came down.

Nothing Paul Bunyan ever did was small. He had an ox named Babe, who used to help him with his logging work. Babe was just about the most phenomenal ox in Michigan. His color was blue, and he stood ninety hands high. If you happened to hang on the tip of one horn, it's doubtful if you could have seen the tip of the other, even on a clear day. One day when Paul had Babe out plowing, the ox was stung by a Michigan deerfly about the size of a bushel basket. Babe took off across the country dragging the plow behind him, right across Indiana, Illinois, and Missouri, with the deerfly bringing up the rear. After a while Babe veered south and didn't stop till he got to the Rio Grande. The plow that Babe was hitched to

From *Ride with the Sun* by Harold Courlander. Copyright © 1983 by Harold Courlander. Reprinted by permission of **The Emma Courlander Trust**.

dug a furrow four miles wide and two hundred miles long. You can check it in your own geography book. They call it Grand Canyon nowadays.

Even the storms that Paul was in were big. The biggest of all was the one they call the Big Blue Snow. It snowed for two months straight, and the way the drifts piled up only the tops of the tallest pines were showing. Lumberjacks went out that winter on their snowshoes and cut off all the pine tops. It saved them a lot of time when spring came around. Babe the blue ox didn't get a wink of sleep, though, from December till the first of March. It seems that standing out there in the weather the way he was, the snow that fell on his back melted and ran down his tail, and once it got there it froze into ice. Babe's tail kept getting heavier and heavier, and it drew on his hide so hard it just pulled his eyelids wide open and kept them that way. Babe never did get his eyes closed until the spring thaw came and melted the ice off his tail.

But the Big Blue Snow wasn't anything compared to the big drought that started in Saginaw County and spread out as far as the Alleghenies in the East and the Rockies in the West. It all started with Paul Bunyan's vegetable garden. Paul planted some corn and some pumpkins. One of those cornstalks was six feet high before the others had sprouted. In two weeks it was tall as a house and growing like crazy. About the time it was as big as a fifty-year-old pine, people began to come in from all over the county to see it. It was growing out of the ground so fast it was pulling up stones that even the frost couldn't heave out. Same kind of thing, more or less, happened to one of the pumpkin vines. It grew so fast it just darted around like a Massauga rattlesnake. It climbed into any place where there was an opening. People had to keep their windows closed. The ones that didn't had to cut their way out of their beds with a brush knife. Sometimes that vine would grow into one window and out another between sunset and sunrise. Things weren't too bad until the vine blossomed and the pumpkins came out. They were about the size of hogsheads—the *little* pumpkins, that is—and when the vine whipped back and forth looking for someplace to grow it just snapped the pumpkins around like crab apples on a string. People had to be mighty alert to keep from getting hit by those pumpkins. One man lost a team of horses that way, and half a dozen good barns and one silo were stove in.

But the real problem started when the corn and pumpkin roots began to soak up all the water out of the ground. Farms for sixty miles around went dry—fields, springs, and wells. The pine woods turned yellow from lack of moisture. The Au Sable River just turned into a trickle, and pretty soon there wasn't anything there but dry mud. The next thing that happened was that the water in the Great Lakes began to go down. It went down so fast in Lake Huron it left the fish hanging in the air. When things began to look real bad, folks came and told Paul Bunyan he'd just have to get rid of his corn and pumpkins. Paul was reasonable about it. First he went after the pumpkin vine. He spent four hours racing around trying to catch hold of the end, and finally did it by trapping it in a barn. He hitched Babe up to the end of the vine, but as fast as Babe pulled the vine grew. Babe ran faster and faster, and he was near Lake Ontario before he had the vine tight enough to pull it out.

Then Paul sized up his cornstalk. He figured he'd have to chop it down. He sharpened up his ax and spit on his hands. He made a good deep cut in that stalk, but before he could chip out a wedge the stalk grew up six feet, cut and all. Every time he made a cut it would shoot up out of reach before he could swing his ax again. Pretty soon he saw there wasn't any use going on this way. "Only way to kill this stalk is to cut off the top," he said. He hung his ax in his belt and started climbing. In about two hours he was completely out of sight. People just stood around and waited. They stood around two and a half days without any sight of Paul. Lars Larson called, "Paul!" but there was no answer. Erik Erikson and Hans Hanson called, "Paul!" But there wasn't any word from Paul Bunyan. So they waited some more. Two more days went by. No word from Paul. They decided that if everyone yelled at once maybe the sound would carry. So all together the two thousand eight hundred men and boys hollered, "Paul!" And sure enough, they heard his faint voice from up above.

"When you going to top that cornstalk?" they yelled back at him.

"Hasn't that top come down yet?" Paul hollered back. "I cut it off three days ago!"

And it was the truth, too. The stalk stopped growing, the water in the Great Lakes stopped falling, the Au Sable River began to run, the springs began to flow again, and things came back to normal. But it was a narrow escape.

■ ■ ■

A general store like the one Billy's grandfather owned was an important place in a small community. Here are some memories of another general store, owned by another grandparent, called "Momma." Can you figure out why, for Angelou, "the Store was my favorite place to be"?

Momma's Store
from I Know Why the Caged Bird Sings
Maya Angelou

Weighing the half-pounds of flour, excluding the scoop, and depositing them dust-free into the thin paper sacks held a simple kind of adventure for me. I developed an eye for measuring how full a silver-looking ladle of flour, mash, meal, sugar or corn had to be to push the scale indicator over to eight ounces or one pound. When I was absolutely accurate our appreciative customers used to admire: "Sister Henderson sure got some smart grandchildrens." If I was off in the Store's favor, the eagle-eyed women would say, "Put some more in that sack, child. Don't you try to make your profit offa me."

Then I would quietly but persistently punish myself. For every bad judgment, the fine was no silver-wrapped Kisses, the sweet chocolate drops that I loved more than anything in the world, except Bailey. And maybe canned pineapples. My obsession with pineapples nearly drove me mad. I dreamt of the days when I would be grown and able to buy a whole carton for myself alone.

Although the syrupy golden rings sat in their exotic cans on our shelves year round, we only tasted them during Christmas. Momma used the juice to make almost-black fruit cakes. Then she lined heavy soot-encrusted iron skillets with the pineapple rings for rich upside-down cakes. Bailey and I received one slice each, and I carried mine around for hours, shredding off the fruit until nothing was left except the perfume on my fingers. I'd like to think that my desire for pineapples was so sacred that I wouldn't allow myself to steal a can (which was possible) and eat it alone out in the garden, but I'm certain that I must have weighed the possibility of the scent exposing me and didn't have the nerve to attempt it.

Until I was thirteen and left Arkansas for good, the Store was my favorite place to be. Alone and empty in the mornings, it looked like an unopened present from a stranger. Opening the front doors was pulling the ribbon off the unexpected gift. The light would come in softly (we faced north), easing itself over the shelves of mackerel, salmon, tobacco, thread. It fell flat on the big vat of lard and by noontime during the summer the grease had softened to a thick soup. Whenever I walked into the Store in the afternoon, I sensed that it was tired. I alone could hear the slow pulse of its job half done. But just before bedtime, after numerous people had walked in and out, had argued over their bills, or joked about their neighbors, or just dropped in "to give Sister Henderson a 'Hi y'all,'" the promise of magic mornings returned to the Store and spread itself over the family in washed life waves.

Momma opened boxes of crispy crackers and we sat around the meat block at the rear of the Store. I sliced onions, and Bailey opened two or even three cans of sardines and allowed their juice of oil and fishing boats to ooze down and around the sides. That was supper. In the evening, when we were alone like that, Uncle Willie didn't stutter or shake or give any indication that he had an "affliction." It seemed that the peace of a day's ending was an assurance that the covenant God made with children, Negroes and the crippled was still in effect.

■ ■ ■

Billy works hard to have dogs of his own. Judy, however, cannot have her own pet and becomes attached to someone else's dog. As you read, think about Princess and the characters in the story. Are they anything like the dogs and characters in Where the Red Fern Grows? *Are they anything like the dogs and people that you know?*

Princess
Nicholasa Mohr

"Can I take Princess for a walk later?" Judy asked. "Please, Don Osvaldo?"

"We'll see . . . later," Don Osvaldo said. "Let me finish now with your order." He checked the handwritten list of groceries against the items stacked on the counter. "A quarter pound of salt butter, fifteen cents' worth of fatback, two pounds of dried red beans . . ."

Judy played with Princess as she waited for him to pack the groceries. "Sit . . . sit up, Princess. That's a good girl. Nice. Now shake hands. Give me your paw. Right paw! Left paw! Good. Good." The little dog wagged her tail and licked Judy's hand.

"O.K., Judy, I got everything your Mama ordered here in the bag."

"Thank you, Don Osvaldo; put it on our bill."

"I already did," he said, closing a large thick ledger. The gray binding on the ledger was worn, frayed, and filthy with grease spots from constant use. Don Osvaldo would jot down whatever his credit customers bought, including how much it cost. Every name was there in the book, in alphabetical order; a clear record for all to see. At the end of each month, before any more credit was extended, customers were obliged to settle accounts according to the ledger.

"Can I come back and take Princess for a walk?" Judy asked again.

"All right," he said.

"I'm coming back to take you for a walk later," she said to the little dog, and patted her on the head.

Princess began to whine and bark after Judy. Don Osvaldo looked at the dog and smiled. "Nereida, Nereida," he called into the back of the store.

"What is it?" his wife asked.

"Princess is crying—she wants to go with Judy for a walk."

"She's too smart for her own good," his wife said, coming into the store. "Give her something to make her feel better. . . . Go on."

Don Osvaldo went over to the meat counter and removed a hunk of boiled ham. Taking a sharp knife, he cut off a small piece and fed it to the dog. Amused, they watched Princess as she chewed the piece of ham, then sat up begging for more.

"She's so clever," said Doña Nereida, and patted the dog affectionately.

Five years ago a customer had given them the white fluffy-haired puppy, which Doña Nereida had decided to call Princess. Princess was loving and friendly, and showed her gratitude by being obedient. Osvaldo and Nereida Negrón lavished all their affection on the little dog and doted on her. They had no children, hobbies, or interests other than their store, Bodega Borinquén, a grocery specializing in tropical foods, which they kept open seven days a week; and Princess. The dog shared the small, sparsely furnished living quarters in the back of the store with her owners. There, she had her own bed and some toys to play with. Doña Nereida knitted sweaters for Princess and shopped for the fanciest collars and leashes she could find. A child's wardrobe unit had been purchased especially for her.

Customers would comment among themselves:

"That dog eats steak and they only eat tuna fish."

"Princess has better furniture than they have."

"I wish my kids ate as well as that mutt. It's not right, you know. God cannot justify this." And so on.

Despite all the gossip and complaints about the dog, no one dared say anything openly to Don Osvaldo or Doña Nereida.

Customers had to agree that Princess herself was a friendly little animal, and pleasant to look at. When children came into the store to shop they would pet her, and she was gentle with them, accepting their attention joyfully.

Princess was especially fond of Judy, who frequently took her out and taught her tricks. At first, Don Osvaldo and Doña Nereida were worried about letting Judy take Princess for walks. "Hold on to that leash. You mustn't let her get near other dogs; especially those male dogs," they warned. But several months had gone by and Judy and the dog always returned safe and sound. Actually, neither owner liked to leave the store, and they were silently grateful that Judy could take Princess out for some air.

"Mami, can I go back downstairs and take Princess for a walk?" Judy asked her mother.

Her mother had emptied the brown grocery bag and was checking the items.

"Look at that! Fifteen cents' worth of fatback and look at the tiny piece he sends. Bendito!" She shook her head. "I have to watch that man, and she's no better. Didn't I tell you to check anything that he has to weigh?" Judy looked at her mother, expecting her to complain as always about Don Osvaldo and Doña Nereida. "Because we have to buy on credit, they think they can cheat us. When I have cash I will not buy there. I cannot trust them. They charge much more than any other store, but they can get away with it because we buy on credit. I would like to see him charge a cash-paying customer what he does me!"

"Mami, can I go to walk Princess now?" Judy asked again.

"Why do you want to walk that dog? You are always walking that dog. What are you, their servant girl, to walk that stupid dog?"

"I'm the one who wants to walk her. . . . I love Princess. Please may I—"

"Go on!" her mother interrupted, waving her hands in a gesture of annoyance.

Before her mother could change her mind, Judy quickly left the apartment. Her little brother, Angel, had had another asthma attack today, and she knew her mother was in a lousy mood. After her father's death, Judy had moved into this neighborhood with her family: her mother, older sister Blanca, older brother William, and little brother Angel. That was three years ago, when she was just eight. The family had been on public assistance since almost immediately after her father had died. Her mother was always worried about making ends meet, but she was especially hard to live with whenever Angel got sick.

She ran toward the grocery store, anxious to take Princess for her walk. Judy had wanted to have a pet ever since she could remember. It was the one thing that she had always prayed for at Christmas and on her birthday, but her mother absolutely refused. Once she had brought home a stray cat and her little brother Angel had had a severe asthma attack. After that, she was positive that she could never ever have a pet. No matter how she had reasoned, her mother could not be persuaded to change her mind.

"I could give the cat my food, Mami. You don't have to spend no money. And during the day I could find a place to keep it until I got home from school."

"No. We cannot make ends meet to feed human beings, and I am not going to worry about animals. Besides, there's Angel and his allergies." Her mother always won out.

If Papi had lived, maybe things would be different, Judy often thought. But since she could play with Princess and take her out, that was almost like having her own dog, and she had learned to be content with that much.

When Judy arrived at the store, Doña Nereida had Princess all ready.

"See, Judy," Doña Nereida said, "she's got a new leash— pale-blue with tiny silver studs. She looks good in blue, don't you think so?" she asked. "It goes with her coloring. Her fur is so nice and white."

The little dog ran, tugging at the leash, and Judy followed, laughing.

Outside in the street, Judy shouted, "Ready, get set . . . go!" Quickly, Judy and Princess began to run, as usual in the direction of the schoolyard. Once they got there, Judy unleashed Princess and she ran freely, chasing her and some of the other children.

They were all used to Princess, and would pet her, run with her, and sometimes even play a game of ball with the little dog. They watched as Princess followed Judy's commands: She could sit up, roll over, play dead, retrieve, and shake hands. Everyone at the schoolyard treated Princess as if she belonged to Judy and asked her permission first before they played or ran with the little dog. And Princess behaved as if she were Judy's dog. She listened and came obediently when Judy called her. After they had finished playing, Judy leashed Princess and they walked back to the store.

"Did you have a good time?" Doña Nereida asked when they returned. "Come inside with Mama. . . . She has a little something for you," she said to Princess.

Judy handed the leash to Doña Nereida. She had never been invited inside where Princess lived. Whenever she came back from her walks she waited around, hoping they would ask her in as well, but they never did. No one was invited into the back rooms where Don Osvaldo, Doña Nereida, and Princess lived.

"Before you leave—Judy, here, have a piece of candy." Doña Nereida opened the cover of a glass display case and removed a small piece of coconut candy that sold for two cents apiece or three for a nickel. She handed it to Judy.

"Thank you," Judy said, taking the candy. She didn't much like it, but she ate it anyway.

"Osvaldo . . . Osvaldo," Doña Nereida called, "come out here; I have to take Princess inside." Turning to Judy, she said, "Goodbye, Judy, see you later."

Judy smiled and left the store. She wished she could see where Princess lived. Shrugging her shoulders, she said to herself, "Maybe tomorrow they'll ask me in."

"There's something wrong with these beans. Smell!" her mother said, handing the can of pork and beans to her children.

"Whew, yeah!" said Blanca. "They smell funny." She handed the can to William, who agreed, and then to Judy.

"They smell funny." Judy nodded.

"Can I smell too?" asked Angel. Judy handed him the can.

"Peeoowee . . . ," he said, making a face. They all laughed.

"It's not funny," her mother said. "If these beans are rotten we could die." She held up the can. "Look—see that? The can is dented and swollen. Sure, he always gives us inferior merchandise. That no-good louse!" She shook her head. "We have to return them, that's all. You go, Judy, bring them back and tell him we want another can that's not spoiled."

"I have to walk Princess, Mami; send somebody else."

"You have to walk to the store and back here. Never mind Princess. Go on!"

"But I'll be too late then," Judy protested, thinking about her friends in the schoolyard.

"How would you like not to walk that mutt at all? What if I say that you cannot walk her anymore?" her mother said, looking severely at Judy.

Quietly, Judy got up and took the can of beans. "Mami, they are already opened."

"Of course. How would I know otherwise if they are rotten? Here is the cover—just place it on top." She put the tin lid back on the opened can. "There . . . don't spill them and come right back here. I have to start supper."

"Can I walk Princess after I come back?"

"Yes," her mother said with exasperation. "Just come back with another can of beans!"

Judy rushed as quickly as she could, at the same time making sure that she did not spill the contents of the can.

"Here she is," said Doña Nereida when she saw Judy, "ready to take you out, Princess." As she fastened the leash, the dog barked and jumped, anxious to go out.

"Doña Nereida, I have to give you something first," Judy said. "What?"

"Here is a can of beans that my brother William brought home before, and they are rotten." She put the can on the counter. "So my mother says could you please give us another can that is not spoiled."

Doña Nereida picked up the can and lifted the lid, sniffing the contents. "What's wrong with them?" she asked.

"They are rotten."

"Who says? They smell just fine to me. Wait a minute. Osvaldo! Osvaldo, come out here please!" Doña Nereida called loudly.

"What do you want? I'm busy." Don Osvaldo came out.

"Smell these beans. Go on." She handed her husband the opened can.

Don Osvaldo sniffed the contents and said, "They are fine. What's wrong?"

"Judy brought them—her mother wants another can. She

says they are spoiled, that they are rotten."

"Tsk . . . ," Don Osvaldo sighed and shook his head. "They are fine. They don't smell spoiled to me, or rotten. Besides, the can is opened. I can't exchange them if she opened the can already." He put the can back on the counter and covered it with the lid. "Here, take it back to your mother and tell her that there is nothing wrong with those beans. I can't change them."

Judy stood there and looked at the couple. She wanted to say that they smelled bad to her, too, but instead she said, "OK, I'll tell her." She picked up the can of beans and returned home.

"What? Do you mean to tell me that he told you that there is nothing wrong with this can of beans?" Her mother's voice was loud and angry. "I don't believe it! Did he smell them?" she asked Judy.

"Yes," Judy said. "They both did."

Her mother shook her head. "I'm not putting up with this anymore. This is the last time that thieving couple do this to me. Come on, Judy. You come with me. I'm taking back the beans myself. Let's see what he will tell me. You too, William; you come with us, since you were the one that bought the beans."

"Can I come too?" asked Angel.

"No," his mother answered, "stay with Blanca till I get back. I don't want you going up and down the stairs. And you, Blanca, start the rice. I'll be back in a little while."

Her mother walked in first, holding the can of beans. Judy and William followed.

"Don Osvaldo, I would like to return this can of beans," her mother said. Don Osvaldo was seated behind the counter, looking through his ledger. He put the book down.

"Mrs. Morales, there is nothing wrong with them beans," he said.

"Did you take a good smell? I sent Judy down before; and I cannot believe that after smelling them, you could refuse to exchange them for another can that is not spoiled!" She put the can on the counter.

Doña Nereida walked in, followed by Princess. When the dog saw Judy, she began to bark and jump up. "Shh . . . ," said Doña Nereida. "Down! Get down, Princess, you are not going out right now. Maybe later. Down!" Princess sat down obediently, wagging her tail and looking at Judy. "What's happening here, Mrs. Morales?" she asked.

"It's about these beans. I refuse to accept them. That can is dented and swollen, that's how it got spoiled. Surely you don't expect me to feed this to my children."

"Why not?" said Doña Nereida. "They smell and look perfectly fine to me."

"Look, Mrs. Morales," said Don Osvaldo, "you probably opened the can and left it open a long time, and that's why they smell funny to you. But they are not spoiled, and I cannot give you another one or any credit for this."

"How could I know they are rotten unless I open up the can? Besides, I did not leave them open a long time. William just bought it here this afternoon," Mrs. Morales said and turned to her son. "Isn't that so, William?"

"Yes. I got them here and the can was already dented," said William.

"That doesn't mean anything," said Don Osvaldo. "You people opened them. There's nothing we can do."

Mrs. Morales looked at Don Osvaldo and Doña Nereida and smiled, remaining silent. After a moment, she asked, "You expect me to eat this and to feed this to my children?"

"You can do what you want with those beans," said Don Osvaldo. "It's not my affair."

"Will you at least give us some credit?" asked Mrs. Morales.

"We already told you, no!" said Doña Nereida. "Listen, you are making a big thing over a can of beans when there is nothing wrong with them."

"Would you eat this, then?" asked Mrs. Morales.

"Of course," said Don Osvaldo.

"Certainly!" Doña Nereida nodded in agreement.

"O.K.," said Mrs. Morales, smiling, "I'll tell you what: You take them. A present from me to you. Eat them and enjoy them."

"All right." Don Osvaldo shrugged his shoulders. "If that's how you feel. It will be your loss. This can is not spoiled."

"Well then, I'll tell you what," said Mrs. Morales. "Why don't you feed it to Princess? Let Judy give it to her—a little present from us."

Don Osvaldo looked at his wife and she returned his glance, shrugging her shoulders.

"We are not going to eat them anyway, so why should they go to waste?" said Mrs. Morales. "Go on, Judy, take the beans and feed them to Princess." Turning toward Doña Nereida, she asked, "Perhaps you could give Judy a little dish?" Doña Nereida did not answer, and looked with uncertainty at her husband. Mrs. Morales continued; this time she spoke to Don Osvaldo. "Why not? Don Osvaldo, if there is nothing wrong with the beans, then let's give them to Princess. She would probably enjoy them. It would be a treat."

"OK," he nodded, "sure. Nereida, get her blue dish from inside. If there is something wrong with the beans, Princess will not eat them."

His wife went into the back and returned, holding a bright-blue bowl with a happy white poodle on it.

"Here, Judy, you do it," said Mrs. Morales, looking at her daughter. "You give it to the dog. She'll take it from you."

Doña Nereida emptied the contents of the can into the bowl

and gave it to Judy. Judy set it down on the floor near Princess.

"Here, girl, here's some beans for you," she said. Quickly, the little dog went over to the bowl and began to eat the beans, wagging her tail.

"See? Mrs. Morales, Princess is eating them beans. . . . There! Nothing was wrong with them. So you gave them away for nothing."

"That's all right, Don Osvaldo," Mrs. Morales responded. "It's not for nothing. Princess is enjoying the beans."

"Do you want another can of pork and beans?" asked Don Osvaldo, laughing. "I'm afraid I'll have to charge you, though!" His wife joined him in laughter as they both watched Princess finish the beans.

"No, thanks. I'll make do with what I have at home." Mrs. Morales turned to leave the store.

"Mami," said Judy, "can I walk Princess now?"

"No," her mother said, "you may not walk her now or later." As Judy followed her mother and brother out of the store, Don Osvaldo and Doña Nereida could still be heard laughing and commenting.

"How about tomorrow, Mami? Can I walk Princess tomorrow?" Judy persisted.

"We'll see . . . tomorrow." her mother answered.

At two the next morning, Osvaldo and Nereida Negrón were awakened by low whining sounds and grunts. When they got up to investigate, they found that Princess was having convulsions. Frightened, they tried to comfort the little dog by giving her water and then warm milk to drink. They even placed a hot-water bottle in her bed, but nothing seemed to help. The whining became softer and lower, until there was no sound at all. Princess lay in her small bed quietly, her eyes wide open, staring. The only visible sign of life was when her body jumped involuntarily, as if she had hiccups.

Don Osvaldo tried to calm his wife; she cried and wrung her hands, on the verge of hysteria. After a while, they decided the best thing to do was to take Princess to a veterinarian. Don Osvaldo found the names of several animal hospitals in the Yellow Pages, and after some telephone calls found one that would take Princess at this time of the morning. They wrapped the dog in a blanket and took a cab to the animal hospital. The doctor examined Princess and told them that her chances of surviving were slim. Whatever she had eaten was already digested and in her bloodstream. However, he promised to do his best and call them, no matter what happened.

The Negróns returned to their store at six A.M., and at six-thirty A.M. they received a phone call from the hospital informing them that Princess was dead. For a small fee they offered to dispose of the remains, and Don Osvaldo agreed.

Doña Nereida took to her bed, refusing to get up. Don Osvaldo opened his store a little late that day. Many of his credit customers had been patiently waiting outside; they had no place else to shop.

No one seemed to notice that Princess was not in the store. Don Osvaldo waited on his customers in silence, checking the back rooms every once in a while to see how his wife was. She remained in her bed, moaning softly and crying quietly.

As usual, that afternoon Judy went to the store to see Princess before going home. She entered and looked around for the little dog. Don Osvaldo was working behind the meat counter.

"Hi, Don Osvaldo," she said. "Where's Princess?"

"She's not here."

"Is she inside with Doña Nereida?" Judy asked and waited for a response. Don Osvaldo continued his work behind the meat counter, not speaking. Judy felt awkward and stepped up a little closer to the counter so that she could see Don Osvaldo. He was carefully cutting small, neat slices from a large side of beef and stacking them evenly on the other side of the chopping block.

After a short while, she said, "I'll be back, then, to walk her later. Goodbye, see you later," and turned to leave.

"Judy," Don Osvaldo said, "please tell your mother that when she sends for her groceries today, she should come herself." He paused. "Did you hear? Tell your mother to come for her groceries herself!"

"Yes," Judy replied, and went home.

Mrs. Morales entered Don Osvaldo's store accompanied by William and Judy.

"Be right with you, Mrs. Morales," Don Osvaldo said, and continued his work on the ledger.

The store was empty, and Judy looked around for Princess. In spite of her concern, she dared not ask Don Osvaldo about the little dog. Her mother's solemn attitude and Don Osvaldo's request this afternoon frightened her. For once, she wished her mother had not asked her to come along.

Don Osvaldo closed the ledger and looked at Mrs. Morales, staring at her without speaking. Finally, he asked, "Do you want anything? Can I get you something?"

"No, thank you," Mrs. Morales answered.

"Nothing?" he asked. "How about you, Judy? Do you want to take Princess for a walk?"

Judy looked at her mother, who reached out and pulled her daughter close to her.

"Do you want me to get her for you, Judy?" Don Osvaldo continued raising his voice loudly. "Do you want to take Princess for a little stroll? Well, answer! Answer!" he yelled.

Judy could feel her mother's body tensing up and trembling slightly.

"What do you want? You sent for me—what is it?" her mother asked.

"Do you know where she is? Where Princess is? She's dead. Dead. You killed her, that's what you did. You, too, Judy, both of you . . . all of you." Don Osvaldo's voice was angry. "She never did anything to you, to any of you. But you!" He pointed at Mrs. Morales. "You had to give that innocent animal, who never harmed you, something that would kill her, on spite! And you knew it—you knew it!"

"What do you want?" Mrs. Morales asked in a loud voice. "You have business with me? Tell me, or I'll leave!"

"Here . . . ," Don Osvaldo said and pushed a white sheet of paper across the counter. "I don't want to touch you. Here is your bill. Pay up by the end of the week, or I'll take you to court. You get no more credit here!"

Mrs. Morales picked up the bill and examined it carefully. "I see, Don Osvaldo, that you have charged me for the beans." Her voice was shaking and she paused, clearing her throat. "I'm glad, real glad you did. It's a small price to pay for the life of my children. As God will judge!" Mrs. Morales made the sign of the cross. "You will get your money, don't worry, Don Osvaldo. It will be my pleasure."

In a moment, Mrs. Morales and her two children left the store.

Judy cried that night and on many other nights whenever she remembered Princess. She wished she had never given the beans to Princess. She stopped going to the schoolyard; she didn't know what to tell the kids there.

Her mother found a grocery store that sold to credit customers. It was farther away—an extra fifteen-minute walk. They had two cats that Judy enjoyed playing with, but it was not the same.

Very often, she would pass by Don Osvaldo's grocery and glance inside, wondering if it had all been a dream and Princess were really in there waiting for her to come and play. She had spoken to several of the kids that shopped there, and all of them told her that the little dog was definitely not in the store. Still, there were times she would walk by and imagine Princess barking and wagging her tail, asking to be taken out to the schoolyard.

Two months went by, and one day, as Judy walked by Don Osvaldo's store on the way home, she heard someone call her name.

"Judy . . . psst, Judy . . . come over here."

She saw Doña Nereida calling her. "Come over here, Judy. . . . I want to talk to you." Judy moved slowly, with some trepidation. "Come on," Doña Nereida insisted. "I just want to see you a minute."

She followed the woman into the store. It was the first time she had set foot inside since the day that Don Osvaldo had spoken to her mother. She could hear her heart pounding, and she wondered what they wanted.

Don Osvaldo was busy waiting on a customer, and did not look in her direction.

"Come on with me," Doña Nereida whispered. "Come on!" Judy followed as she led her behind the counter and over to the back of the store.

They entered a medium-sized room with an old gas stove, a sink, a small refrigerator, and several kitchen cabinets. The room was furnished with an old armchair in need of upholstering and a kitchen table with four chairs.

"Sit . . . sit down, Judy." They both sat down.

"I suppose you are wondering why I asked you in," she said. Judy nodded. "It's that . . . I just want to talk to you. About . . . Princess." Doña Nereida lowered her eyes and sighed. "You miss her too, I'll bet." Judy blushed. Being here with Doña Nereida embarrassed her. "Don't you?"

"Yes . . . ," Judy said.

"She was so good; such a fine little dog. Almost like a person. We had her for five years. She was so obedient." Doña Nereida paused and, choking back the tears, wiped her eyes. "It's not the same anymore, you know. And he . . ." She gestured into the store. "He doesn't understand and expects me to forget! I can't. You understand, don't you?"

Judy nodded.

"See—I knew it. I told him. Judy—Judy knows. She loved Princess. She'll understand. I don't want another dog. You see, it wouldn't be fair to Princess. I have all her things, and he wants me to give them away!" She paused. "Would you like to see them? Would you?"

Judy shrugged her shoulders, feeling uncomfortable.

"Don't be shy. I know you want to see where Princess slept. Come on, now." Doña Nereida stood up and took Judy into a small adjoining room. It had a large double bed and a dresser. Over in a corner was a child's colorful yellow-and-blue wardrobe unit. Next to it, on the floor, was what appeared to Judy to be a flat kind of wicker basket with a pillow. Inside were a rubber ball, a teething ring, and a toy telephone. "That's her little bed. We bought it at the pet shop on Third Avenue."

The room was stuffy and unkempt. Judy tried not to show her displeasure at the way the room smelled.

"It's been very hard on me." Judy wished that Doña Nereida would stop talking.

"Doña Nereida," Judy said, "I have to go home now. My mother is waiting."

"Of course. What will you think of me?" She led Judy back out through the front. Don Osvaldo was busy looking at his ledger. "Here, Judy. . . ." Doña Nereida reached into the glass display case and took a piece of white coconut candy. "Here."

"Thank you," said Judy.

"I know how you used to like this candy." She smiled.

"Goodbye," said Judy.

"Tomorrow. Come back tomorrow, Judy, and we'll talk some more!" She smiled.

"OK," Judy said, leaving the store. She put the candy in her mouth and decided that she definitely did not like it.

As she walked home, she felt strange about what had just happened. The back of the store didn't seem to have anything to do with the Princess she remembered—barking wildly, jumping, running, playing in the schoolyard, and chasing all the kids.

Judy made sure that on her way home from school, she did not pass by Don Osvaldo's store the next day, or any other day.

■   ■   ■

*What would Billy Colman think of a dog that avoided the woods?
Here is that dog's story—a story that has more in common with
Billy's world than you might guess.*

The Saddest Day the Summer Had
Dick Perry

Now I must write about the saddest day the summer had. It will
be hard to write it and I may not write it well. It's about Sarah's
dog. I haven't told you much about him, hardly mentioned him at
all in fact, but I have my reasons. To write about him will break
my heart.

But Raymond said this has to do with the summer, too. He said
I should tell everything, not just the sunny parts. So I'm going to
tell you about Sarah's dog.

As I said, his name was Eleanor Roosevelt, which was a dumb
name to give a dog that's a boy. I had nothing against the name
itself. Mr. Roosevelt was a nice President. I had nothing against his
wife. I'd never met the lady. But I must be honest. I didn't care for
Eleanor Roosevelt the dog. He was dumb. He didn't know enough
to come in out of the rain. That's true. He would stand dripping wet
in a cloudburst and wonder where the water was coming from. He
wouldn't go inside. He figured it was raining everywhere.

Another thing: Sarah kept wanting him to bite us.

"Go bite 'em!" she'd shout at Eleanor. "Sic Raymond! Sic
George! Sic, sic, sic!"

But Eleanor was too dumb. He'd look at her, bemused, and wag
his tail. Any dog that doesn't know enough to come in out of the
rain doesn't know enough to bite people, either. All he knew was
that Sarah loved him. That was all he wanted to know. She was his
universe. He'd tag after her—or sleep and wait for her return. He
wasn't an angry dog. He was a lazy dog.

He was a red-haired dog who stared at other dogs in disbelief; he thought he was people. Once Sarah said he was a River collie but Raymond looked up River collies at the library and said he wasn't. Then Sarah said he was an English springer spaniel, then a Chesapeake Bay retriever, then an Irish setter, then a combination bloodhound, basset, and beagle. Raymond looked these up, too, and said she was nuts. She shouted she had papers to prove it. When Raymond demanded to see the papers she threw a stone and told Eleanor to bite Raymond on the leg, but Eleanor didn't. It was beginning to rain and Eleanor was staring puzzled at the sky wondering what was making him wet.

Other dogs—and our neighborhood had lots of them—chased streetcars, snarled at the mailman, and pursued bank robbers through the woods, but not Eleanor. No wood-running for him. He wanted no part of the forest. The idea of walking where there were no sidewalks was distasteful and uncivilized. He didn't know what a tree was. He used a fireplug. Whenever Sarah took him in the woods to play she had to carry him every step of the way. Otherwise Eleanor wouldn't budge. It was dumb. Raymond and I would be horsing in the woods, and along the path would come Sarah, her dog in her arms.

"I'm taking him for a walk," she would say.

"Then why don't you let him walk," I said one time.

She glared at me and stomped away. She was touchy where Eleanor was concerned. But the next time I saw her, she hit me on the jaw. That was three days later, but her memory and her left hook were fierce.

Raymond, of course, was forever teasing about the dog's name.

"Eleanor Roosevelt is a *girl's* name," he said one day. "You can't give a girl's name to a boy dog."

"A fat lot you know," Sarah said. "I happen to like Eleanor Roosevelt."

She looked for a rock to throw.

"It's not legal," Raymond said. "There's probably something in the Constitution that says you can't name a boy dog after a president's wife."

"The only thing the Constitution doesn't allow," said Sarah, "is drinking beer. And they're even changing *that!*"

"Don't come running to me," said Raymond, "when Secret Service agents come and shoot you."

"My dog will bite them all," Sarah sneered.

"He doesn't know how to bite," Raymond sneered back.

"Someday he's going to bite you something awful," Sarah said, sticking out her tongue.

"You still can't call him Eleanor Roosevelt," Raymond said while her tongue was out. "People think you're loony. What other girl stands around, whistling through her teeth, snapping her fingers, and yelling 'Eleanor Roosevelt'?"

"A fat lot you know," she bellowed.

Raymond threw up his hands in despair. "They're going to come after you with a net!"

Before she heaved a stone, Raymond ran.

Eleanor Roosevelt—the dog, not the First Lady; see how Sarah confused things—didn't chase Raymond. He had been sleeping throughout their whole argument. When Raymond ran, the dog woke up, stared after Raymond, yawned, checked to see if Sarah was near, and promptly went back to sleep again. He worried about Sarah, but the rest of the world he took as it came. When freight trains rattled by our tenements, he dozed. Unable to solve rain, he didn't try to solve why the ground shook. He worried about Sarah. That was all. He didn't worry about streetcars, dogs, automobiles, rain, where his next meal was coming from, or fleas, which is one reason he had so many.

Sarah was his moon and his sun. When she was away he dozed fitfully, troubled, wondering when she would come back to him. He lay in the sun and dreamed worried dreams of a world without

Sarah. But when she called or whistled, his worry vanished. His universe was complete again. He perked up, stretched, shook his head because her whistle hurt, wagged his tail, and ran to her—that is, he ran to her if she was on a sidewalk. If she was in the woods, that was another matter. He couldn't go there. Only animals ran in the woods. There were no sidewalks to run on. If that happened, he would crumble back to sleep and worry some more.

Oh, he crossed the street, of course. There was a sidewalk on the other side. But beyond the sidewalk was the woods. He would never venture there. To him, crossing the street held no danger. Automobiles slammed on their brakes, honked wildly, and swerved around him. He didn't give them the time of day. Streetcar motormen hated to travel his section of the street. They couldn't make their streetcars swerve and he ignored their clanging bells. So streetcars moved slowly through his domain. He had no time to think of traffic. He spent all his time thinking of Sarah.

But I have been avoiding the day I was supposed to write about. I can't avoid it any longer. It wouldn't be fair.

Well, nothing much happened that morning. We played baseball in Mount Echo Park and almost won. Sarah, naturally, hit three home runs, whistled through her teeth, and got dirty looks from both teams. That afternoon, after lunch, the three of us—her, Raymond, and me—sat in a tree and discussed the game.

"You freaks," said Sarah, "have got to keep your eye on the ball. That's the only way you'll learn to hit."

"Ha," I said, and meant it.

She looked at me with scorn. "The strikeout king," she snorted, and made a face at me. "You shut your eyes before the pitcher even pitches."

"I don't!"

"You do!"

There was a pause. I had to be honest.

"Well, not *all* the time," I said.

"See what I mean," Sarah said. "The strikeout king!"

"Quit picking on him," Raymond said. "He's the best outfielder we got."

I felt better.

"He's the only outfielder we got," Sarah said.

I felt bad again.

"Pick on somebody your own size," Raymond said.

That shut her up a minute.

"Anyway," Raymond said, "you got no reason to brag. Your dumb dog is afraid to get his feet dirty. He won't walk in the woods. He's afraid to." Raymond looked at me with pride. "George is braver that *that*."

I didn't know whether to feel complimented or not. I'd rather have been compared to Babe Ruth. I was about to tell Raymond this but I didn't get the chance.

"A fat lot you know," Sarah seethed. "Eleanor Roosevelt is afraid of *nothing*!" She glared at me. "You hide from thunder. Eleanor doesn't."

"Yes, but Eleanor is a dog and I'm . . ." I tried to say, wishing they'd leave me out of it. But Sarah didn't let me finish.

"Scaredy-cat," she brayed. "I'd rather have a dog than a scaredy-cat!"

"You don't have a dog," Raymond said. He was getting angry. "Real dogs go walking in the woods. You have to carry yours!"

"A fat lot you know," Sarah said. She was getting angry, too.

"*I* don't have to carry George," Raymond shouted.

I wished he hadn't shouted that. I wasn't his dog. I was his friend.

"*Eleanor* wouldn't shut his eyes when he's at bat!" Sarah shouted.

"*George* doesn't have fleas!" Raymond shouted back.

They argued like that for a half hour. Sometimes I was ahead, sometimes her dog was. Sometimes Sarah offered to fist fight

Raymond. Sometimes he offered to fist fight her. They were careful not to offer to fist fight at the same time.

"I won't fight a girl," Raymond would say.

Another time Sarah would say:

"I won't fight a boy. I hate to see boys cry."

It was an awful afternoon.

"I'll bet," said Raymond, "your dumb dog doesn't know enough to save your life. I'll bet . . ."

"He's fierce as a tiger," Sarah said. "Watch your mouth."

"On *sidewalks*," Raymond sneered. "He scares people with his snores!"

"A fat lot you know!"

"If you were *really* in trouble," Raymond said, "here in the woods he wouldn't lift a finger. There are no sidewalks here."

Sarah put her hands on her hips. She almost fell out of the tree doing it.

"He'll save my life whenever I want," she said.

Raymond laughed at her.

"Not here," he said. "No sidewalks."

"Up here, too!"

"Prove it!"

She looked at him, furious. But her glance wavered. I saw it and so did Raymond. We knew why. Right then, at that exact moment, her dog was asleep on a sidewalk somewhere, waiting for her to come back to him. Sarah could whistle and he'd cross the street like a blur and zoom to her, unnerving motorists and making streetcar motormen cringe. But would he run into the woods and seek her out? That was the question. He was a sidewalk dog. Would he, perhaps, wait where the sidewalk ended, whining for someone to carry him to the rescue in the woods? This was why Sarah's glance wavered. Raymond had backed her into a corner she didn't want to be in.

"Why should I prove it?" she said. "There's nothing but sissybritches here. There's nothing to be scared of."

"If you call him and he comes," said Raymond. "I'll eat dirt."

That was the supreme challenge. Sarah couldn't refuse. Raymond had put his honor on the line and was waiting for hers.

"Tomorrow," she hedged.

"Now," said Raymond.

He climbed down from the tree.

"Well?" he said.

There was an awful pause.

"I hate you," she said.

She was distressed. But when she looked at Raymond her distress went away. Anger returned. She climbed down from the tree and started along the path.

"Get ready to eat dirt," she said.

We followed her.

Moments later, Sarah, Raymond, and me stood in the shadows at the forest's edge. Our tenements were down the path and across the street. I watched Sarah as she looked from behind a bush and saw, across the street, her dog sleeping fitfully in the sun.

This was her put-up-or-shut-up hour. Would Eleanor Roosevelt come to her—or stop where the sidewalk stopped?

Her eyes narrowed with worry.

"It's your move," said Raymond. "Whistle for Eleanor."

She closed her eyes.

Was she praying?

"I'll show you how wonderful my dog is," she said, putting two fingers to her mouth, and the neighborhood was deafened by the force of her whistle. "Watch," she said. "Now just you watch."

We did.

Her dog stirred, raised up, cocked his head, and with a look of surprise and doubt searched the hillside for the whistle's source. First his tail thumped with gladness. Sarah had come back. Then it slowed and thumped with hesitation. Sarah had never called him to the woods before, his tail said. He got up, shook himself, and studied the hillside some more. She's never called me to the hill before, his look said.

"Well," said Raymond. "He's not coming."

"He is!" said Sarah—and whistled again.

Her dog couldn't locate Sarah but he knew she was there and she wanted him. Love replaced doubt. Need replaced reason. He was a red smear—tail wagging, body low, feet flying—as he zoomed across the street, ignoring cars, ignoring everything, following his heart to seek his one true north: Sarah behind a tree.

"There!" she shouted gleefully.

But her shout died on her lips.

I can still hear the thud. The car that hit her dog wasn't going fast. The thud was noisier than any noise that ever was. I can still see her dog sailing through the air to crash against a curbstone, dead.

Her shout died when her dog did.

I can still see her running down the path, stumbling, and I can still hear the moan she moaned. I can still see her pick up her lifeless dog, cradle him in her arms, and talk to him words of regret he didn't hear.

As Raymond and I approached, the driver of the car approached. He was a nice man, shaken; he didn't mean harm. I heard him say:

"I'm sorry, I'm sorry. . . ."

Other people came. They always do. They recited where they had been when it happened. They attached great importance to this. They recited what each had seen. They compared notes. They managed to turn the death of Sarah's dog into an event as ordinary as rain. They indexed and catalogued the happening and were done with it. Then they stood and talked of other things.

But Raymond, his face white and his soul in torment, said:

"It was my fault."

Sarah looked at him. The hurt in her eyes showed the hurt in her heart.

She shook her head.

"No," she said. "I called him when I shouldn't have."

She gazed around at neighbors who had ceased to talk of her dog's death.

"I better bury him," she said.

No one moved forward.

They compared the death of this dog with other animal deaths they had witnessed and filed.

"I'll help you," said Raymond.

"No!" she cried, stricken.

Then she looked surprised. She shook her head and tried to smile. It wasn't the day for smiling.

"Please," she said. "But no."

She walked away from the crowd. They hardly noticed her go. She carried her dog across the street into the woods. She walked slowly. There was no need to hurry. It was their last walk in the woods together. Last walks require goodbyes.

I started after her but Raymond touched my arm.

"Not yet," he said.

She vanished in the shadows of the trees. The driver drove away. The people laughed and talked of other things. A streetcar passed, slowed, then speeded up. Soon motormen would spread the word: No need to slow down there again; the dog is gone.

Raymond and I sat on the curb and watched the hill.

Finally, Raymond sighed a terrible sigh.

"Let's go to her," he said.

We didn't know exactly where she was. We took the main path up the hill. We didn't go too far. Raymond, in front of me, motioned me to stop. He pointed.

But I had seen it, too. It was a fresh-dug grave, fresh-covered. It was a little grave but he had been a little dog.

I looked up—and there she was.

Sarah, forlorn, sat in a tree on the highest branch that would hold her. Her hands, black from digging, were in her lap. She didn't swing her feet. She didn't say hello. She stared up to where God was. She didn't look down at us. We were of the world and the world hadn't been too good to her. It had taken her dog away.

Raymond motioned me to follow him. We went along a path. Once out of her sight, he stopped. He looked around. He found some sticks and made them into a cross. He tied the cross together with grass. He worked swiftly and silently. I stood by and said nothing. Then we walked back to where the dog was buried.

Without a word, Raymond forced the cross into the ground to make the grave complete.

Sarah, hearing this, looked down.

"I tried," she said lonesomely. "But I didn't know how to make a cross."

Raymond and Sarah stared at each other the longest time.

Then Raymond said:

"Come on. I'll take you home."

No doubt about it—Billy's coon hounds are smart dogs. But how would they stack up against Hank the Cowdog, Head of Ranch Security?

Bloody Murder
from The Original Adventures of Hank the Cowdog
John R. Erickson

It's me again, Hank the Cowdog. I just got some terrible news. There's been a murder on the ranch.

I know I shouldn't blame myself. I mean, a dog is only a dog. He can't be everywhere at once. When I took this job as Head of Ranch Security, I knew that I was only flesh and blood, four legs, a tail, a couple of ears, a pretty nice kind of nose that the women really go for, two bushels of hair and another half-bushel of Mexican sandburs.

You add that all up and you don't get Superman, just me, good old easy-going Hank who works hard, tries to do his job, and gets very little cooperation from anyone else around here.

I'm not complaining. I knew this wouldn't be an easy job. It took a special kind of dog—strong, fearless, dedicated, and above all, smart. Obviously Drover didn't fit. The job fell on my shoulders. It was my destiny. I couldn't escape the broom of history that swept through . . . anyway, I took the job.

Head of Ranch Security. Gee, I was proud of that title. Just the sound of it made my tail wag. But now this, a murder, right under my nose. I know I shouldn't blame myself, but I do.

I got the report this morning around dawn. I had been up most of the night patrolling the northern perimeter of ranch headquarters. I had heard some coyotes yapping up there and I went up to check it out. I told Drover where I was going and he came up lame all of a sudden, said he needed to rest his right front leg.

I went alone, didn't find anything. The coyotes stayed out in the pasture. I figured there were two, maybe three of them. They yapped for a couple of hours, making fun of me, calling me ugly names, and daring me to come out and fight.

Well, you know me. I'm no dummy. There's a thin line between heroism and stupidity, and I try to stay on the south side of it. I didn't go out and fight, but I answered them bark for bark, yap for yap, name for name.

The coyote hasn't been built who can outyap Hank the Cowdog.

A little before dawn, Loper, one of the cowboys on this outfit, stuck his head out the door and bellered, "Shut up that yapping, you idiot!" I guess he thought there was only one coyote out there.

They kept it up and I gave it back to them. Next time Loper came to the door, he was armed. He fired a gun into the air and squalled, something about how a man couldn't sleep around here with all the dad-danged noise. I agreed.

Would you believe it? Them coyotes yipped louder than ever, and I had no choice but to give it back to them.

Loper came back out on the porch and fired another shot. This one came so close to me that I heard the hum. Loper must have lost his bearings or something, so I barked louder than ever to give him my position, and, you know, to let him know that I was out there protecting the ranch.

The next bullet just derned near got me. I mean, I felt the wind of it as it went past. That was enough for me. I shut her down for the night. If Loper couldn't aim any better than that, he was liable to hurt somebody.

I laid low for a while, hiding in the shelter belt, until I was sure the artillery had gone back to bed. Then I went down for a roll in the sewer, cleaned up, washed myself real good, came out feeling refreshed and ready to catch up on my sleep. Trotted down to the gas tanks and found Drover curled up in my favorite spot.

I growled him off my gunny sack. "Beat it, son. Make way for the night patrol."

He didn't want to move so I went to sterner measures, put some fangs on him. That moved him out, and he didn't show no signs of lameness either. I have an idea that where Drover is lamest is between his ears.

I did my usual bedtime ritual of walking in a tight circle around my bed until I found just exactly the spot I wanted, and then I flopped down. Oh, that felt good! I wiggled around and finally came to rest with all four paws sticking up in the air. I closed my eyes and had some wonderful twitching dreams about . . . don't recall exactly the subject matter, but most likely they were about Beulah, the neighbor's collie. I dream about her a lot.

What a woman! Makes my old heart pound just to think about her. Beautiful brown and white hair, big eyes, nose that tapers down to a point (not quite as good as mine, but so what?), and nice ears that flap when she runs.

Only trouble is that she's crazy about a spotted bird dog, without a doubt the ugliest, dumbest, worthlessest cur I ever met. What could be uglier than a spotted short-haired dog with a long skinny tail? And what could be dumber or more worth-less than a dog that goes around chasing *birds*?

They call him Plato. I don't know why, except maybe because his eyes look like plates half the time, empty plates. He don't know a cow from a sow, but do you think that makes him humble? No sir. He thinks that birdchasing is hot stuff. What really hurts, though, is that Beulah seems to agree.

Don't understand that woman, but I dream about her a lot.

Anyway, where was I? Under the gas tanks, catching up on my sleep. All at once Drover was right there beside me, jumping up and down and giving off that high-pitched squeal of his that kind of bores into your eardrums. You can't ignore him when he does that.

Well, I throwed open one eye, kept the other one shut so that I could get some halfway sleep. "Will you please shut up?"

"Hank, oh Hankie, it's just terrible, you wouldn't believe, hurry and wake up, I seen his tracks down on the creek, get up before he escapes!"

I throwed open the other eye, pushed myself up, and went nose-to-nose with the noisemaker. "Quit hopping around. Quit making all that racket. Hold still and state your business."

"Okay, Hank, all right, I'll try." He tried and was none too successful, but he did get the message across. "Oh Hank, there's been a killing, right here on the ranch, and we slept through it!"

"Huh?" I was coming awake by then, and the word *killing* sent a jolt clean out to the end of my tail. "Who's been killed?"

"They hit the chickenhouse, Hank. I don't know how they got in but they did, busted in there and killed one of those big leghorn hens, killed her dead, Hank, and oh, the blood!"

Well, that settled it. I had no choice but to go back on duty. A lot of dogs would have just turned over and gone back to sleep, but I take this stuff pretty serious.

We trotted up to the chickenhouse, and Drover kept jumping up and down and talking. "I found some tracks down by the creek. I'm sure they belong to the killer, Hank, I'm just sure they do."

"What kind of tracks?"

"Coyote."

"Hmm." We reached the chickenhouse and, sure enough, there was the hen lying on the ground, and she was still dead. I walked around the body, sniffing it good and checking the signs.

I noticed the position of the body and memorized every detail. The hen was lying on her left side, pointing toward the northeast, with one foot out and the other one curled up under her wing. Her mouth was open and it appeared to me that she had lost some tail feathers.

"Uh huh, I'm beginning to see the pattern."

"What, tell me, Hank, who done it?"

"Not yet. Where'd you see them tracks?" There weren't any tracks around the corpse, ground was too hard. Drover took off in a run and I followed him down into the brush along the creek.

He stopped and pointed to some fresh tracks in the mud. "There they are, Hank, just where I found them. Are you proud of me?"

I pushed him aside and studied the sign, looked it over real careful, sniffed it, gave it the full treatment. Then I raised up.

"Okay, I've got it now. It's all clear. Them's coon tracks, son, not coyote. I can tell from the scent. Coons must have attacked while I was out on patrol. They're sneaky, you've got to watch 'em every minute."

Drover squinted at the tracks. "Are you sure those are coon tracks? They sure look like coyote to me."

"You don't go by the *look*, son, you go by the *smell*. This nose of mine don't lie. If it says coon, you better believe there's a coon at the end of them tracks. And I'm fixing to clean house on him. Stay behind me and don't get hurt."

I threaded my way through the creek willows, over the sand, through the water. I never lost the scent. In the heat of a chase, all my senses come alive and point like a blazing arrow toward the enemy.

In a way I felt sorry for the coon, even though he'd committed a crime and become my mortal enemy. With me on his trail, the little guy just didn't have a chance. One of the disadvantages of being as big and deadly as I am is that you sometimes find yourself in sympathy with the other guy.

But part of being Head of Ranch Security is learning to ignore that kind of emotion. I mean, to hold down this job, you have to be cold and hard.

The scent was getting stronger all the time, and it didn't smell exactly like any coon I'd come across before. All at once I saw him. I stopped dead still and Drover, the little dummy, ran right into me and almost had a heart attack. I guess he thought I was a giant coon or something. It's hard to say what he thinks.

The coon was hiding in some bushes about five feet in front of me. I could hear him chewing on something, and that smell was real strong now.

"What's that?" Drover whispered, sniffing the air.

"Coon, what do you think?" I glanced back at him. He was shaking with fear. "You ready for some combat experience?"

"Yes," he squeaked.

"All right, here's the plan. I'll jump him and try to get him behind the neck. You come in the second wave and take what you can. If you run away like you did last time, I'll sweep the corral with you and give you a whupping you won't forget. All right, let's move out."

I crouched down and crept forward, every muscle in my highly conditioned body taut and ready for action. Five feet, four feet, three feet, two. I sprang through the air and hit right in the middle of the biggest porcupine I ever saw.

It was kind of a short fight. Coming down, I seen them quills aimed up at me and tried to change course. Too late. I don't move so good in mid-air.

I lit right in the middle of him and *bam*, he slapped me across the nose with his tail, sure did hurt too, brought tears to my eyes. I hollered for Drover to launch the second wave but he had disappeared.

Porcupine took another shot at me but I dodged, tore up half an acre of brush, and got the heck out of there. As I limped back up to the house on pin-cushion feet, my thoughts went back to the murder scene and the evidence I had committed to memory.

It was clear now. The porcupine had had nothing at all to do with the murder because porcupines don't eat anything but trees. Drover had found the first set of tracks he had come to and had started hollering about coyotes. I had been duped into believing the runt.

Yes, it was all clear. I had no leads, no clues, no idea who had killed the hen. What I *did* have was a face-full of porcupine quills, as well as several in my paws. . . .

■ ■ ■

Wilson Rawls

■ (1913–1984) ■

Woodrow Wilson Rawls grew up in northeastern
Oklahoma, on a small farm in the foothills of the Ozark
Mountains. With no schools in the area for him to attend,
young Rawls learned from his mother how to read and write.
Later, when a school was built for the local children, Wilson
and his sisters attended for only a few months every summer.
It was not until the family moved to the town of Tahlequah
that the boy first visited a library or attended a regular school.
When the Great Depression struck, however, Rawls was
forced to leave school without completing eighth grade. He
began traveling the United States in search of work, and he
always sent to his family half of whatever money he earned.

While he still was a teenager, Rawls worked on a construction job in Mexico for a time and then took a better-paying
job in South America. Later, he headed north to work on the
Alcan Highway in Alaska and on five of the largest dams
in the United States. Rawls also did construction work for
the Navy in Oregon, held a job with a lumber company in
western Canada, and worked in various shipyards along the
West Coast.

Wherever he traveled, whatever else he was doing, Rawls
found time to write. Even though he did not think that his
work was worth publishing, Rawls never stopped putting his
stories down on paper. Storing his manuscripts in a trunk at his
parents' house, Rawls relocated to Idaho in 1956 in search of
construction work. There he met Sophie Styczinski, a budget
analyst for the Atomic Energy Commission. Promising to settle
down, Rawls began to spend less of his free time writing and
more at his favorite leisure activities of hunting and fishing.

Shortly before marrying Sophie, Rawls visited his parents'

home in New Mexico. There, he found and re-read his old manuscripts. Very disappointed in them, Rawls decided to give up his lifetime ambition and to get rid of his early writings. He burned five complete novels.

Fortunately, Sophie refused to let him abandon his dream. With her support and encouragement, Rawls rewrote his auto-biographical story "The Secret of the Red Fern" from memory. Sophie edited the manuscript and submitted it to the *Saturday Evening Post.* The magazine wanted the story and published it in three installments under the title "Hounds of Youth." The entire story was published by Doubleday in 1961 as *Where the Red Fern Grows.*

Despite excellent reviews, the novel did not begin to sell well until Rawls accepted an invitation to speak at a summer workshop for teachers at the University of Utah. The teachers were so impressed by Rawls's remarks that they began urging their students to read his novel. Sales began to take off. Soon thereafter, the story was filmed. Rawls's second novel, *Summer of the Monkeys,* was published in 1976. That novel tells of a fourteen-year-old boy from the Oklahoma Ozarks who tracks down some escaped circus monkeys with the help of his grandfather and his loyal dog Rowdy.

As a celebrated author, Rawls visited more than two thousand schools in twenty-two states. He also addressed many teacher and librarian conferences. His speaking engagements continued until 1983, when illness prevented him from traveling. He died at the age of seventy-one on December 16, 1984.